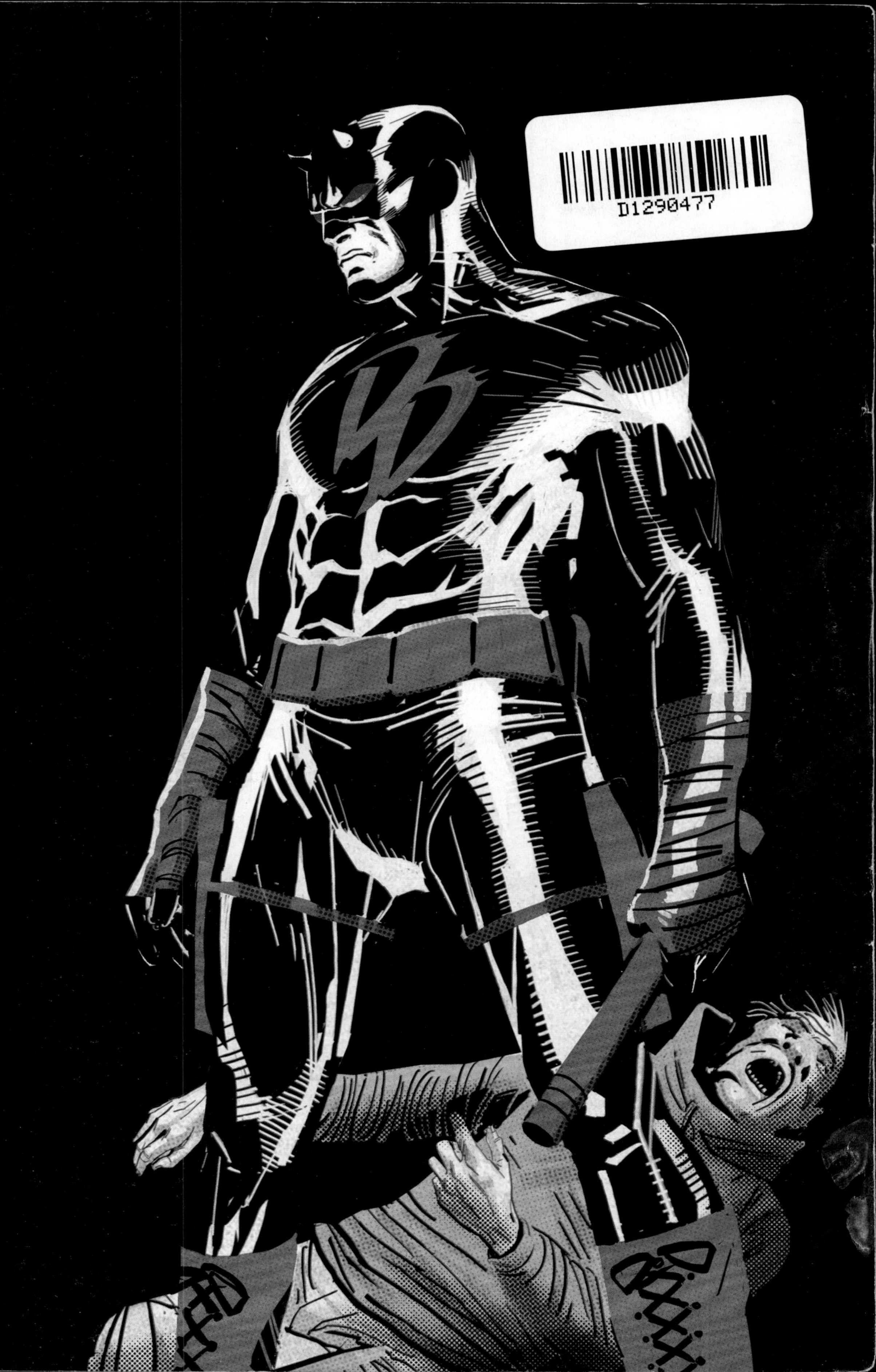

WHEN MATT MURDOCK WAS A KID, HE LOST HIS SIGHT IN AN ACCIDENT INVOLVING A TRUCK CARRYING RADIOACTIVE CHEMICALS. THOUGH HE COULD NO LONGER SEE, THE CHEMICALS HEIGHTENED MURDOCK'S OTHER SENSES AND IMBUED HIM WITH AN AMAZING 360-RADAR SENSE. NOW MATT USES HIS ABILITIES TO FIGHT FOR HIS CITY. HE IS THE *MAN WITHOUT FEAR.* HE IS...

DAREDEVIL

CHINATOWN

CHARLES SOULE
WRITER

RON GARNEY WITH **GORAN SUDŽUKA** (*No.4*)
ARTISTS

MATT MILLA
COLOR ARTIST

VC's CLAYTON COWLES WITH
JOE CARAMAGNA (*ALL-NEW, ALL-DIFFERENT POINT ONE No.1*)
LETTERERS

RON GARNEY & MATT MILLA
COVER ART

CHARLES BEACHAM
ASSISTANT EDITOR

SANA AMANAT
EDITOR

COLLECTION EDITOR JENNIFER GRÜNWALD
ASSOCIATE EDITOR SARAH BRUNSTAD
ASSOCIATE MANAGING EDITOR ALEX STARBUCK
EDITOR, SPECIAL PROJECTS MARK D. BEAZLEY
VP, PRODUCTION & SPECIAL PROJECTS JEFF YOUNGQUIST
SVP PRINT, SALES & MARKETING DAVID GABRIEL
BOOK DESIGNER ADAM DEL RE

EDITOR IN CHIEF AXEL ALONSO
CHIEF CREATIVE OFFICER JOE QUESADA
PUBLISHER DAN BUCKLEY
EXECUTIVE PRODUCER ALAN FINE

DAREDEVIL: BACK IN BLACK VOL. 1 — CHINATOWN. Contains material originally published in magazine form as DAREDEVIL #1-5 and ALL-NEW, ALL-DIFFERENT POINT ONE #1. First printing 2016. ISBN# 978-0-7851-9644-0. Published by MARVEL WORLDWIDE, INC., a subsidiary of MARVEL ENTERTAINMENT, LLC. OFFICE OF PUBLICATION: 135 West 50th Street, New York, NY 10020.

Printed in Canada. ALAN FINE, President, Marvel Entertainment; DAN BUCKLEY, President, TV, Publishing & Brand Management; JOE QUESADA, Chief Creative Officer; TOM BREVOORT, SVP of Publishing; DAVID BOGART, SVP of Business Affairs & Operations, Publishing & Partnership; C.B. CEBULSKI, VP of Brand Management & Development, Asia; DAVID GABRIEL, SVP of Sales & Marketing, Publishing; JEFF YOUNGQUIST, VP of Production & Special Projects; DAN CARR, Executive Director of Publishing Technology; ALEX MORALES, Director of Publishing Operations; SUSAN CRESPI, Production Manager; STAN LEE, Chairman Emeritus. For information regarding advertising in Marvel Comics or on Marvel.com, please contact Vit DeBellis, Integrated Sales Manager, at vdebellis@marvel.com. For Marvel subscription inquiries, please call 888-511-5480. **Manufactured between 3/18/2016 and 4/25/2016 by SOLISCO PRINTERS, SCOTT, QC, CANADA.**

10 9 8 7 6 5 4 3 2 1

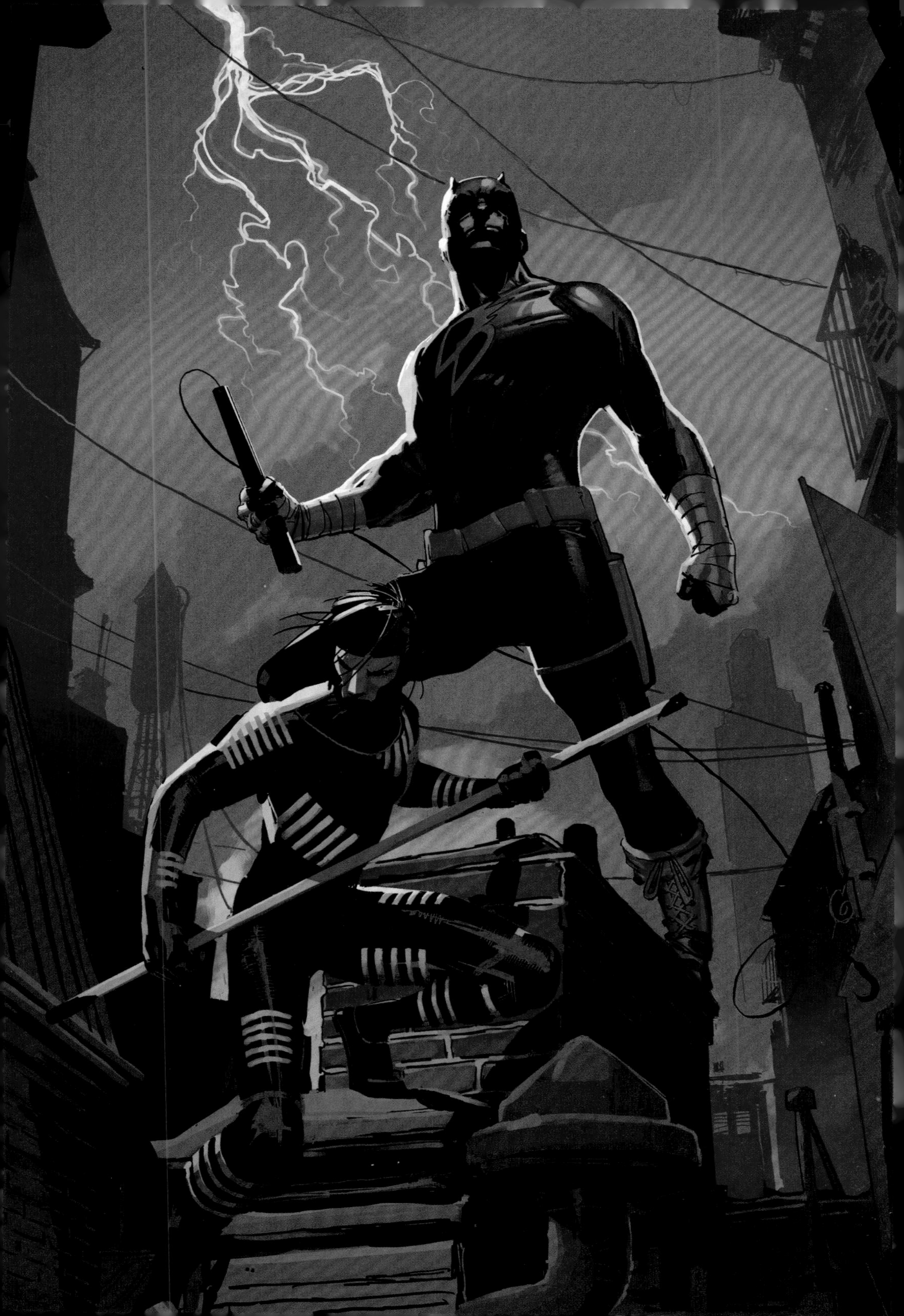

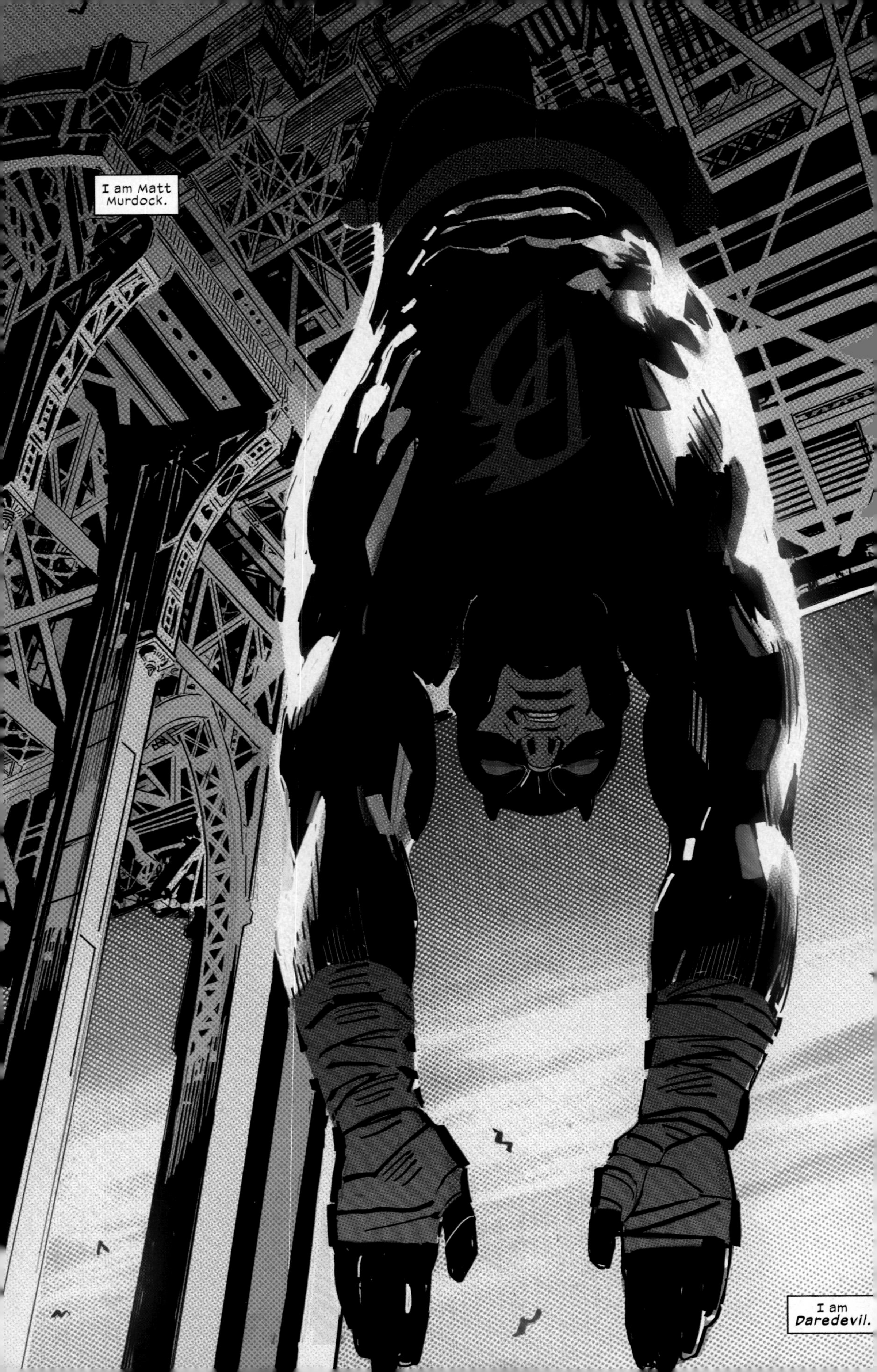
I am Matt Murdock.
I am *Daredevil.*

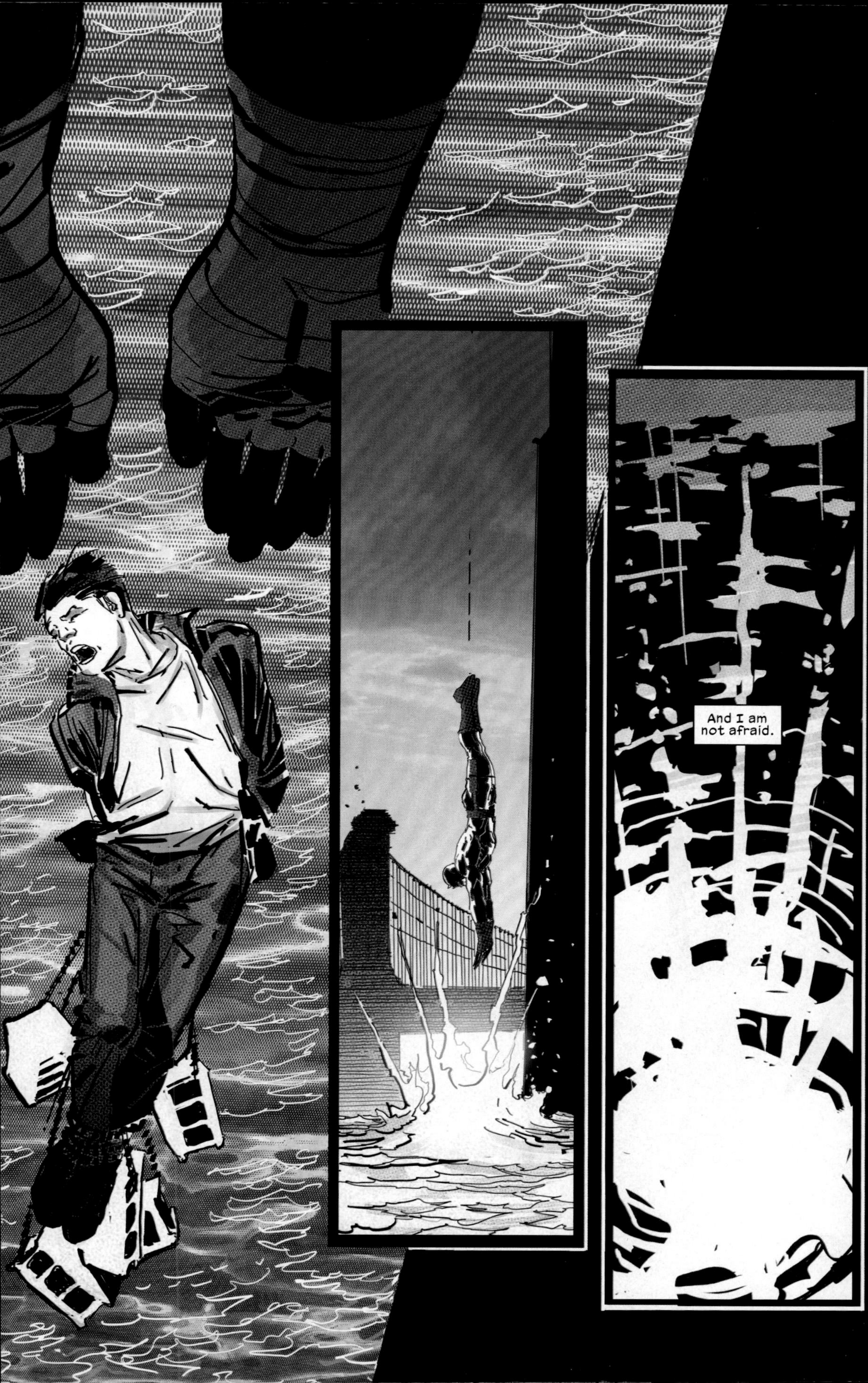
And I am not afraid.

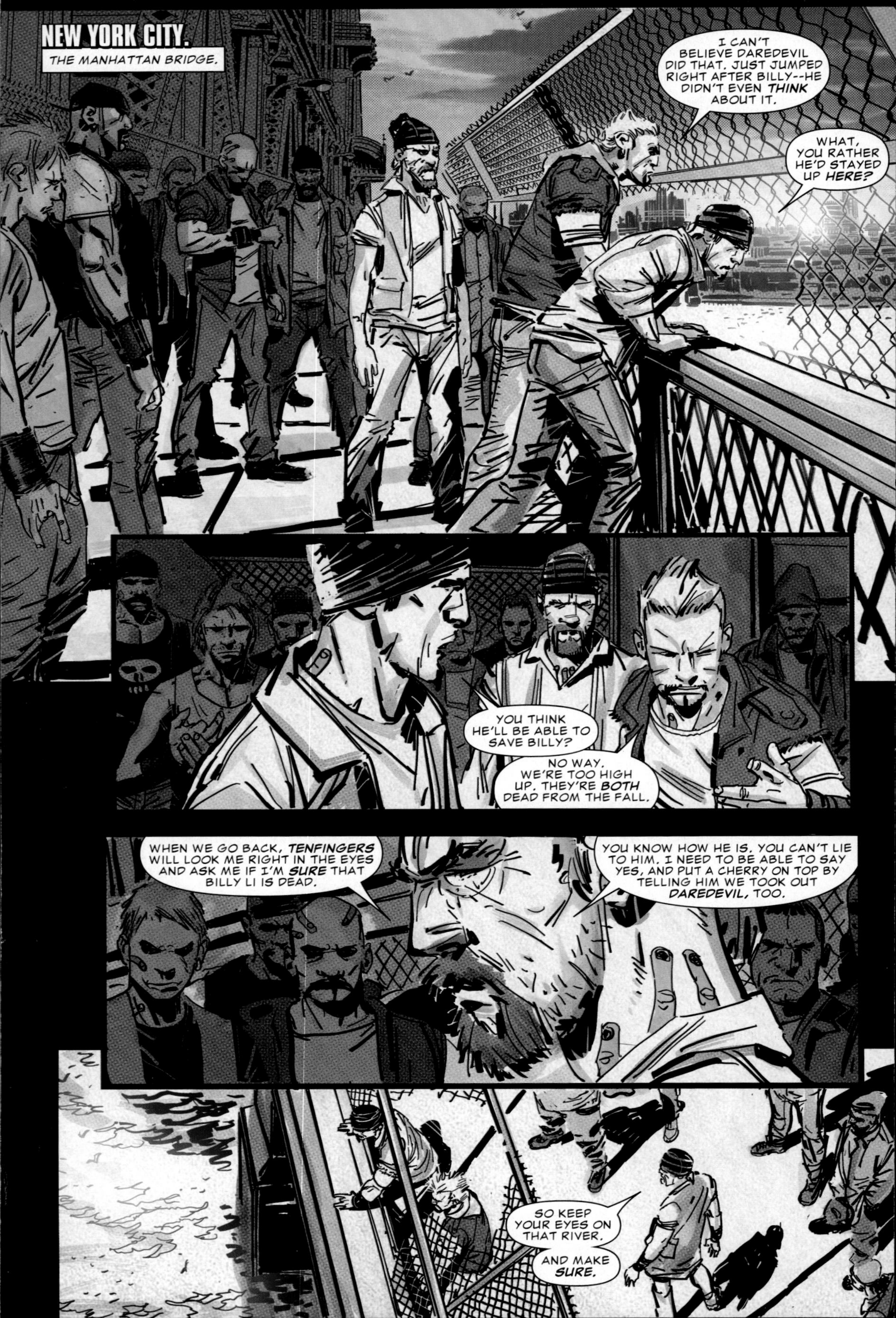
NEW YORK CITY.
THE MANHATTAN BRIDGE.
I CAN'T BELIEVE DAREDEVIL DID THAT. JUST JUMPED RIGHT AFTER BILLY--HE DIDN'T EVEN THINK ABOUT IT.
WHAT, YOU RATHER HE'D STAYED UP HERE?
YOU THINK HE'LL BE ABLE TO SAVE BILLY?
NO WAY. WE'RE TOO HIGH UP. THEY'RE BOTH DEAD FROM THE FALL.
WHEN WE GO BACK, TENFINGERS WILL LOOK ME RIGHT IN THE EYES AND ASK ME IF I'M SURE THAT BILLY LI IS DEAD.
YOU KNOW HOW HE IS. YOU CAN'T LIE TO HIM. I NEED TO BE ABLE TO SAY YES, AND PUT A CHERRY ON TOP BY TELLING HIM WE TOOK OUT DAREDEVIL, TOO.
SO KEEP YOUR EYES ON THAT RIVER.
AND MAKE SURE.

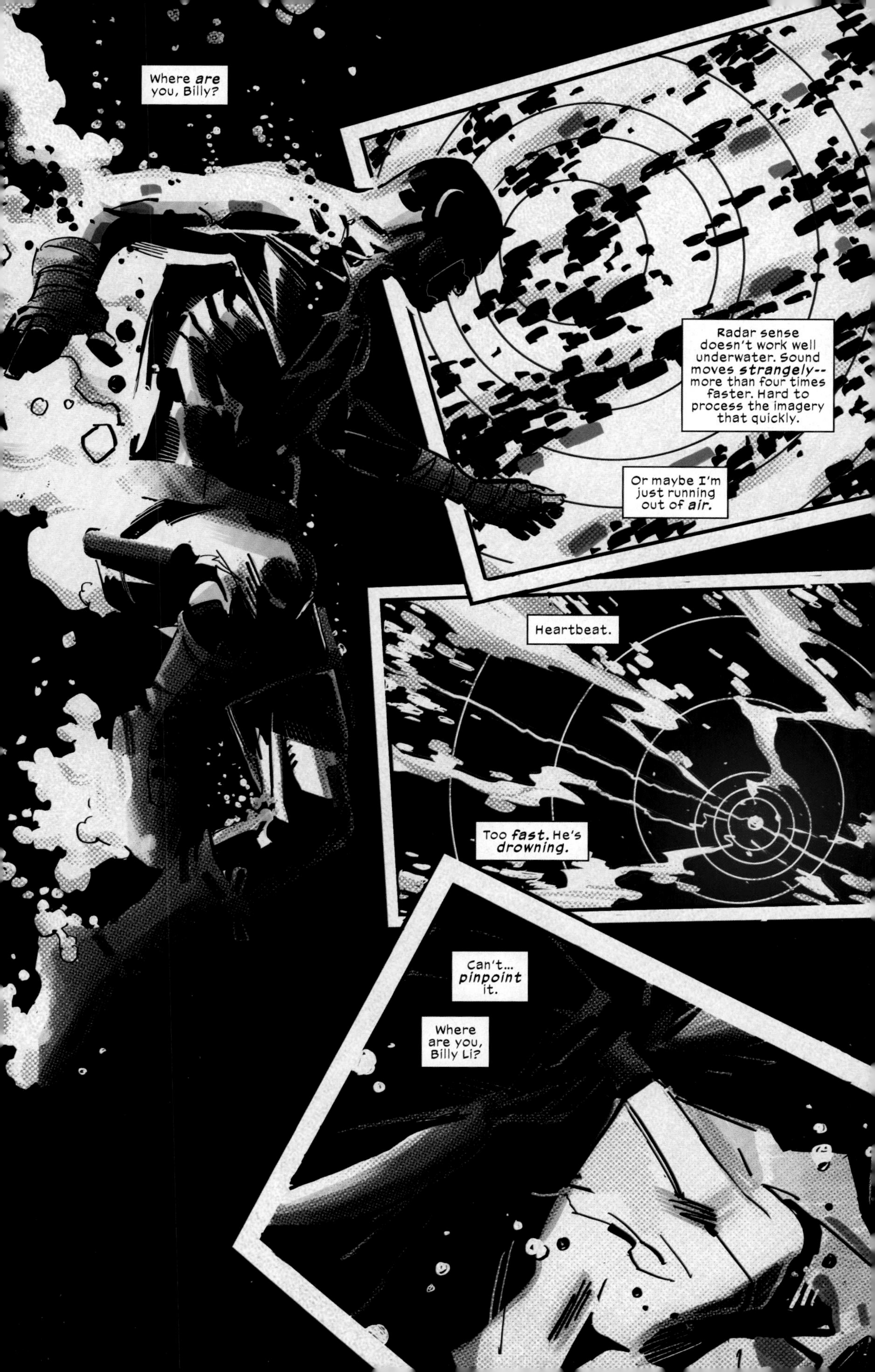
Where are you, Billy?
Radar sense doesn't work well underwater. Sound moves strangely-- more than four times faster. Hard to process the imagery that quickly.
Or maybe I'm just running out of air.
Heartbeat.
Too fast. He's drowning.
Can't... pinpoint it.
Where are you, Billy Li?

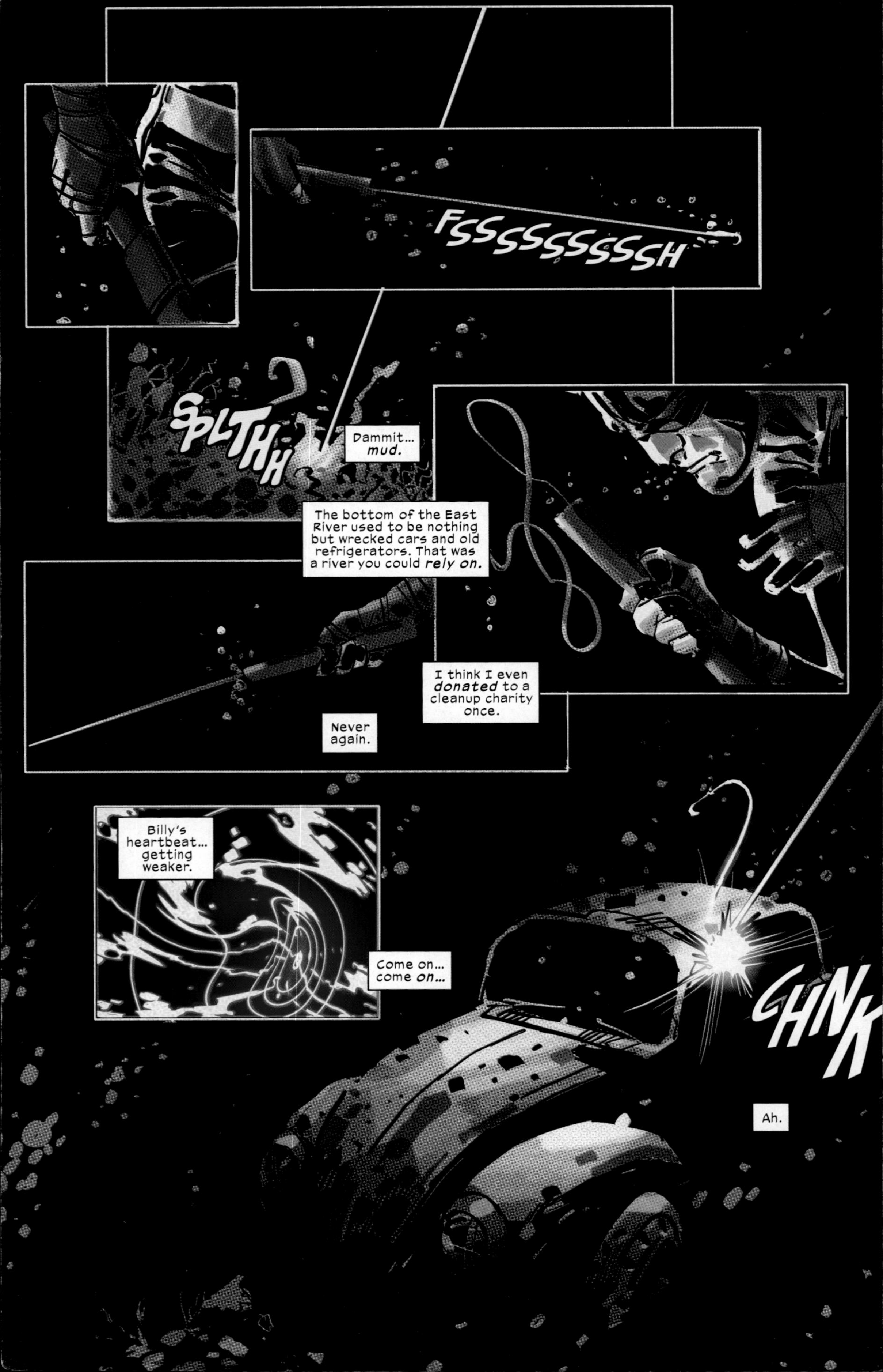

FSSSSSSSSSSH
SPLTHH
Dammit... mud.
The bottom of the East River used to be nothing but wrecked cars and old refrigerators. That was a river you could rely on.
I think I even donated to a cleanup charity once.
Never again.
Billy's heartbeat... getting weaker.
Come on... come on...
CHINK
Ah.

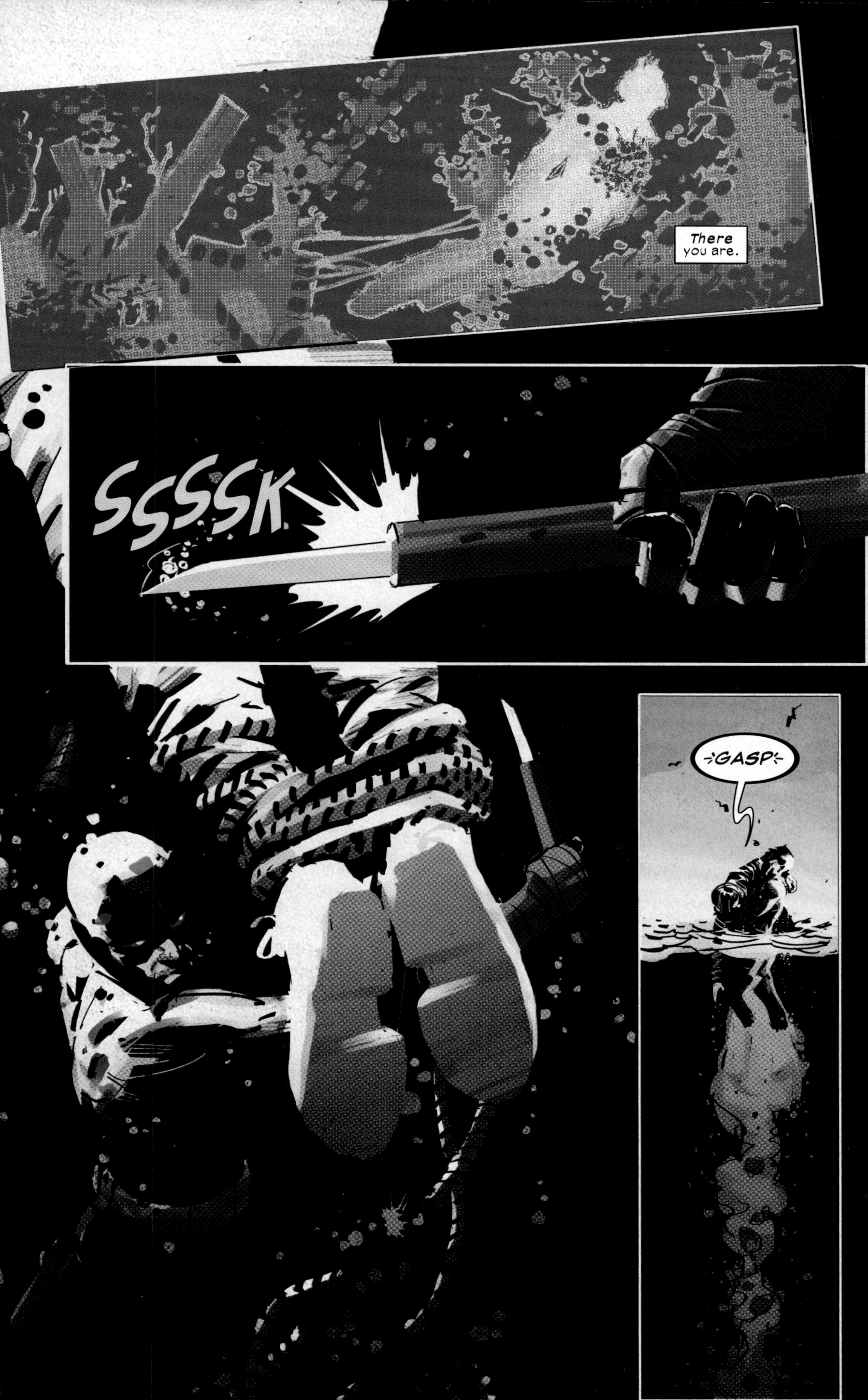
There you are.
SSSSK
GASP

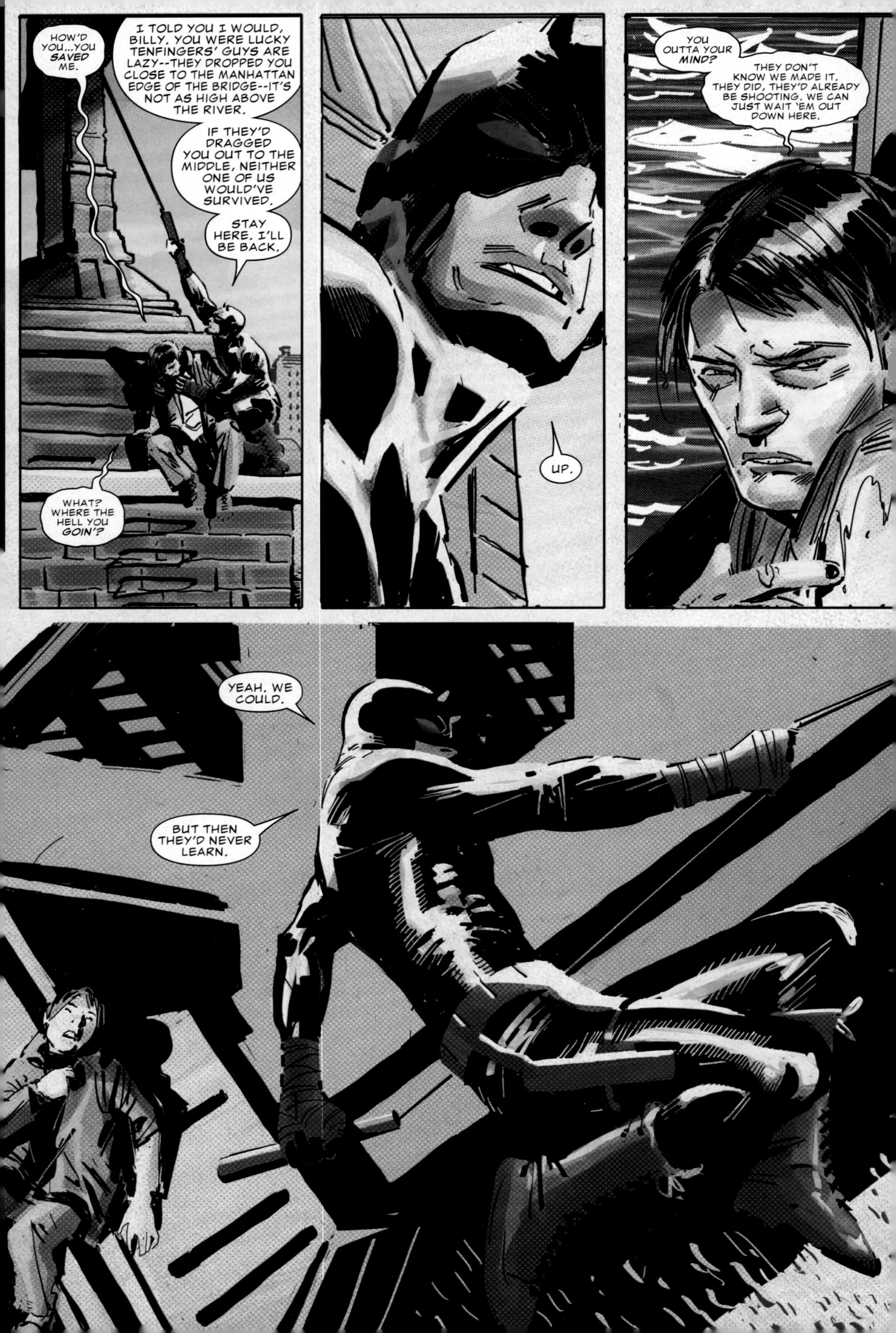
HOW'D YOU...YOU SAVED ME.
I TOLD YOU I WOULD, BILLY. YOU WERE LUCKY TENFINGERS' GUYS ARE LAZY--THEY DROPPED YOU CLOSE TO THE MANHATTAN EDGE OF THE BRIDGE--IT'S NOT AS HIGH ABOVE THE RIVER.
IF THEY'D DRAGGED YOU OUT TO THE MIDDLE, NEITHER ONE OF US WOULD'VE SURVIVED.
STAY HERE. I'LL BE BACK.
WHAT? WHERE THE HELL YOU GOIN'?
UP.
YOU OUTTA YOUR MIND?
THEY DON'T KNOW WE MADE IT. THEY DID, THEY'D ALREADY BE SHOOTING. WE CAN JUST WAIT 'EM OUT DOWN HERE.
YEAH, WE COULD.
BUT THEN THEY'D NEVER LEARN.

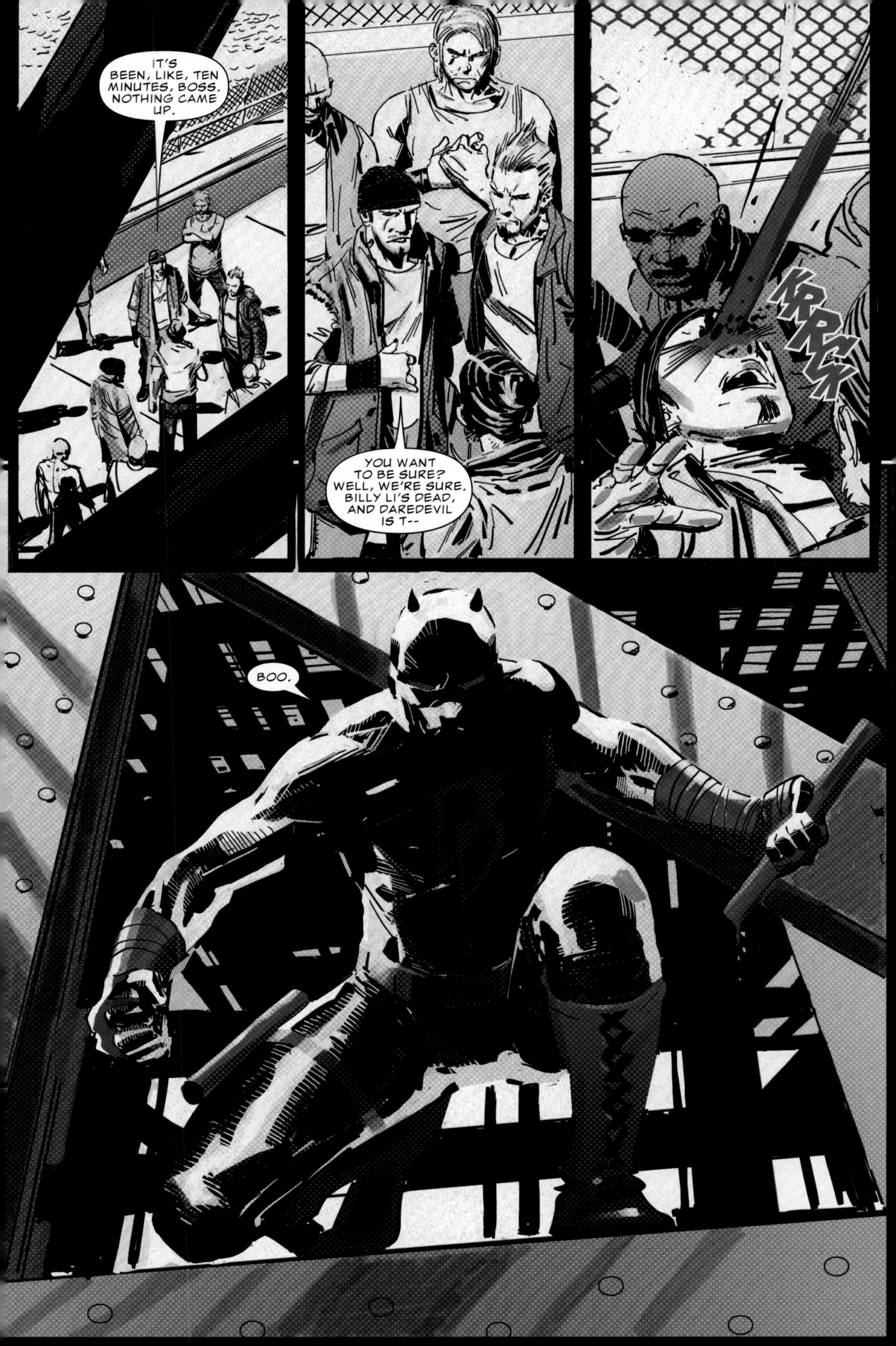
IT'S BEEN, LIKE, TEN MINUTES, BOSS. NOTHING CAME UP.
YOU WANT TO BE SURE? WELL, WE'RE SURE. BILLY LI'S DEAD, AND DAREDEVIL IS T--
KRRCK
BOO.

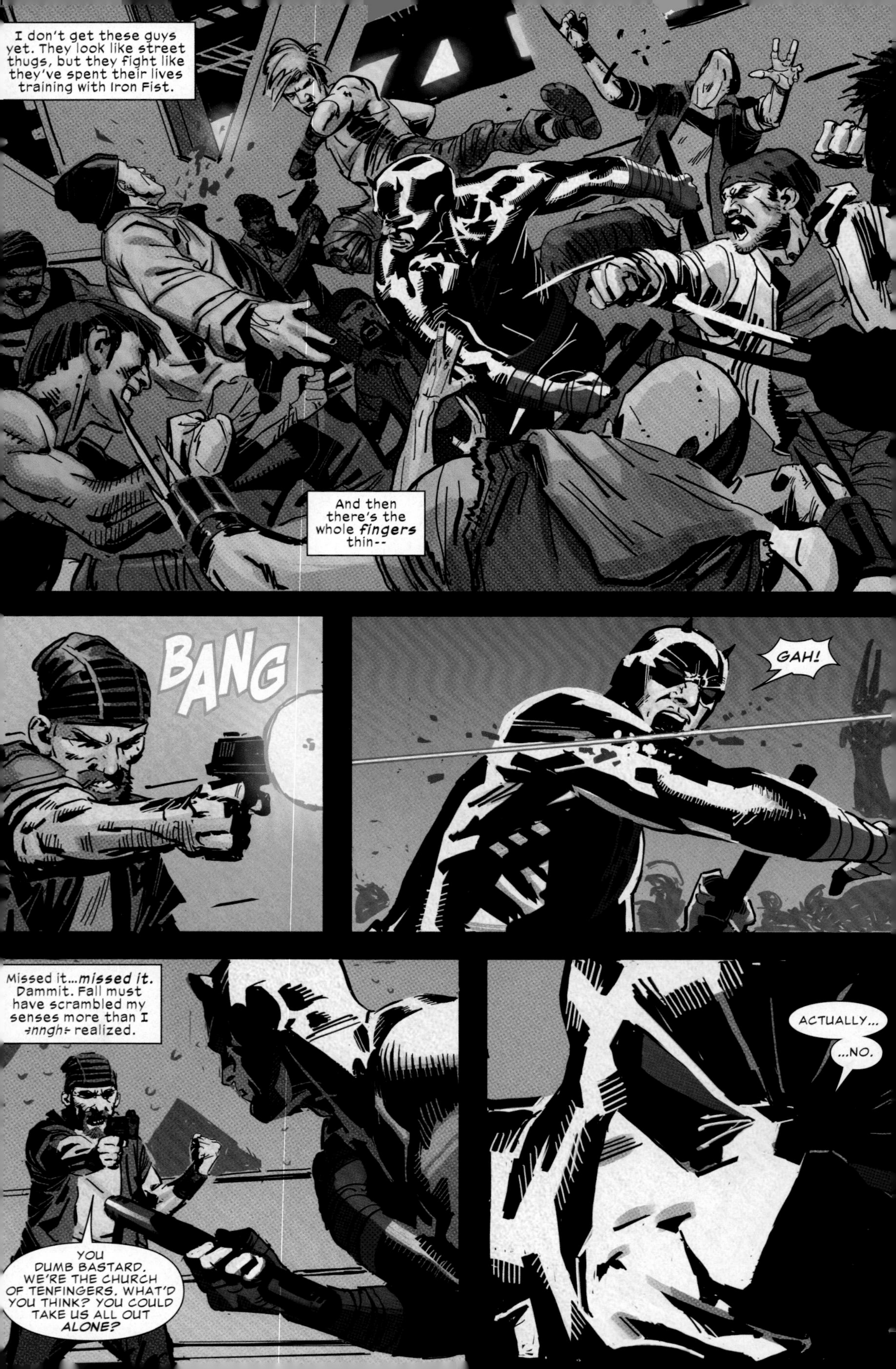
I don't get these guys yet. They look like street thugs, but they fight like they've spent their lives training with Iron Fist.
And then there's the whole fingers thin--
BANG
GAH!
Missed it...missed it. Dammit. Fall must have scrambled my senses more than I -nngh- realized.
YOU DUMB BASTARD. WE'RE THE CHURCH OF TENFINGERS. WHAT'D YOU THINK? YOU COULD TAKE US ALL OUT ALONE?
ACTUALLY...
...NO.

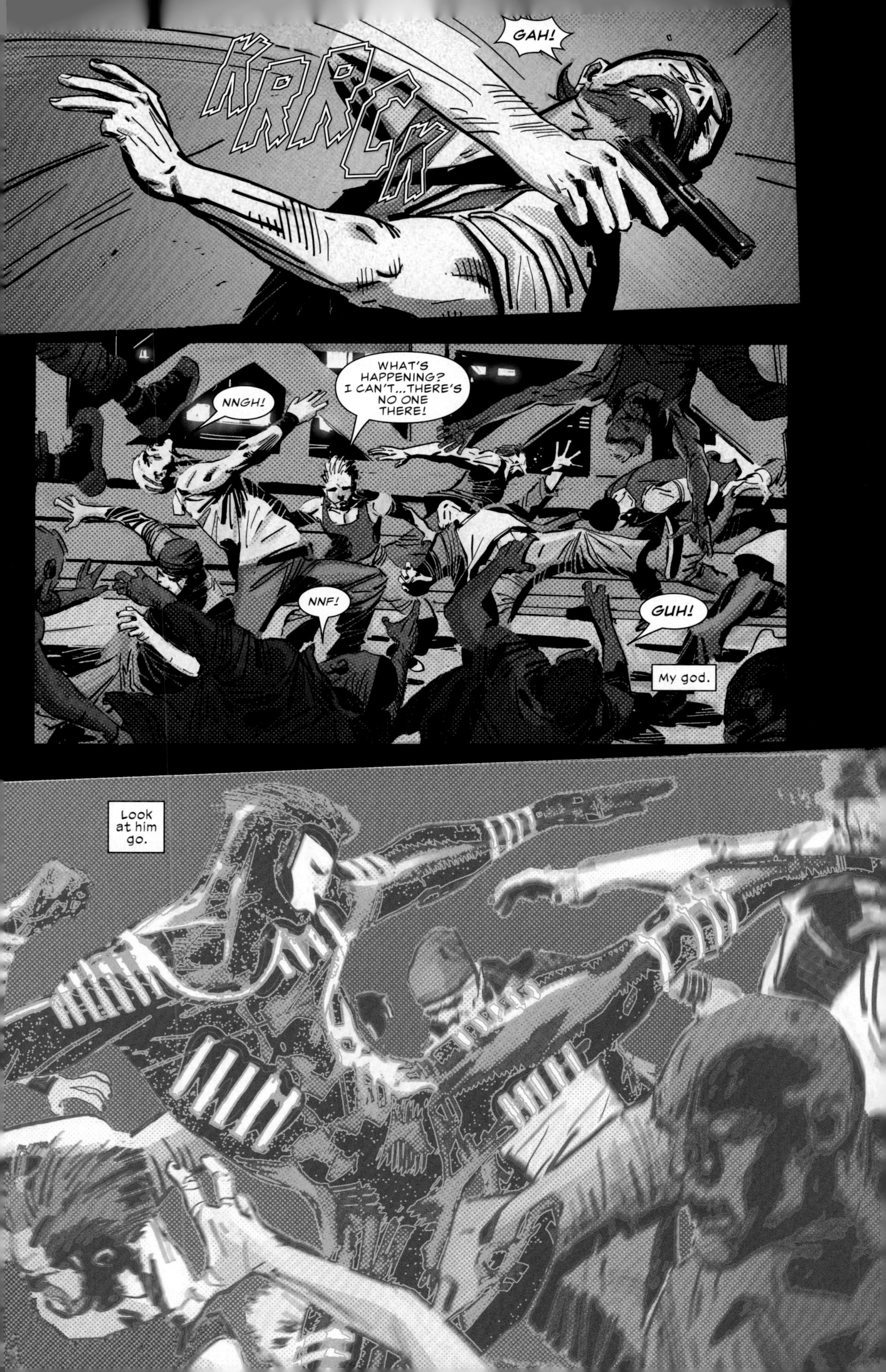
GAH!
KRRCK
NNGH!
WHAT'S HAPPENING? I CAN'T...THERE'S NO ONE THERE!
NNF!
GUH!
My god.
Look at him go.

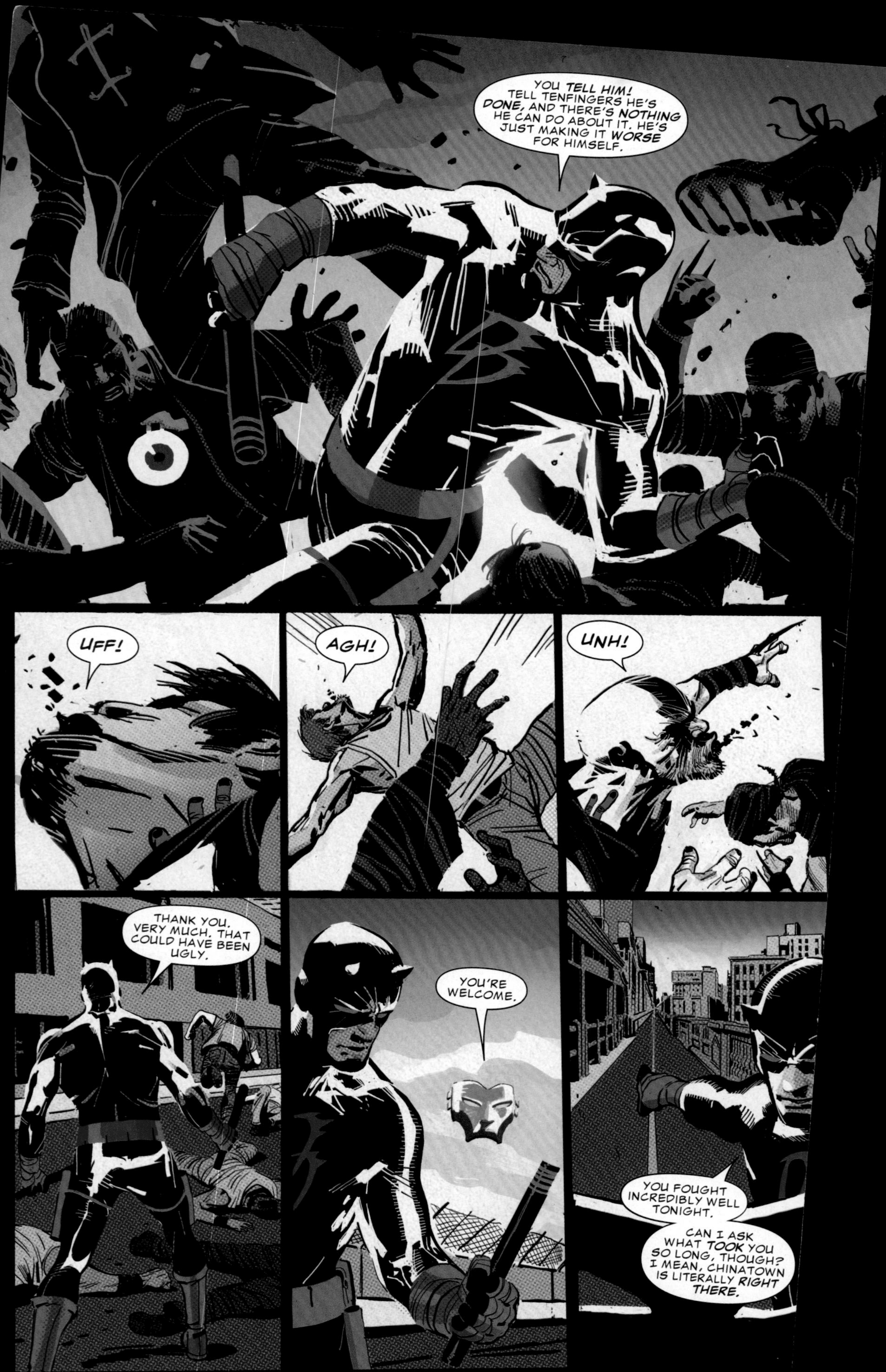
YOU TELL HIM! TELL TENFINGERS HE'S DONE, AND THERE'S NOTHING HE CAN DO ABOUT IT. HE'S JUST MAKING IT WORSE FOR HIMSELF.
UFF!
AGH!
UNH!
THANK YOU. VERY MUCH. THAT COULD HAVE BEEN UGLY.
YOU'RE WELCOME.
YOU FOUGHT INCREDIBLY WELL TONIGHT.
CAN I ASK WHAT TOOK YOU SO LONG, THOUGH? I MEAN, CHINATOWN IS LITERALLY RIGHT THERE.

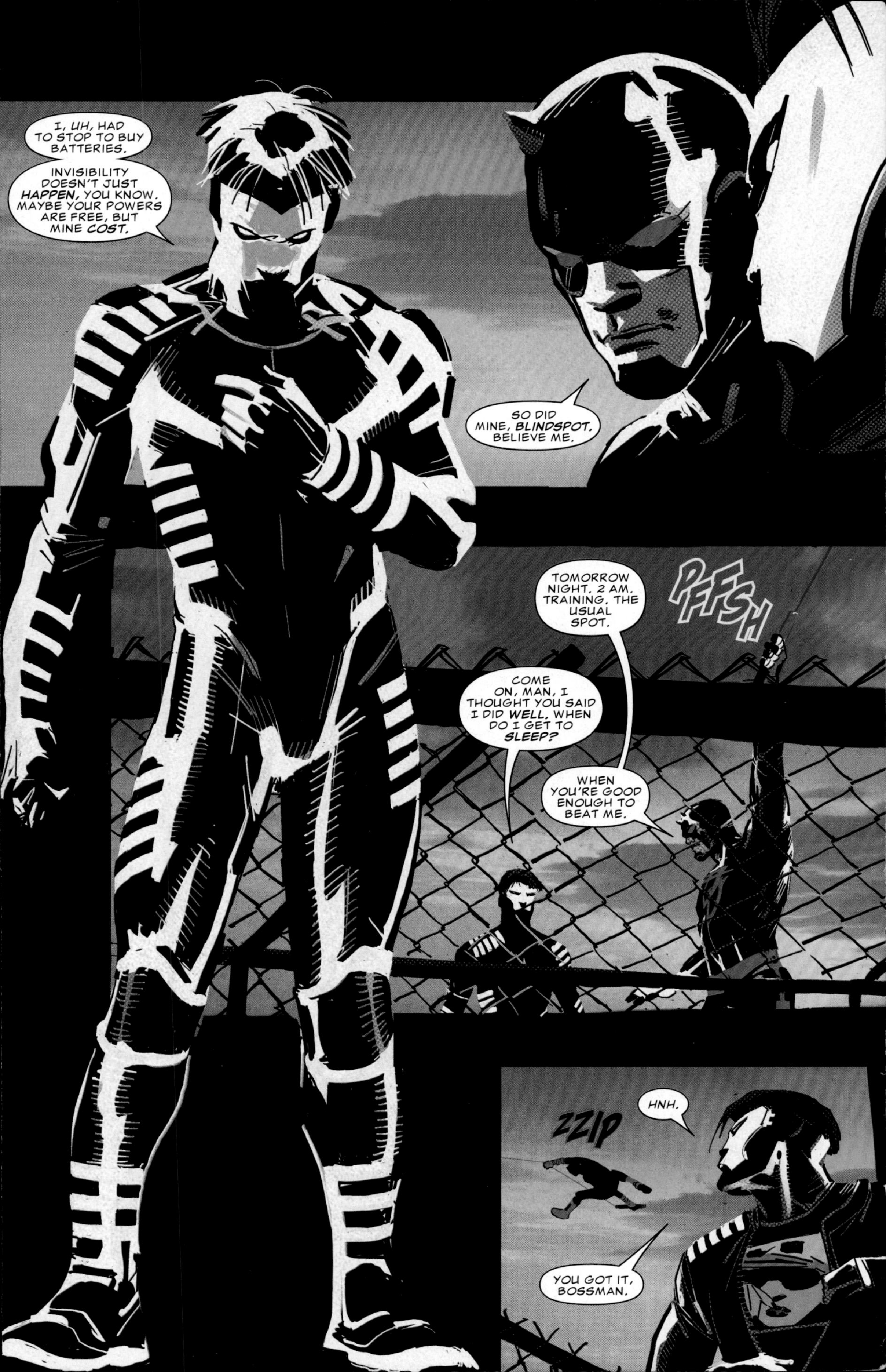
I, UH, HAD TO STOP TO BUY BATTERIES.
INVISIBILITY DOESN'T JUST HAPPEN, YOU KNOW. MAYBE YOUR POWERS ARE FREE, BUT MINE COST.
SO DID MINE, BLINDSPOT. BELIEVE ME.
TOMORROW NIGHT, 2 AM. TRAINING, THE USUAL SPOT.
PFFSH
COME ON, MAN, I THOUGHT YOU SAID I DID WELL. WHEN DO I GET TO SLEEP?
WHEN YOU'RE GOOD ENOUGH TO BEAT ME.
ZZIP
HNH.
YOU GOT IT, BOSSMAN.

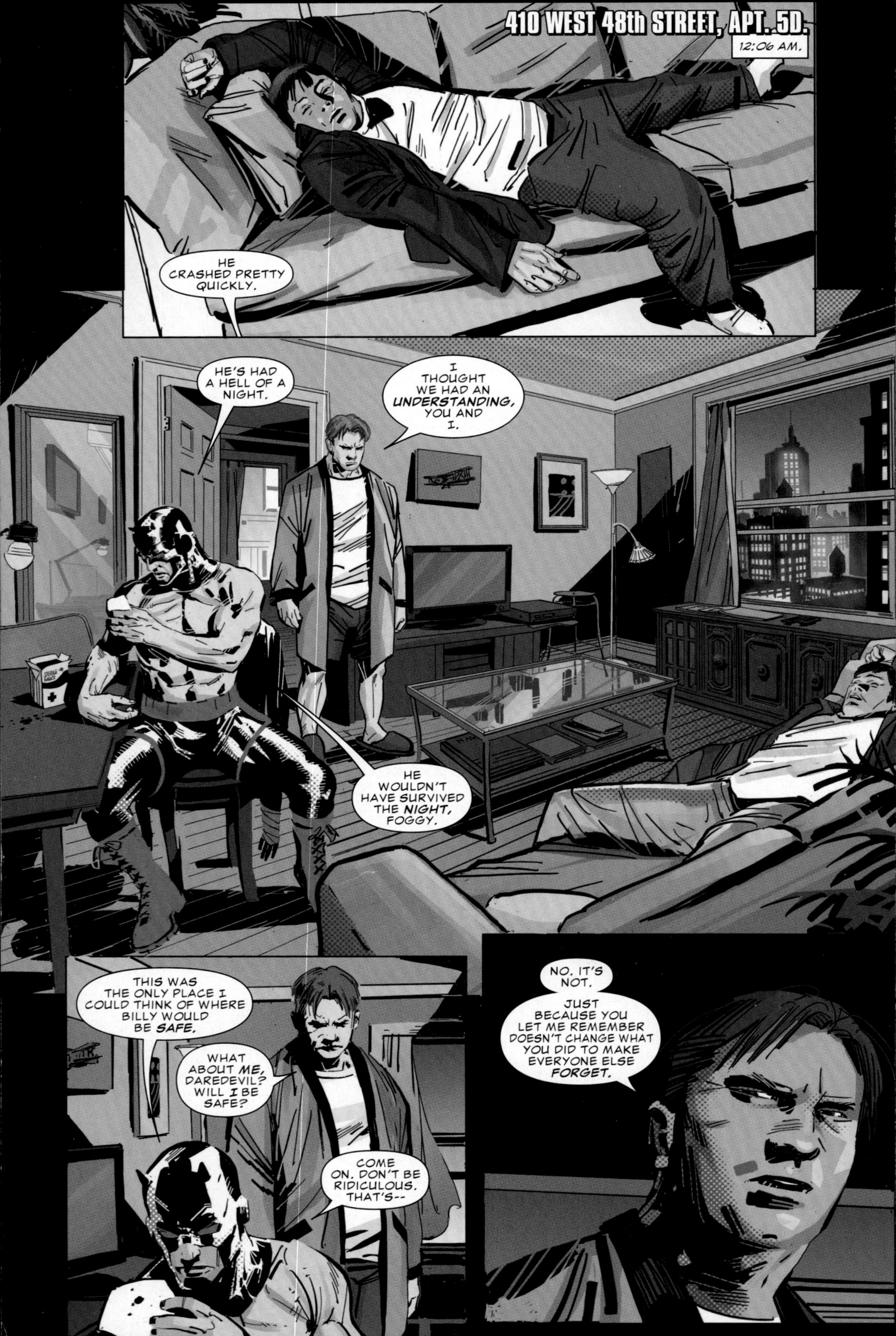
410 WEST 48th STREET, APT. 5D.
12:06 AM.
HE CRASHED PRETTY QUICKLY.
HE'S HAD A HELL OF A NIGHT.
I THOUGHT WE HAD AN UNDERSTANDING, YOU AND I.
HE WOULDN'T HAVE SURVIVED THE NIGHT, FOGGY.
THIS WAS THE ONLY PLACE I COULD THINK OF WHERE BILLY WOULD BE SAFE.
WHAT ABOUT ME, DAREDEVIL? WILL I BE SAFE?
COME ON. DON'T BE RIDICULOUS. THAT'S--
NO. IT'S NOT.
JUST BECAUSE YOU LET ME REMEMBER DOESN'T CHANGE WHAT YOU DID TO MAKE EVERYONE ELSE FORGET.

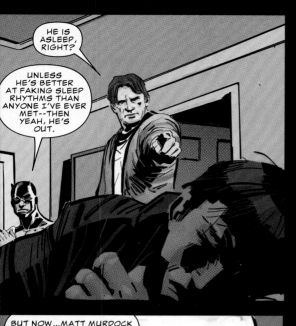

HE IS ASLEEP, RIGHT?

UNLESS HE'S BETTER AT FAKING SLEEP RHYTHMS THAN ANYONE I'VE EVER MET--THEN YEAH, HE'S OUT.

GOOD. LISTEN, I DIDN'T *ASK* TO BE THE ONLY PERSON LEFT WHO KNOWS DAREDEVIL'S REAL NAME. I DON'T WANT TO BE YOUR *CONSCIENCE*. I DON'T WANT TO BE YOUR *SAFE HARBOR*.

I *HAD* TO, FOGGY. MATT MURDOCK AND DAREDEVIL-- THEY WERE BECOMING EACH OTHER'S WORST ENEMIES.

BUT NOW...MATT MURDOCK CAN LIVE HIS LIFE, AND DAREDEVIL CAN TAKE RISKS AGAIN.

EVERYTHING I HAD TO DO TO GET HERE WAS WORTH IT.

AND THAT *KID* YOU'RE WORKING WITH? YOU DON'T KNOW ANYTHING *ABOUT* HIM. YOU'RE TRUSTING HIM WITH YOUR *LIFE*. WHY?

YOU JUST SAID IT, FOGGY. BECAUSE I *TRUST* HIM. AND HE NEEDS ME. I'M FEELING THIS OUT AS I GO, BUT BLINDSPOT IS THE ONE THING I'M *SURE* IS RIGHT.

THIS IS THE LAST TIME I HELP YOU. NEVER AGAIN.

MATT.

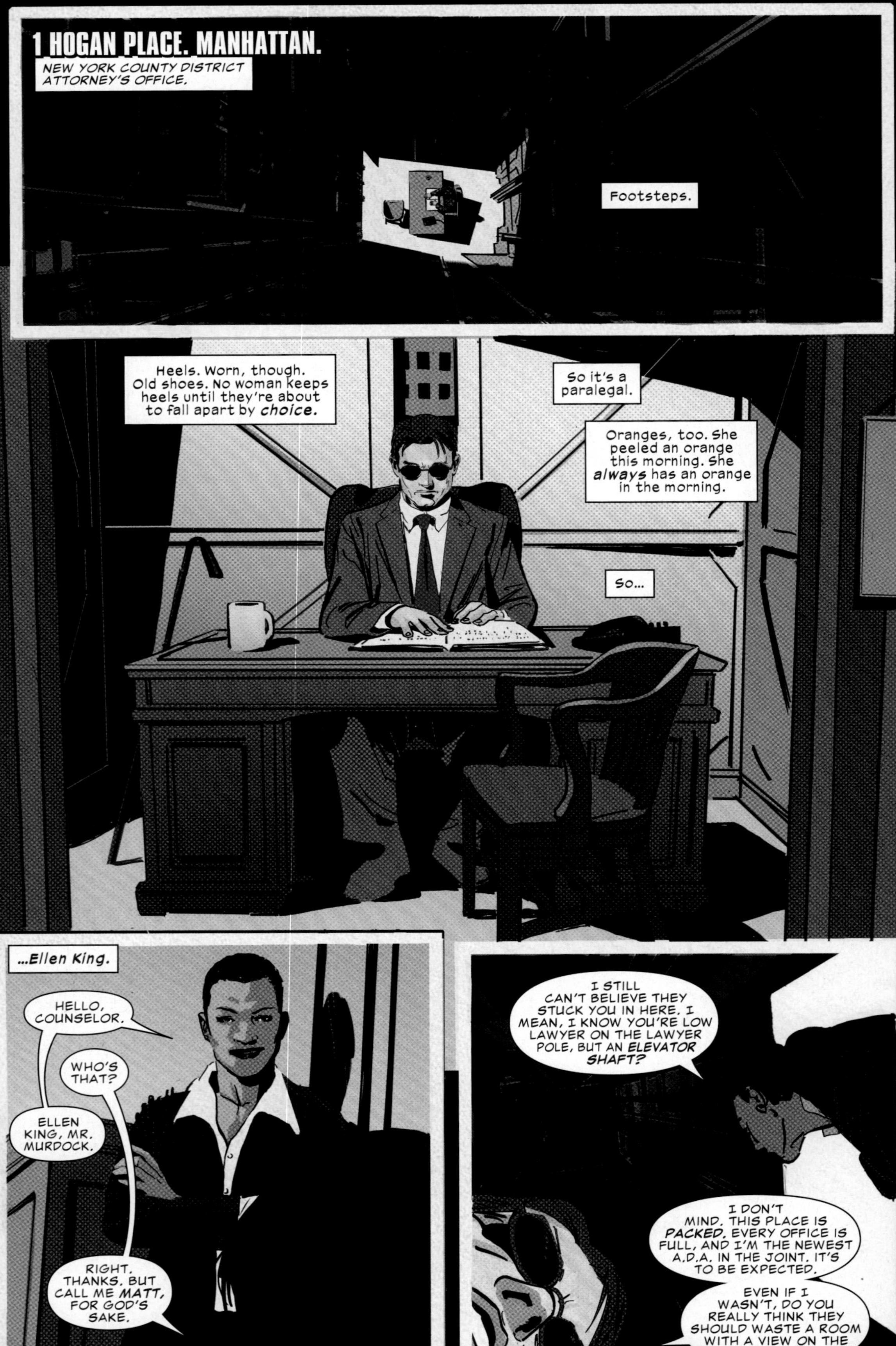
1 HOGAN PLACE. MANHATTAN.
NEW YORK COUNTY DISTRICT ATTORNEY'S OFFICE.
Footsteps.
Heels. Worn, though. Old shoes. No woman keeps heels until they're about to fall apart by *choice.*
So it's a paralegal.
Oranges, too. She peeled an orange this morning. She *always* has an orange in the morning.
So...
...*Ellen King.*
HELLO, COUNSELOR.
WHO'S THAT?
ELLEN KING, MR. MURDOCK.
RIGHT. THANKS. BUT CALL ME *MATT*, FOR GOD'S SAKE.
I STILL CAN'T BELIEVE THEY STUCK YOU IN HERE. I MEAN, I KNOW YOU'RE LOW LAWYER ON THE LAWYER POLE, BUT AN *ELEVATOR SHAFT?*
I DON'T MIND. THIS PLACE IS *PACKED.* EVERY OFFICE IS FULL, AND I'M THE NEWEST A.D.A. IN THE JOINT. IT'S TO BE EXPECTED.
EVEN IF I WASN'T, DO YOU REALLY THINK THEY SHOULD WASTE A ROOM WITH A VIEW ON THE *BLIND GUY?*

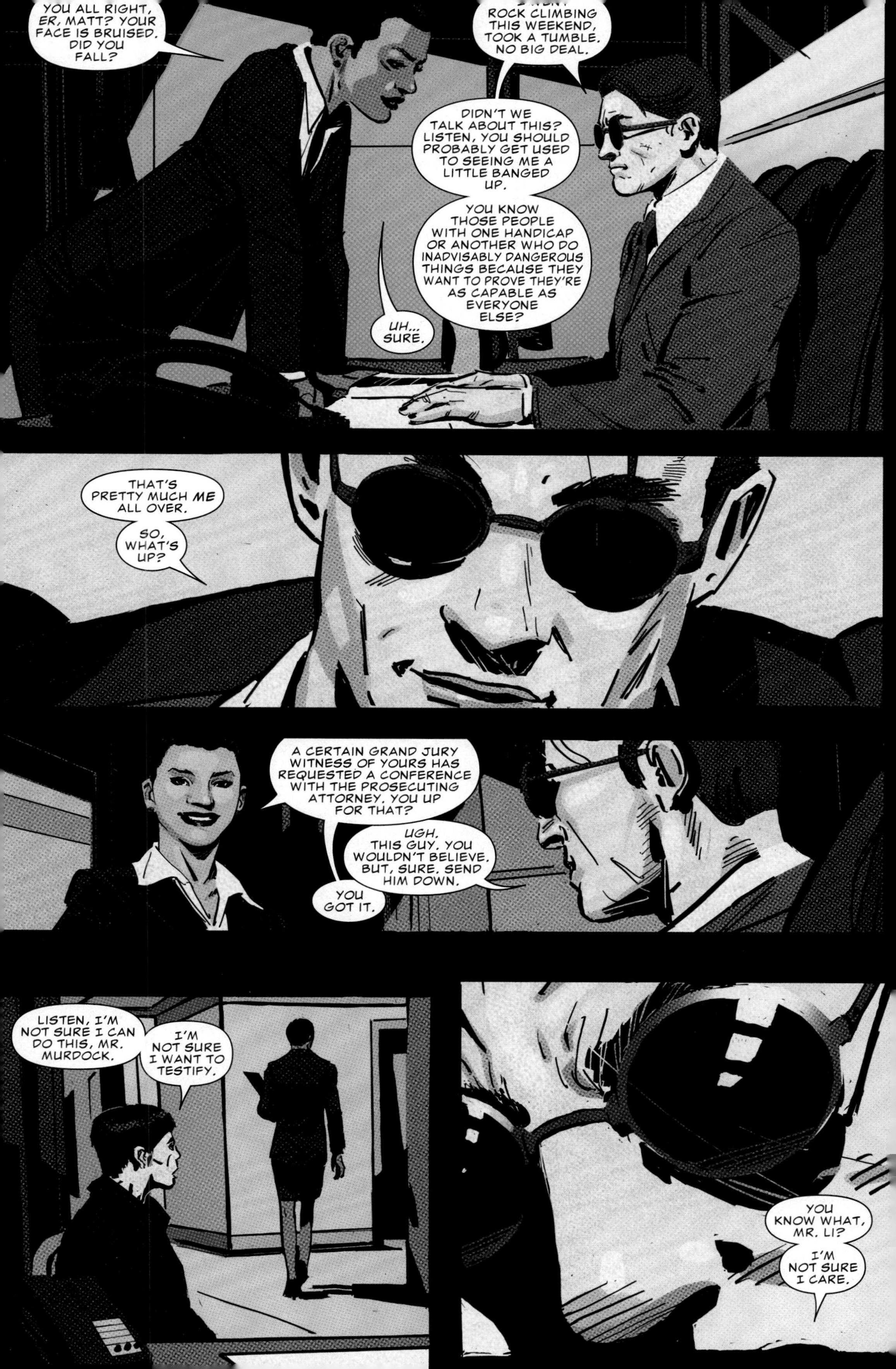
YOU ALL RIGHT, ER, MATT? YOUR FACE IS BRUISED. DID YOU FALL?
ROCK CLIMBING THIS WEEKEND, TOOK A TUMBLE. NO BIG DEAL.
DIDN'T WE TALK ABOUT THIS? LISTEN, YOU SHOULD PROBABLY GET USED TO SEEING ME A LITTLE BANGED UP.
YOU KNOW THOSE PEOPLE WITH ONE HANDICAP OR ANOTHER WHO DO INADVISABLY DANGEROUS THINGS BECAUSE THEY WANT TO PROVE THEY'RE AS CAPABLE AS EVERYONE ELSE?
UH... SURE.
THAT'S PRETTY MUCH ME ALL OVER.
SO, WHAT'S UP?
A CERTAIN GRAND JURY WITNESS OF YOURS HAS REQUESTED A CONFERENCE WITH THE PROSECUTING ATTORNEY. YOU UP FOR THAT?
UGH. THIS GUY. YOU WOULDN'T BELIEVE. BUT, SURE. SEND HIM DOWN.
YOU GOT IT.
LISTEN, I'M NOT SURE I CAN DO THIS, MR. MURDOCK.
I'M NOT SURE I WANT TO TESTIFY.
YOU KNOW WHAT, MR. LI?
I'M NOT SURE I CARE.

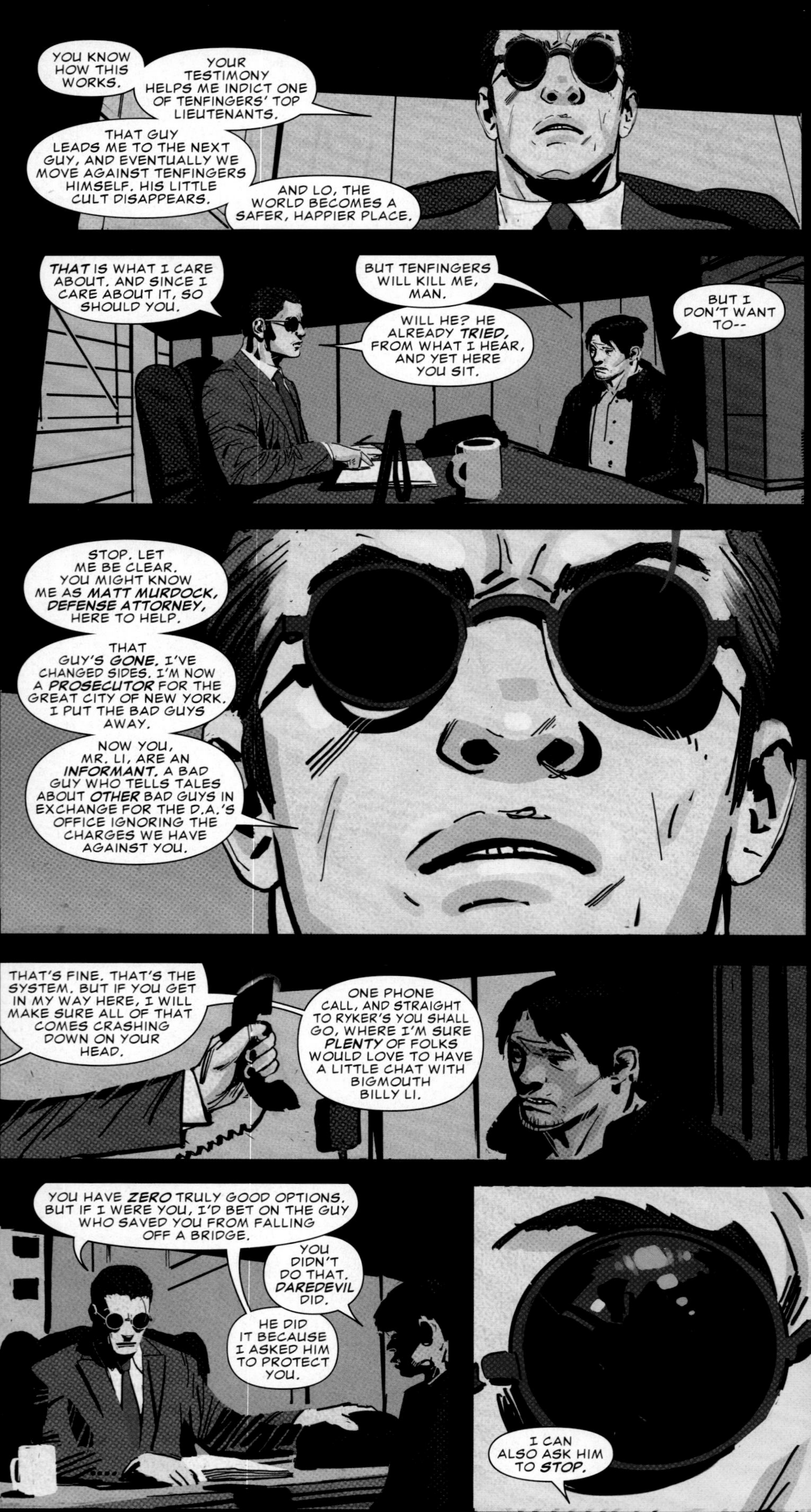
YOU KNOW HOW THIS WORKS.
YOUR TESTIMONY HELPS ME INDICT ONE OF TENFINGERS' TOP LIEUTENANTS.
THAT GUY LEADS ME TO THE NEXT GUY, AND EVENTUALLY WE MOVE AGAINST TENFINGERS HIMSELF. HIS LITTLE CULT DISAPPEARS.
AND LO, THE WORLD BECOMES A SAFER, HAPPIER PLACE.
THAT IS WHAT I CARE ABOUT. AND SINCE I CARE ABOUT IT, SO SHOULD YOU.
BUT TENFINGERS WILL KILL ME, MAN.
WILL HE? HE ALREADY TRIED, FROM WHAT I HEAR, AND YET HERE YOU SIT.
BUT I DON'T WANT TO--
STOP. LET ME BE CLEAR. YOU MIGHT KNOW ME AS MATT MURDOCK, DEFENSE ATTORNEY, HERE TO HELP.
THAT GUY'S GONE. I'VE CHANGED SIDES. I'M NOW A PROSECUTOR FOR THE GREAT CITY OF NEW YORK. I PUT THE BAD GUYS AWAY.
NOW YOU, MR. LI, ARE AN INFORMANT. A BAD GUY WHO TELLS TALES ABOUT OTHER BAD GUYS IN EXCHANGE FOR THE D.A.'S OFFICE IGNORING THE CHARGES WE HAVE AGAINST YOU.
THAT'S FINE. THAT'S THE SYSTEM. BUT IF YOU GET IN MY WAY HERE, I WILL MAKE SURE ALL OF THAT COMES CRASHING DOWN ON YOUR HEAD.
ONE PHONE CALL, AND STRAIGHT TO RYKER'S YOU SHALL GO, WHERE I'M SURE PLENTY OF FOLKS WOULD LOVE TO HAVE A LITTLE CHAT WITH BIGMOUTH BILLY LI.
YOU HAVE ZERO TRULY GOOD OPTIONS. BUT IF I WERE YOU, I'D BET ON THE GUY WHO SAVED YOU FROM FALLING OFF A BRIDGE.
YOU DIDN'T DO THAT. DAREDEVIL DID.
HE DID IT BECAUSE I ASKED HIM TO PROTECT YOU.
I CAN ALSO ASK HIM TO STOP.

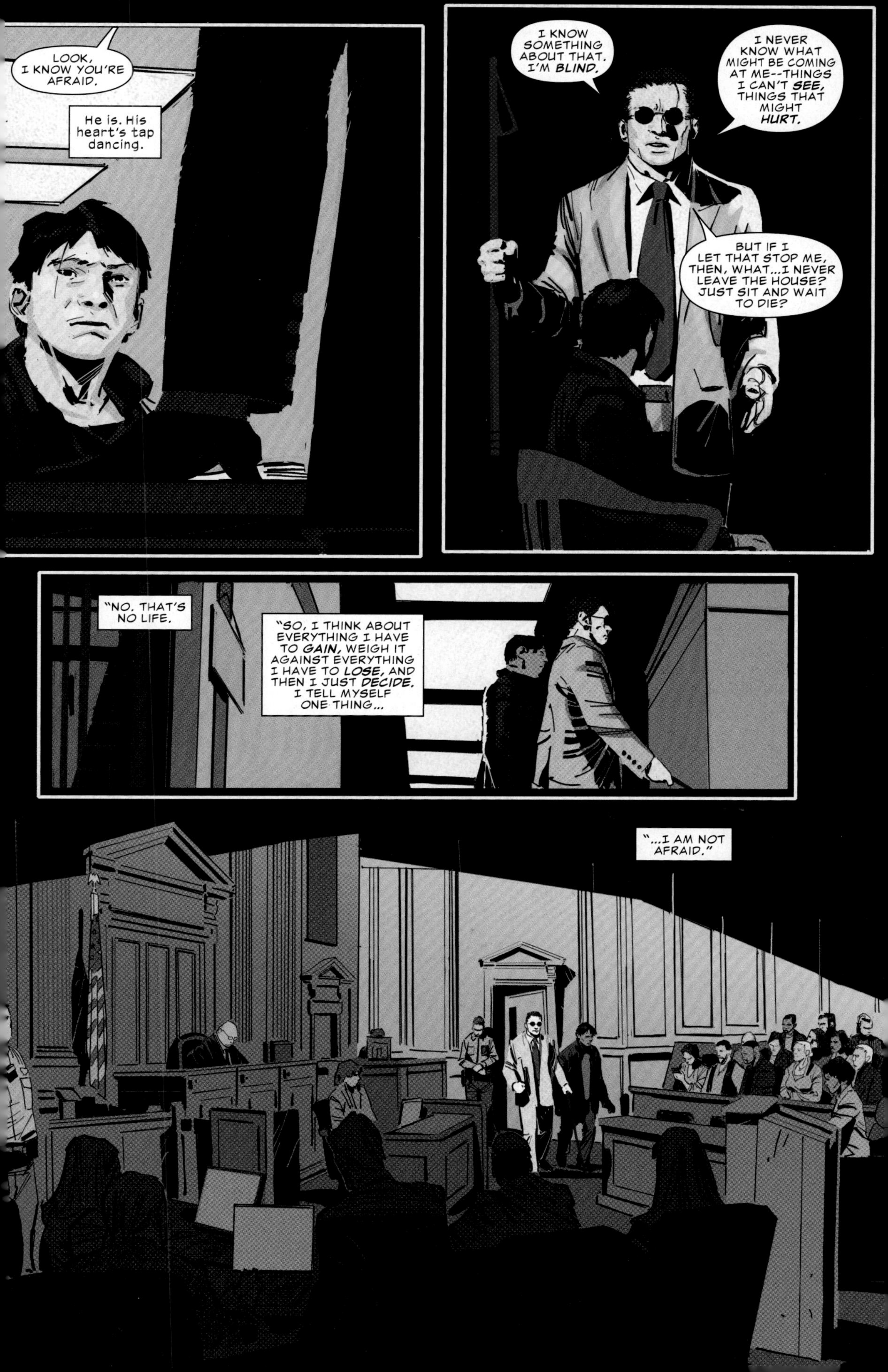
LOOK, I KNOW YOU'RE AFRAID.
He is. His heart's tap dancing.
I KNOW SOMETHING ABOUT THAT. I'M BLIND.
I NEVER KNOW WHAT MIGHT BE COMING AT ME--THINGS I CAN'T SEE, THINGS THAT MIGHT HURT.
BUT IF I LET THAT STOP ME, THEN, WHAT...I NEVER LEAVE THE HOUSE? JUST SIT AND WAIT TO DIE?
"NO. THAT'S NO LIFE.
"SO, I THINK ABOUT EVERYTHING I HAVE TO GAIN, WEIGH IT AGAINST EVERYTHING I HAVE TO LOSE, AND THEN I JUST DECIDE. I TELL MYSELF ONE THING...
"...I AM NOT AFRAID."

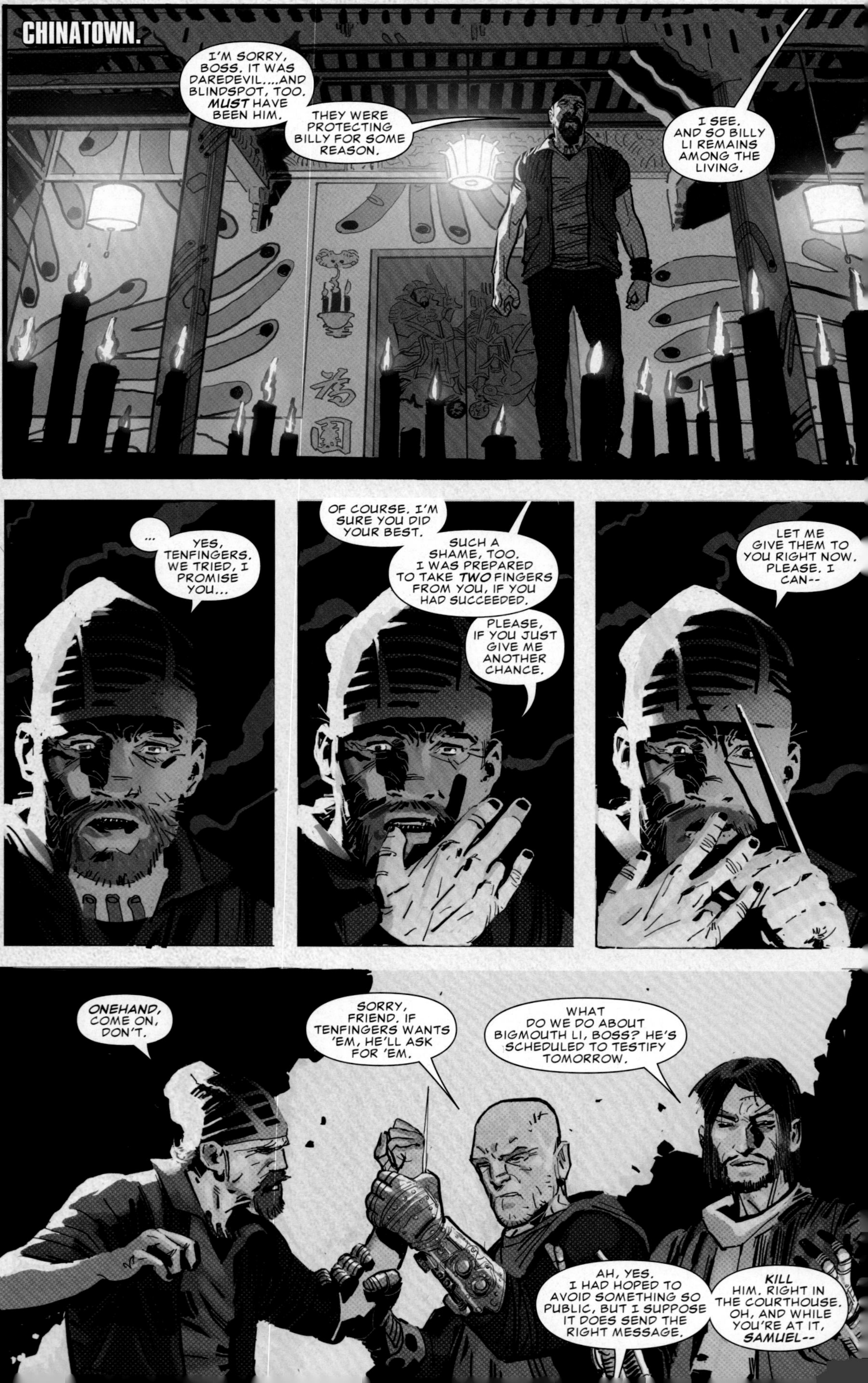
CHINATOWN.
I'M SORRY, BOSS. IT WAS DAREDEVIL....AND BLINDSPOT, TOO. MUST HAVE BEEN HIM.
THEY WERE PROTECTING BILLY FOR SOME REASON.
I SEE. AND SO BILLY LI REMAINS AMONG THE LIVING.
...
YES, TENFINGERS. WE TRIED, I PROMISE YOU...
OF COURSE. I'M SURE YOU DID YOUR BEST.
SUCH A SHAME, TOO. I WAS PREPARED TO TAKE TWO FINGERS FROM YOU, IF YOU HAD SUCCEEDED.
PLEASE, IF YOU JUST GIVE ME ANOTHER CHANCE.
LET ME GIVE THEM TO YOU RIGHT NOW. PLEASE. I CAN--
ONEHAND, COME ON, DON'T.
SORRY, FRIEND. IF TENFINGERS WANTS 'EM, HE'LL ASK FOR 'EM.
WHAT DO WE DO ABOUT BIGMOUTH LI, BOSS? HE'S SCHEDULED TO TESTIFY TOMORROW.
AH, YES. I HAD HOPED TO AVOID SOMETHING SO PUBLIC, BUT I SUPPOSE IT DOES SEND THE RIGHT MESSAGE.
KILL HIM. RIGHT IN THE COURTHOUSE. OH, AND WHILE YOU'RE AT IT, SAMUEL--

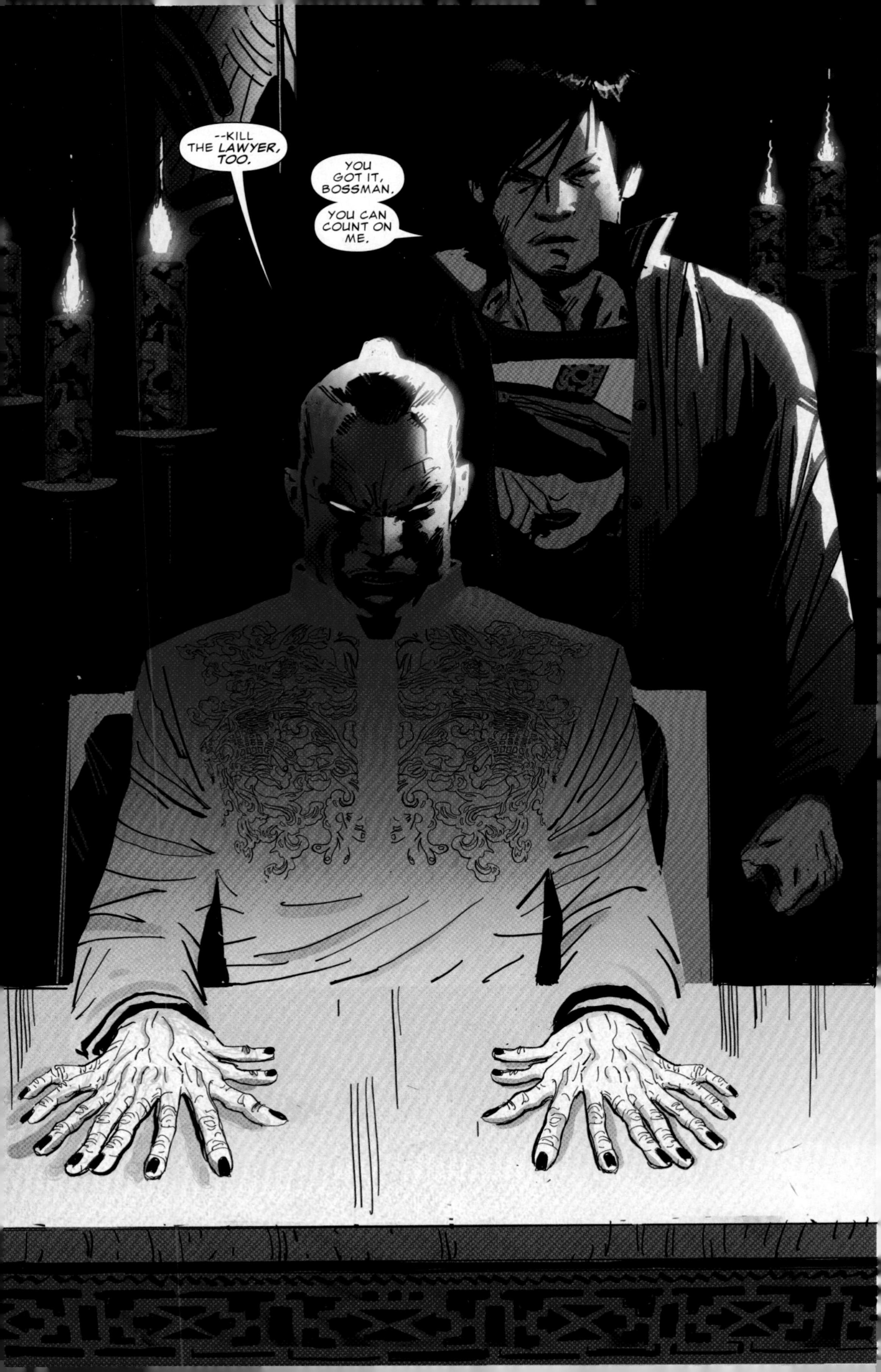
--KILL THE LAWYER, TOO.
YOU GOT IT, BOSSMAN.
YOU CAN COUNT ON ME.

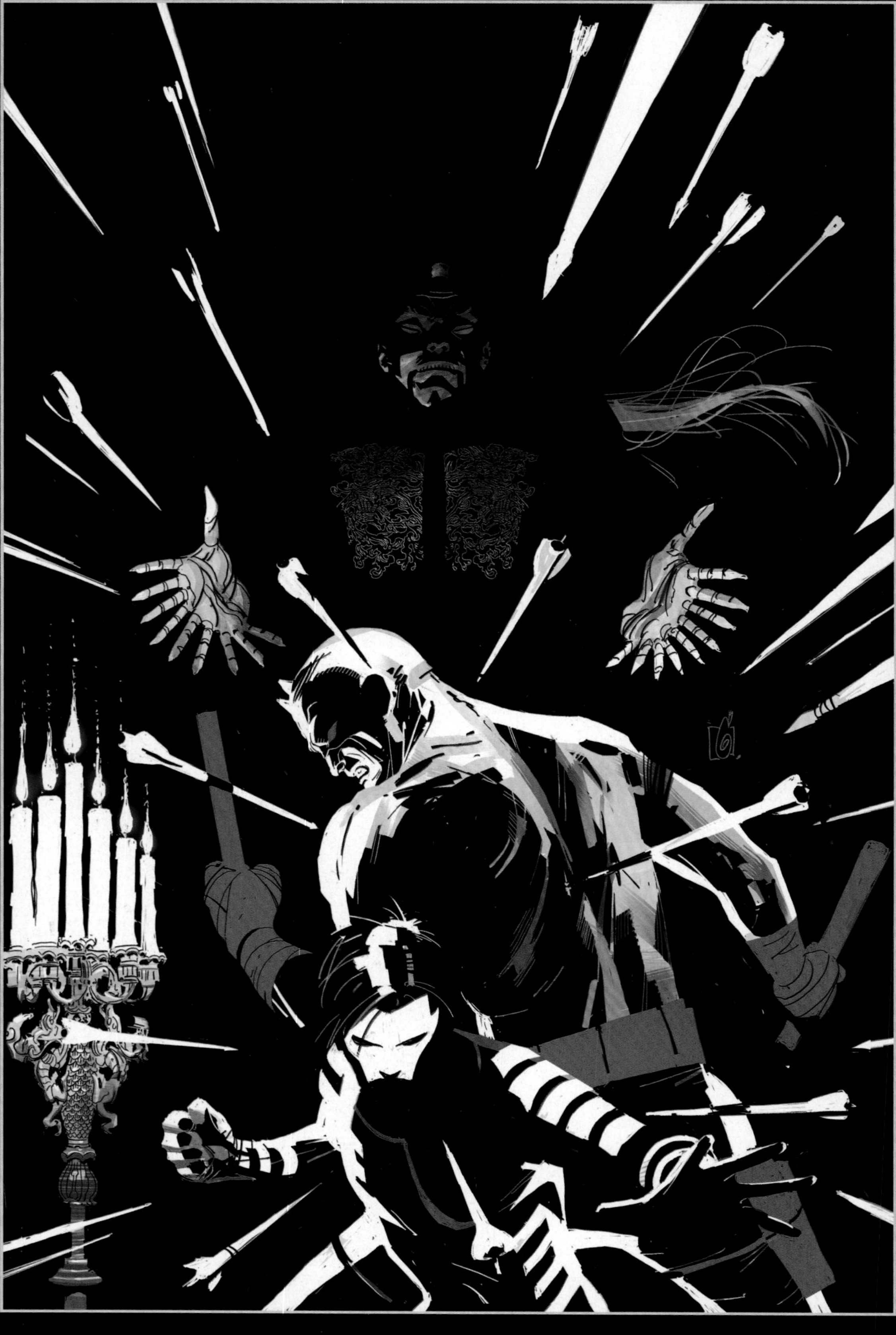

7

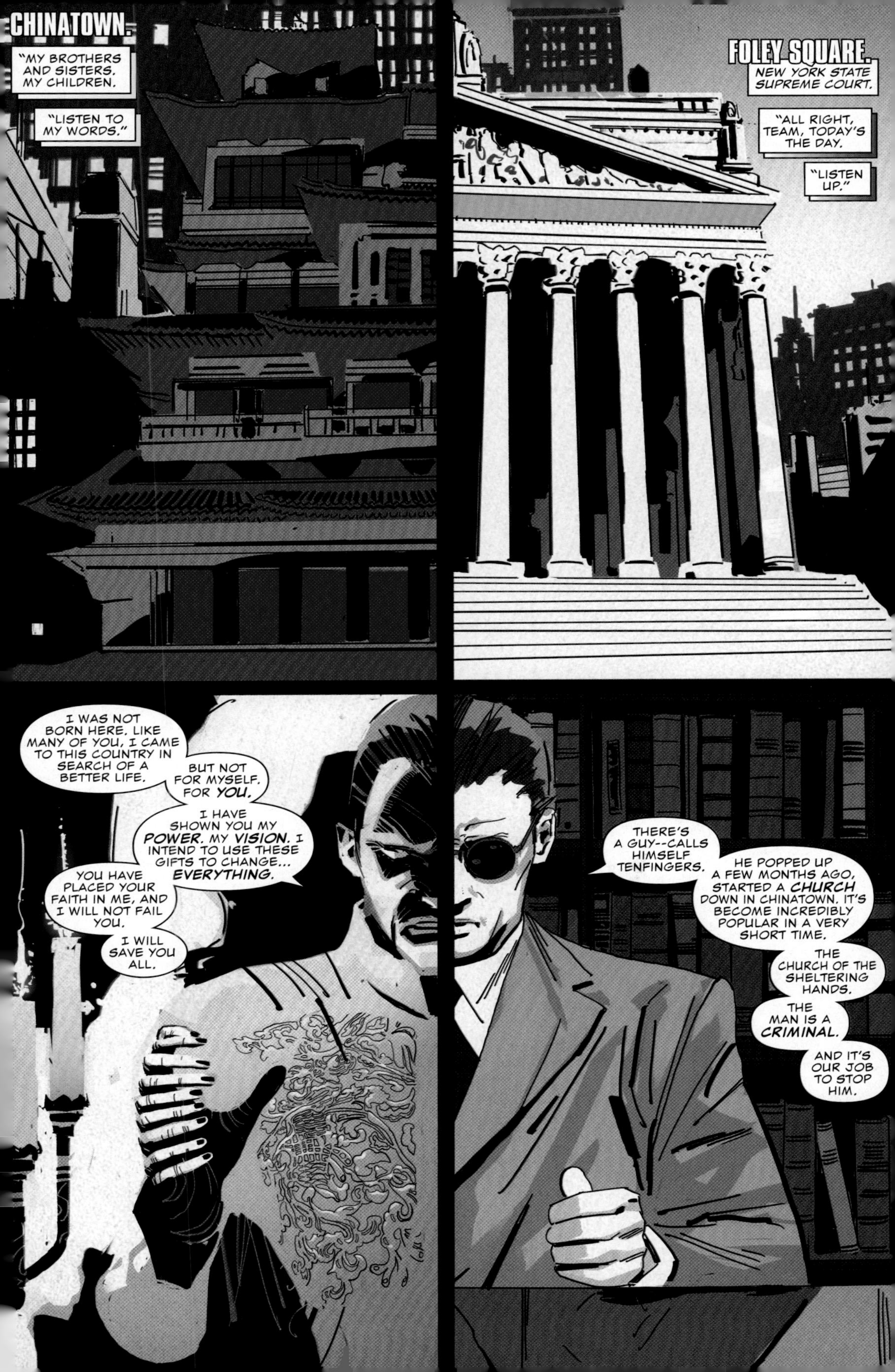
CHINATOWN.
"MY BROTHERS AND SISTERS. MY CHILDREN.
"LISTEN TO MY WORDS."
FOLEY SQUARE. NEW YORK STATE SUPREME COURT.
"ALL RIGHT, TEAM, TODAY'S THE DAY.
"LISTEN UP."
I WAS NOT BORN HERE. LIKE MANY OF YOU, I CAME TO THIS COUNTRY IN SEARCH OF A BETTER LIFE.
BUT NOT FOR MYSELF. FOR YOU.
I HAVE SHOWN YOU MY POWER. MY VISION. I INTEND TO USE THESE GIFTS TO CHANGE... EVERYTHING.
YOU HAVE PLACED YOUR FAITH IN ME, AND I WILL NOT FAIL YOU.
I WILL SAVE YOU ALL.
THERE'S A GUY--CALLS HIMSELF TENFINGERS.
HE POPPED UP A FEW MONTHS AGO, STARTED A CHURCH DOWN IN CHINATOWN. IT'S BECOME INCREDIBLY POPULAR IN A VERY SHORT TIME.
THE CHURCH OF THE SHELTERING HANDS.
THE MAN IS A CRIMINAL.
AND IT'S OUR JOB TO STOP HIM.

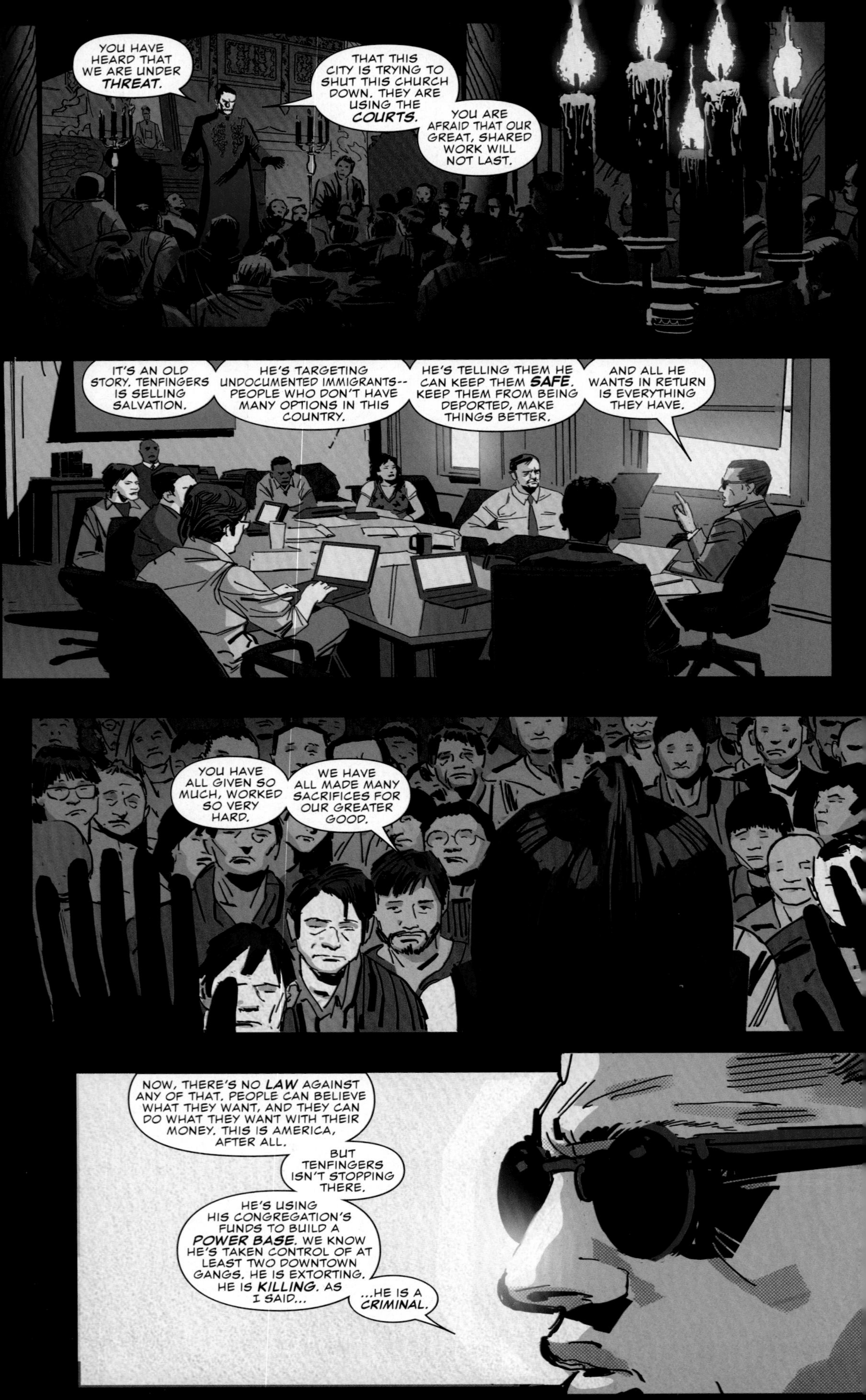
YOU HAVE HEARD THAT WE ARE UNDER THREAT.
THAT THIS CITY IS TRYING TO SHUT THIS CHURCH DOWN. THEY ARE USING THE COURTS.
YOU ARE AFRAID THAT OUR GREAT, SHARED WORK WILL NOT LAST.
IT'S AN OLD STORY. TENFINGERS IS SELLING SALVATION.
HE'S TARGETING UNDOCUMENTED IMMIGRANTS-- PEOPLE WHO DON'T HAVE MANY OPTIONS IN THIS COUNTRY.
HE'S TELLING THEM HE CAN KEEP THEM SAFE. KEEP THEM FROM BEING DEPORTED, MAKE THINGS BETTER.
AND ALL HE WANTS IN RETURN IS EVERYTHING THEY HAVE.
YOU HAVE ALL GIVEN SO MUCH, WORKED SO VERY HARD.
WE HAVE ALL MADE MANY SACRIFICES FOR OUR GREATER GOOD.
NOW, THERE'S NO LAW AGAINST ANY OF THAT. PEOPLE CAN BELIEVE WHAT THEY WANT, AND THEY CAN DO WHAT THEY WANT WITH THEIR MONEY. THIS IS AMERICA, AFTER ALL.
BUT TENFINGERS ISN'T STOPPING THERE.
HE'S USING HIS CONGREGATION'S FUNDS TO BUILD A POWER BASE. WE KNOW HE'S TAKEN CONTROL OF AT LEAST TWO DOWNTOWN GANGS. HE IS EXTORTING. HE IS KILLING. AS I SAID...
...HE IS A CRIMINAL.

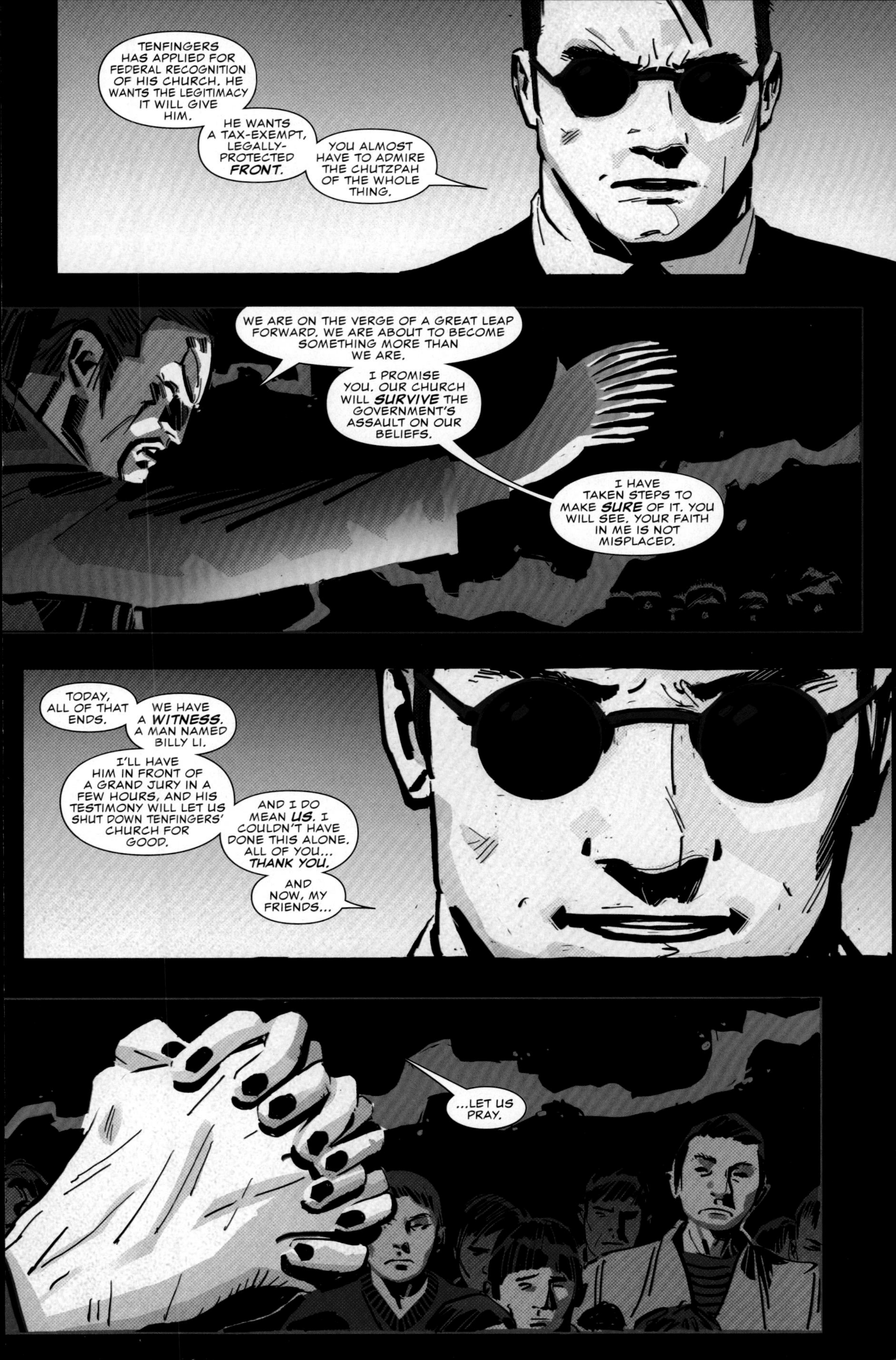
TENFINGERS HAS APPLIED FOR FEDERAL RECOGNITION OF HIS CHURCH. HE WANTS THE LEGITIMACY IT WILL GIVE HIM.
HE WANTS A TAX-EXEMPT, LEGALLY-PROTECTED ***FRONT.***
YOU ALMOST HAVE TO ADMIRE THE CHUTZPAH OF THE WHOLE THING.
WE ARE ON THE VERGE OF A GREAT LEAP FORWARD. WE ARE ABOUT TO BECOME SOMETHING MORE THAN WE ARE.
I PROMISE YOU. OUR CHURCH WILL ***SURVIVE*** THE GOVERNMENT'S ASSAULT ON OUR BELIEFS.
I HAVE TAKEN STEPS TO MAKE ***SURE*** OF IT. YOU WILL SEE. YOUR FAITH IN ME IS NOT MISPLACED.
TODAY, ALL OF THAT ENDS.
WE HAVE A ***WITNESS.*** A MAN NAMED BILLY LI.
I'LL HAVE HIM IN FRONT OF A GRAND JURY IN A FEW HOURS, AND HIS TESTIMONY WILL LET US SHUT DOWN TENFINGERS' CHURCH FOR GOOD.
AND I DO MEAN ***US.*** I COULDN'T HAVE DONE THIS ALONE. ALL OF YOU... ***THANK YOU.***
AND NOW, MY FRIENDS...
...LET US PRAY.

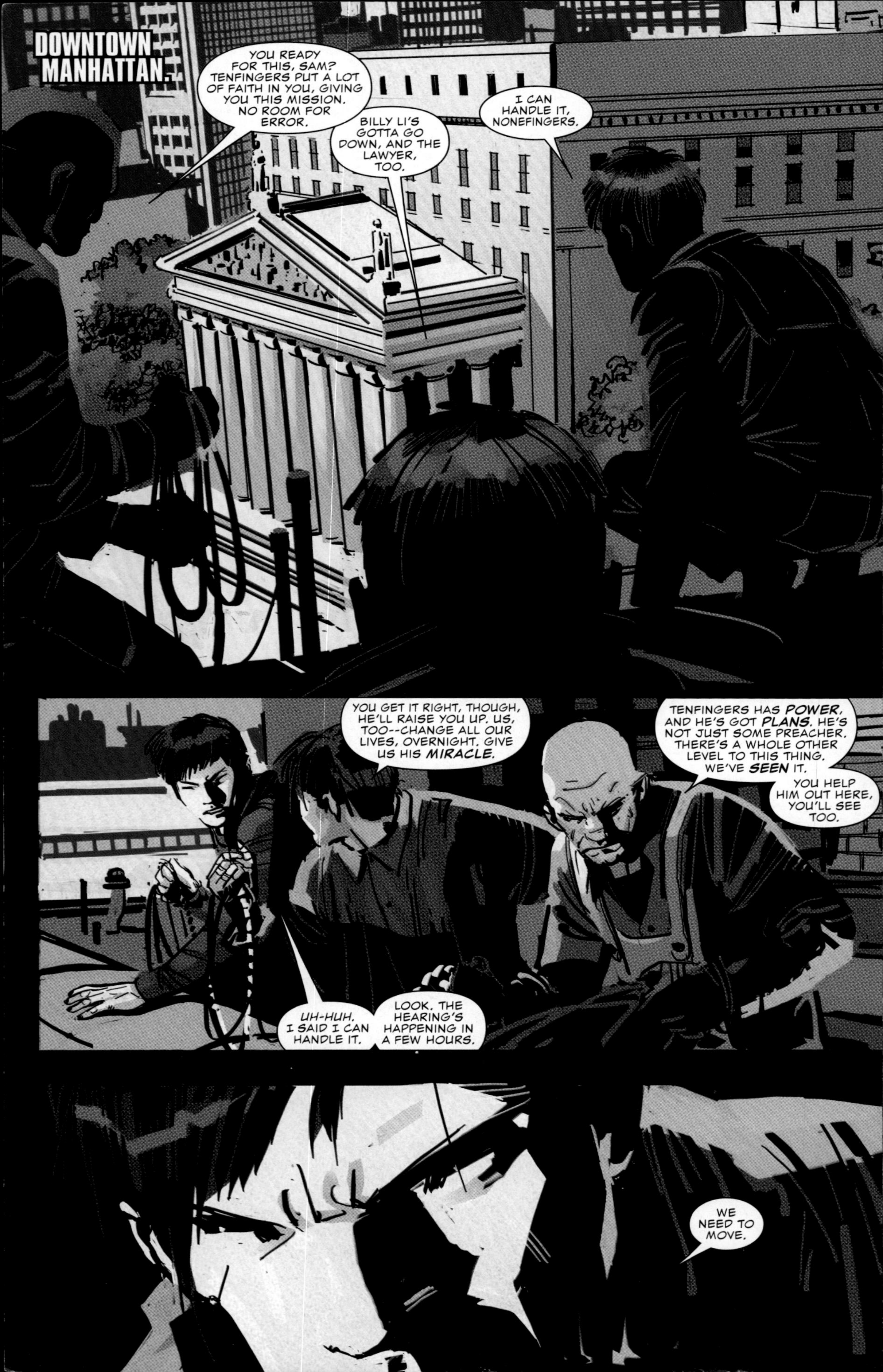
DOWNTOWN MANHATTAN.
YOU READY FOR THIS, SAM? TENFINGERS PUT A LOT OF FAITH IN YOU, GIVING YOU THIS MISSION. NO ROOM FOR ERROR.
BILLY LI'S GOTTA GO DOWN, AND THE LAWYER, TOO.
I CAN HANDLE IT, NONEFINGERS.
YOU GET IT RIGHT, THOUGH, HE'LL RAISE YOU UP. US, TOO--CHANGE ALL OUR LIVES, OVERNIGHT. GIVE US HIS MIRACLE.
TENFINGERS HAS POWER, AND HE'S GOT PLANS. HE'S NOT JUST SOME PREACHER. THERE'S A WHOLE OTHER LEVEL TO THIS THING. WE'VE SEEN IT.
YOU HELP HIM OUT HERE, YOU'LL SEE TOO.
UH-HUH. I SAID I CAN HANDLE IT.
LOOK. THE HEARING'S HAPPENING IN A FEW HOURS.
WE NEED TO MOVE.

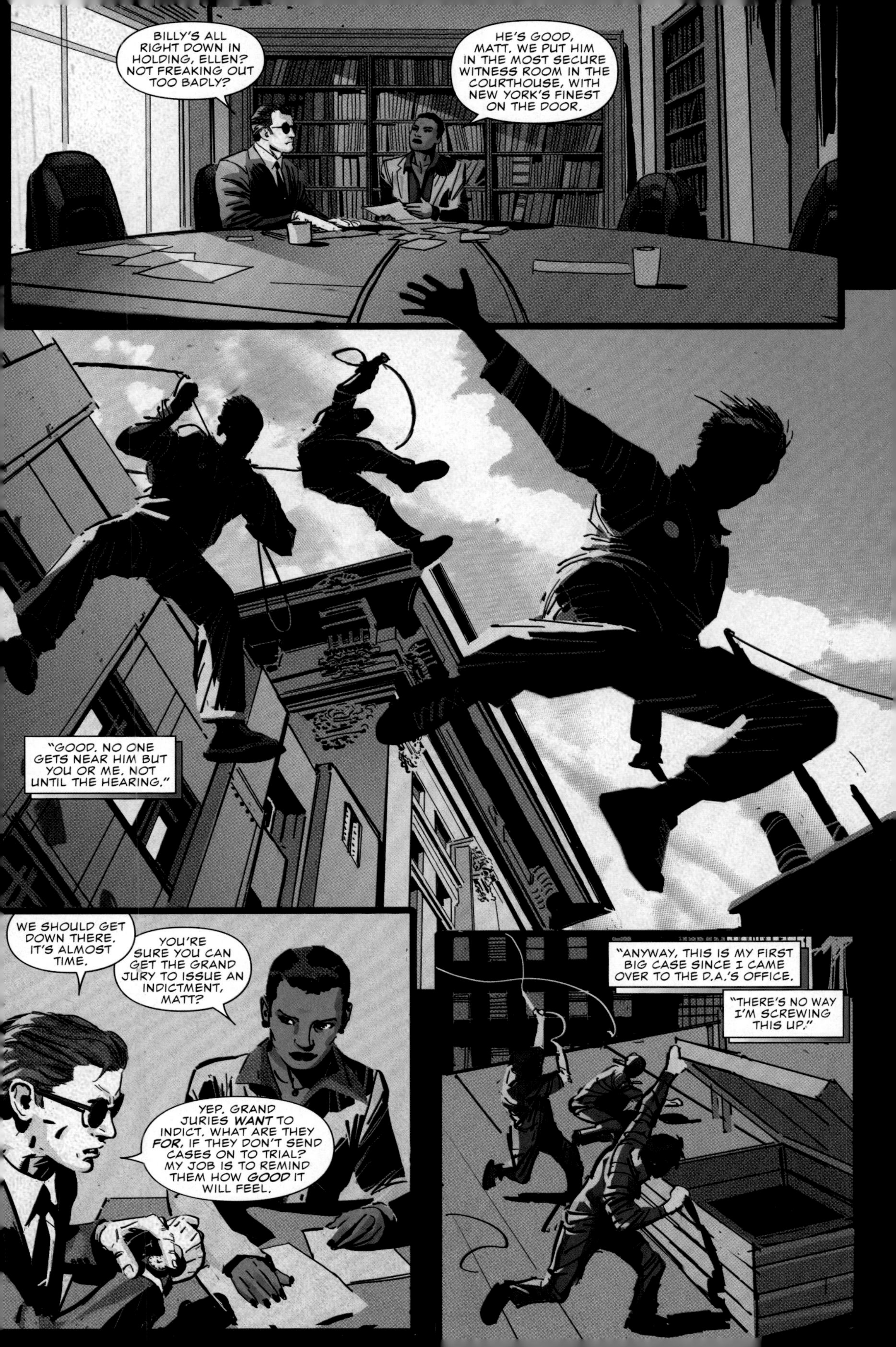
BILLY'S ALL RIGHT DOWN IN HOLDING, ELLEN? NOT FREAKING OUT TOO BADLY?
HE'S GOOD, MATT. WE PUT HIM IN THE MOST SECURE WITNESS ROOM IN THE COURTHOUSE, WITH NEW YORK'S FINEST ON THE DOOR.
"GOOD. NO ONE GETS NEAR HIM BUT YOU OR ME. NOT UNTIL THE HEARING."
WE SHOULD GET DOWN THERE. IT'S ALMOST TIME.
YOU'RE SURE YOU CAN GET THE GRAND JURY TO ISSUE AN INDICTMENT, MATT?
YEP. GRAND JURIES *WANT* TO INDICT. WHAT ARE THEY *FOR*, IF THEY DON'T SEND CASES ON TO TRIAL? MY JOB IS TO REMIND THEM HOW *GOOD* IT WILL FEEL.
"ANYWAY, THIS IS MY FIRST BIG CASE SINCE I CAME OVER TO THE D.A.'S OFFICE.
"THERE'S NO WAY I'M SCREWING THIS UP."

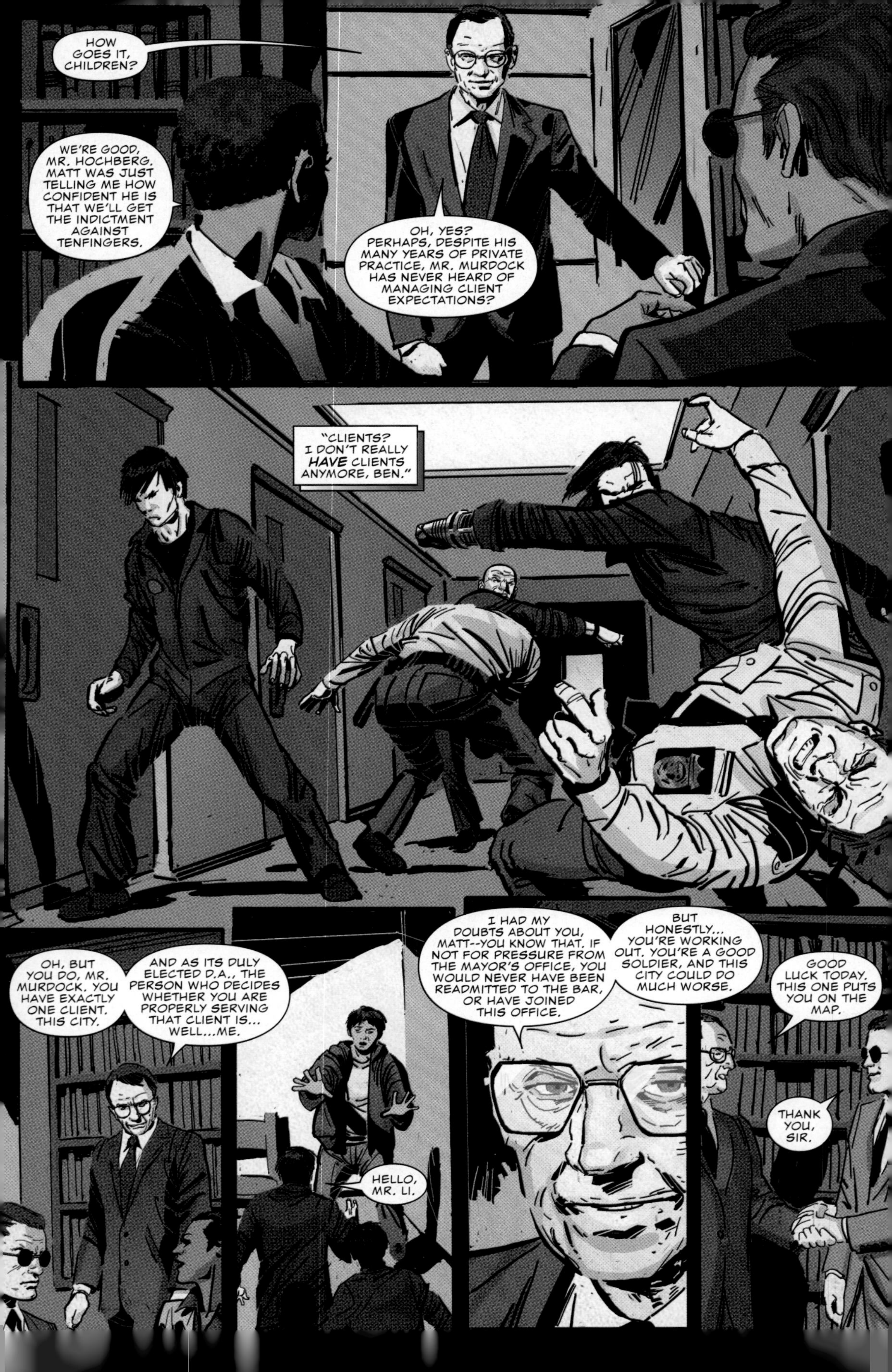

HOW GOES IT, CHILDREN?
WE'RE GOOD, MR. HOCHBERG. MATT WAS JUST TELLING ME HOW CONFIDENT HE IS THAT WE'LL GET THE INDICTMENT AGAINST TENFINGERS.
OH, YES? PERHAPS, DESPITE HIS MANY YEARS OF PRIVATE PRACTICE, MR. MURDOCK HAS NEVER HEARD OF MANAGING CLIENT EXPECTATIONS?
"CLIENTS? I DON'T REALLY HAVE CLIENTS ANYMORE, BEN."
OH, BUT YOU DO, MR. MURDOCK. YOU HAVE EXACTLY ONE CLIENT. THIS CITY.
AND AS ITS DULY ELECTED D.A., THE PERSON WHO DECIDES WHETHER YOU ARE PROPERLY SERVING THAT CLIENT IS... WELL...ME.
HELLO, MR. LI.
I HAD MY DOUBTS ABOUT YOU, MATT--YOU KNOW THAT. IF NOT FOR PRESSURE FROM THE MAYOR'S OFFICE, YOU WOULD NEVER HAVE BEEN READMITTED TO THE BAR, OR HAVE JOINED THIS OFFICE.
BUT HONESTLY... YOU'RE WORKING OUT. YOU'RE A GOOD SOLDIER, AND THIS CITY COULD DO MUCH WORSE.
GOOD LUCK TODAY. THIS ONE PUTS YOU ON THE MAP.
THANK YOU, SIR.

DETENTION LEVEL.

This whole floor reeks of fear.

Behind every one of these doors is a person waiting to go up on the stand and swear to tell the truth, the whole truth and nothing but.

I don't care who you are--that's intimidating.

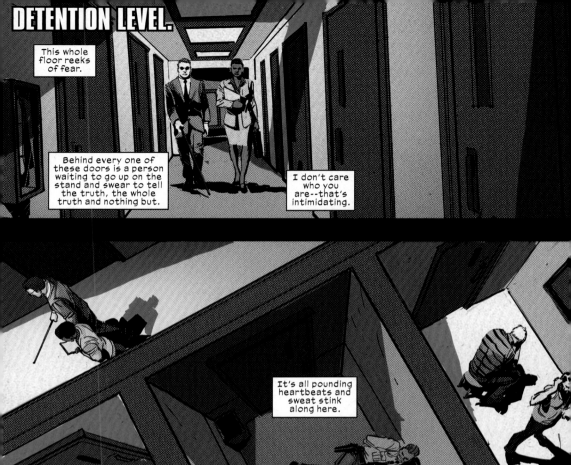

It's all pounding heartbeats and sweat stink along here.

Which I get.

Not in here, though. Billy's pulse is nice and regular. He's cool as a cuke.

That's a good sign.

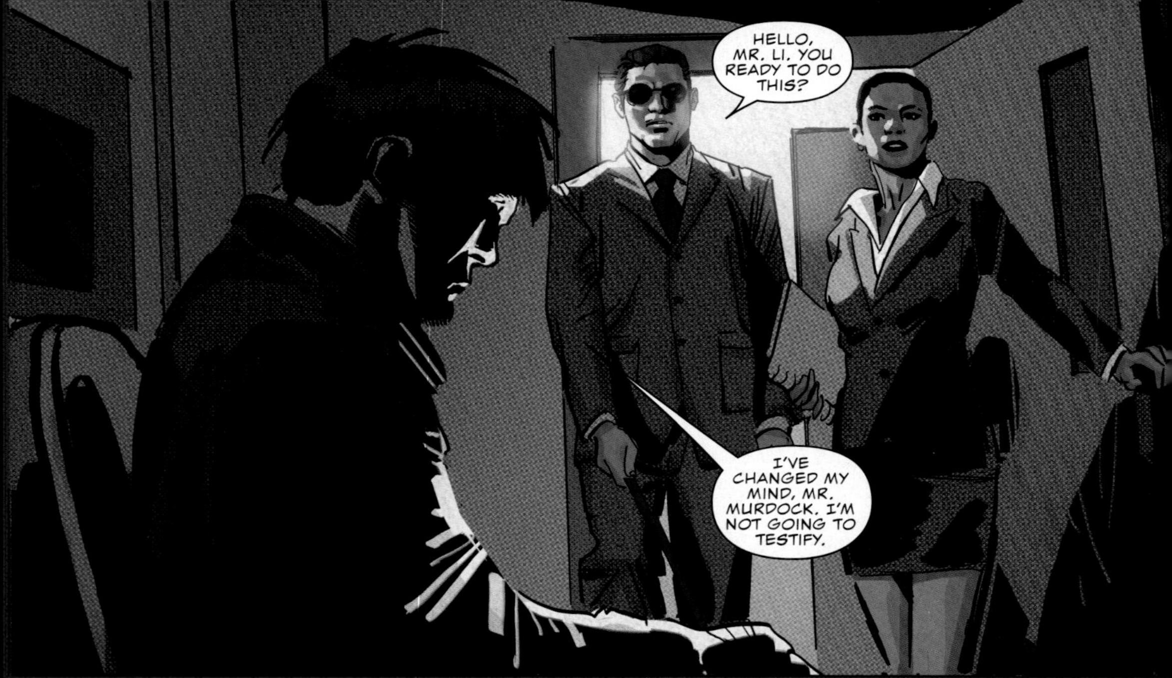
HELLO, MR. LI. YOU READY TO DO THIS?
I'VE CHANGED MY MIND, MR. MURDOCK. I'M NOT GOING TO TESTIFY.

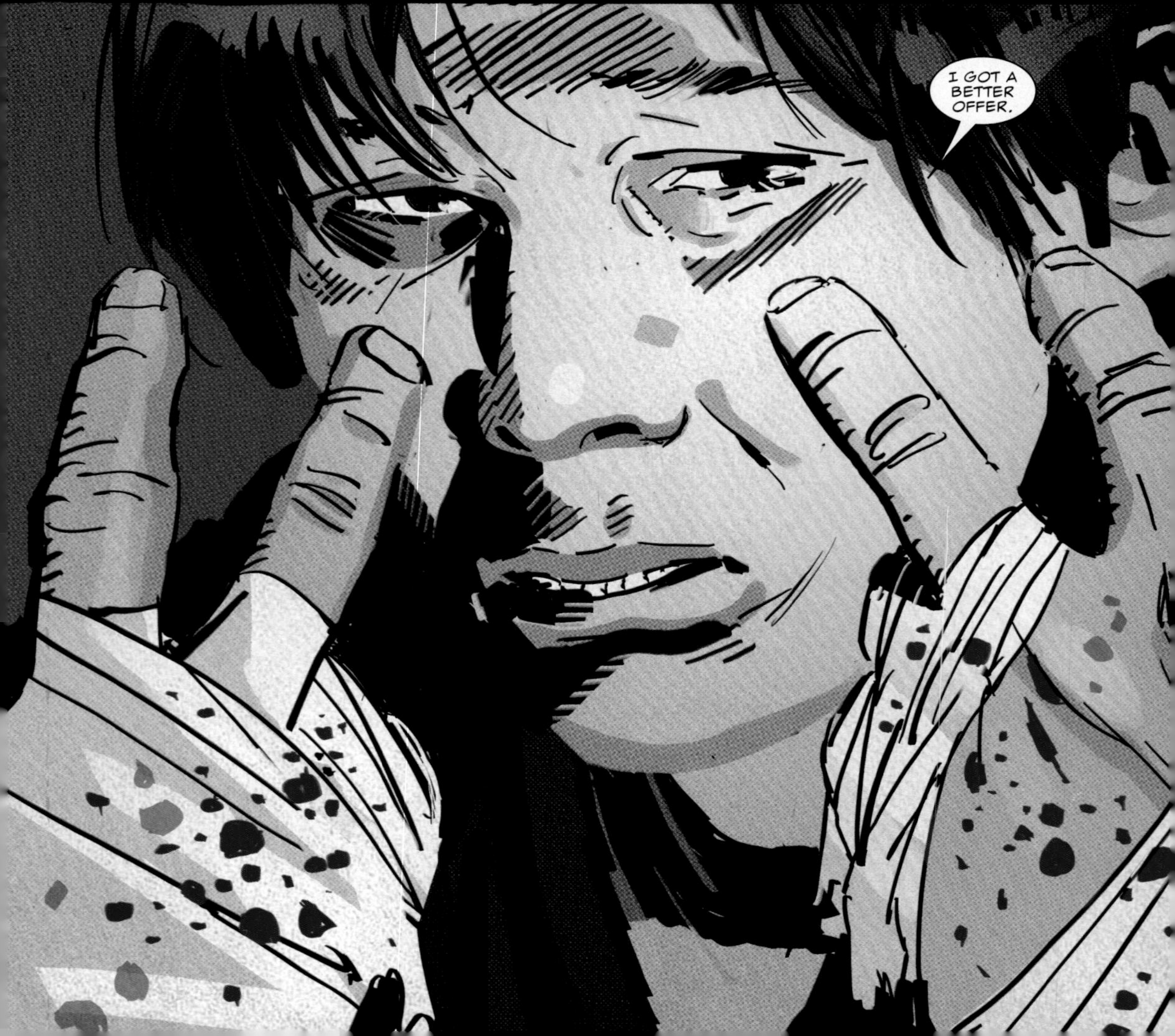
I GOT A BETTER OFFER.

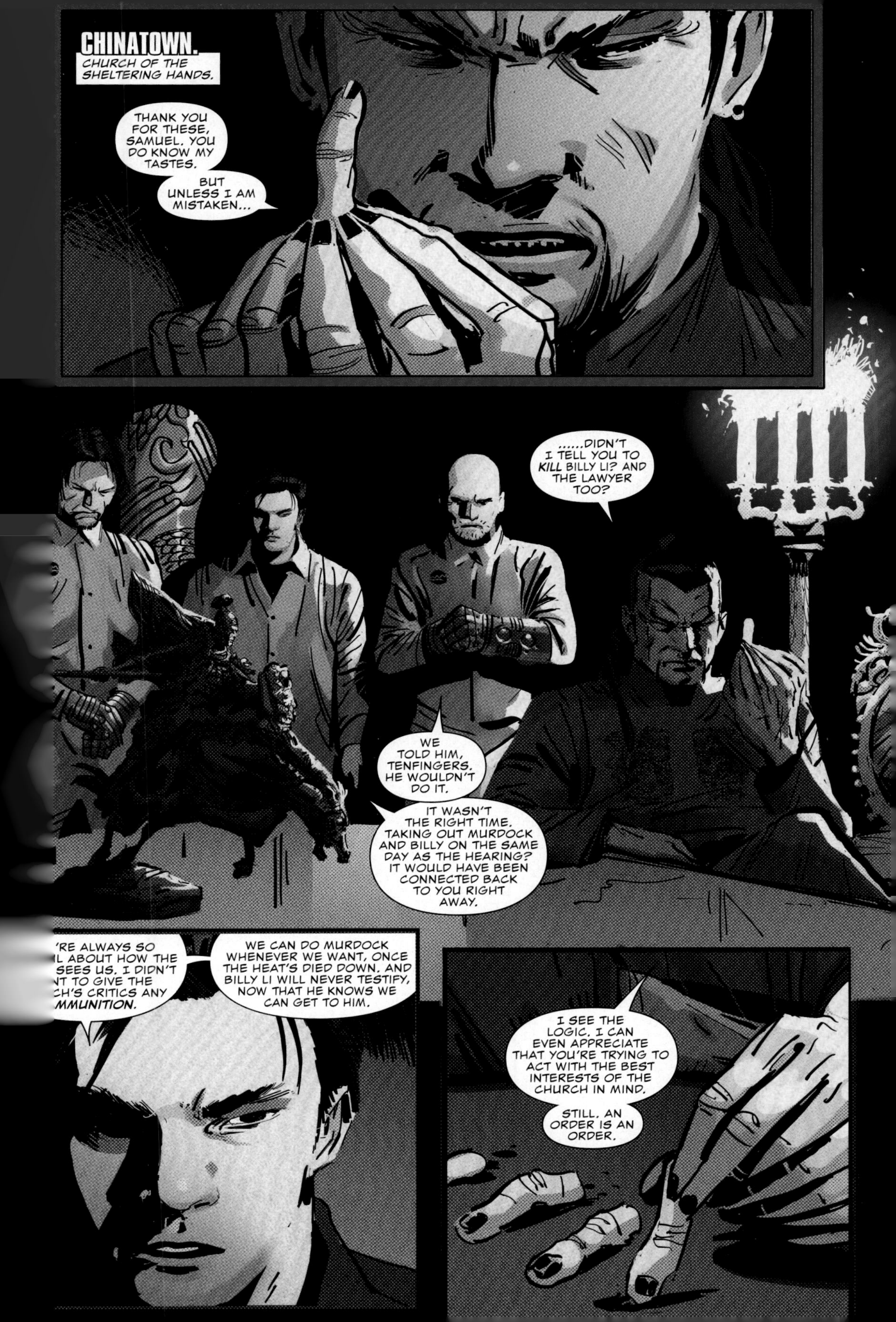

CHINATOWN.
CHURCH OF THE SHELTERING HANDS.
THANK YOU FOR THESE, SAMUEL. YOU DO KNOW MY TASTES.
BUT UNLESS I AM MISTAKEN...
......DIDN'T I TELL YOU TO KILL BILLY LI? AND THE LAWYER TOO?
WE TOLD HIM, TENFINGERS. HE WOULDN'T DO IT.
IT WASN'T THE RIGHT TIME. TAKING OUT MURDOCK AND BILLY ON THE SAME DAY AS THE HEARING? IT WOULD HAVE BEEN CONNECTED BACK TO YOU RIGHT AWAY.
'RE ALWAYS SO L ABOUT HOW THE SEES US. I DIDN'T NT TO GIVE THE CH'S CRITICS ANY MMUNITION.
WE CAN DO MURDOCK WHENEVER WE WANT, ONCE THE HEAT'S DIED DOWN. AND BILLY LI WILL NEVER TESTIFY, NOW THAT HE KNOWS WE CAN GET TO HIM.
I SEE THE LOGIC. I CAN EVEN APPRECIATE THAT YOU'RE TRYING TO ACT WITH THE BEST INTERESTS OF THE CHURCH IN MIND.
STILL, AN ORDER IS AN ORDER.

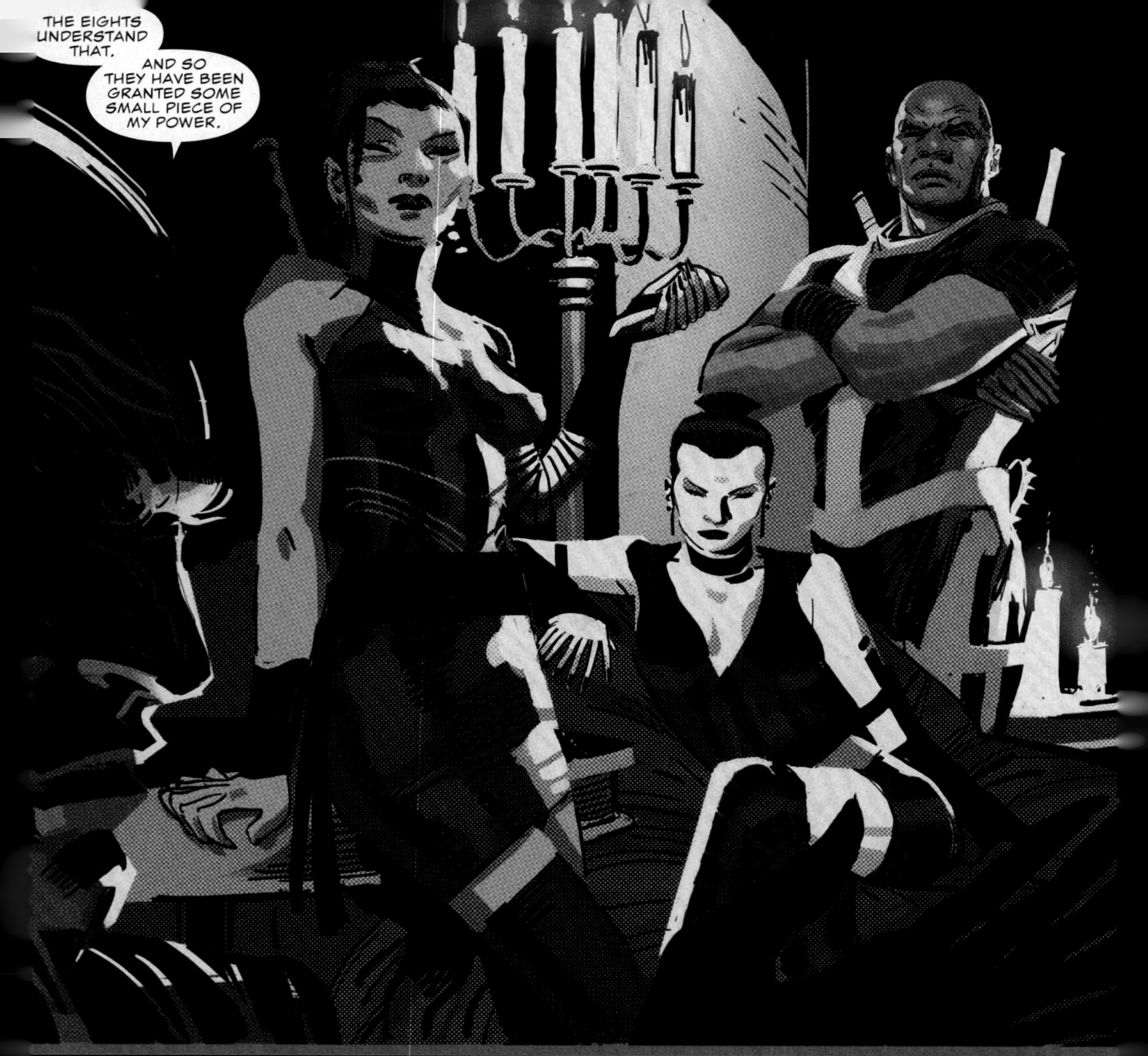
THE EIGHTS UNDERSTAND THAT.
AND SO THEY HAVE BEEN GRANTED SOME SMALL PIECE OF MY POWER.

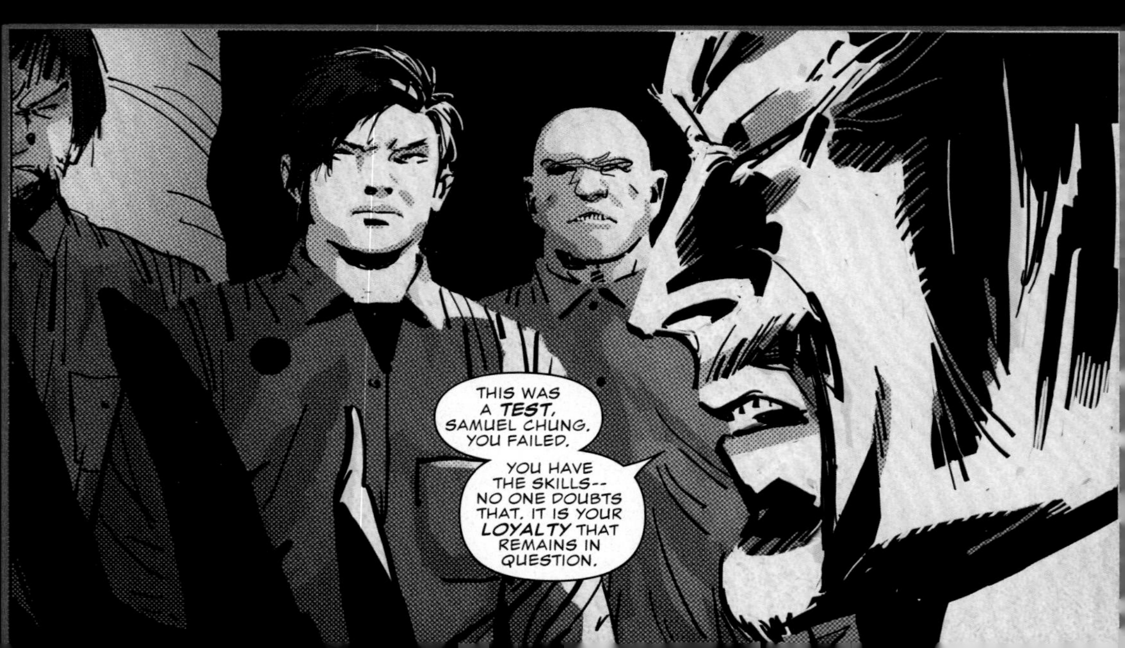
THIS WAS A TEST, SAMUEL CHUNG. YOU FAILED.
YOU HAVE THE SKILLS-- NO ONE DOUBTS THAT. IT IS YOUR LOYALTY THAT REMAINS IN QUESTION.

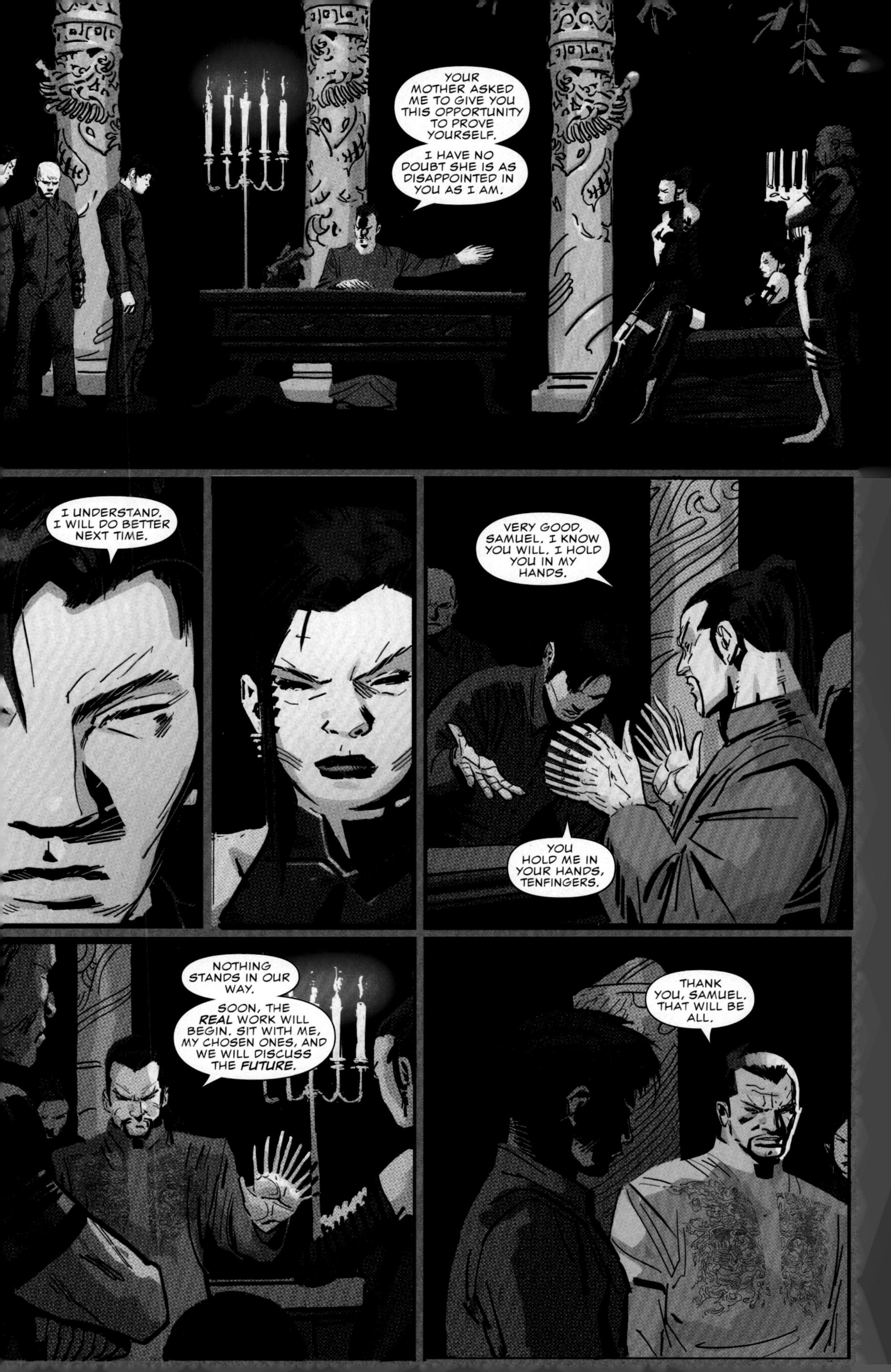
YOUR MOTHER ASKED ME TO GIVE YOU THIS OPPORTUNITY TO PROVE YOURSELF.
I HAVE NO DOUBT SHE IS AS DISAPPOINTED IN YOU AS I AM.
I UNDERSTAND. I WILL DO BETTER NEXT TIME.
VERY GOOD, SAMUEL. I KNOW YOU WILL. I HOLD YOU IN MY HANDS.
YOU HOLD ME IN YOUR HANDS, TENFINGERS.
NOTHING STANDS IN OUR WAY.
SOON, THE REAL WORK WILL BEGIN. SIT WITH ME, MY CHOSEN ONES, AND WE WILL DISCUSS THE FUTURE.
THANK YOU, SAMUEL. THAT WILL BE ALL.

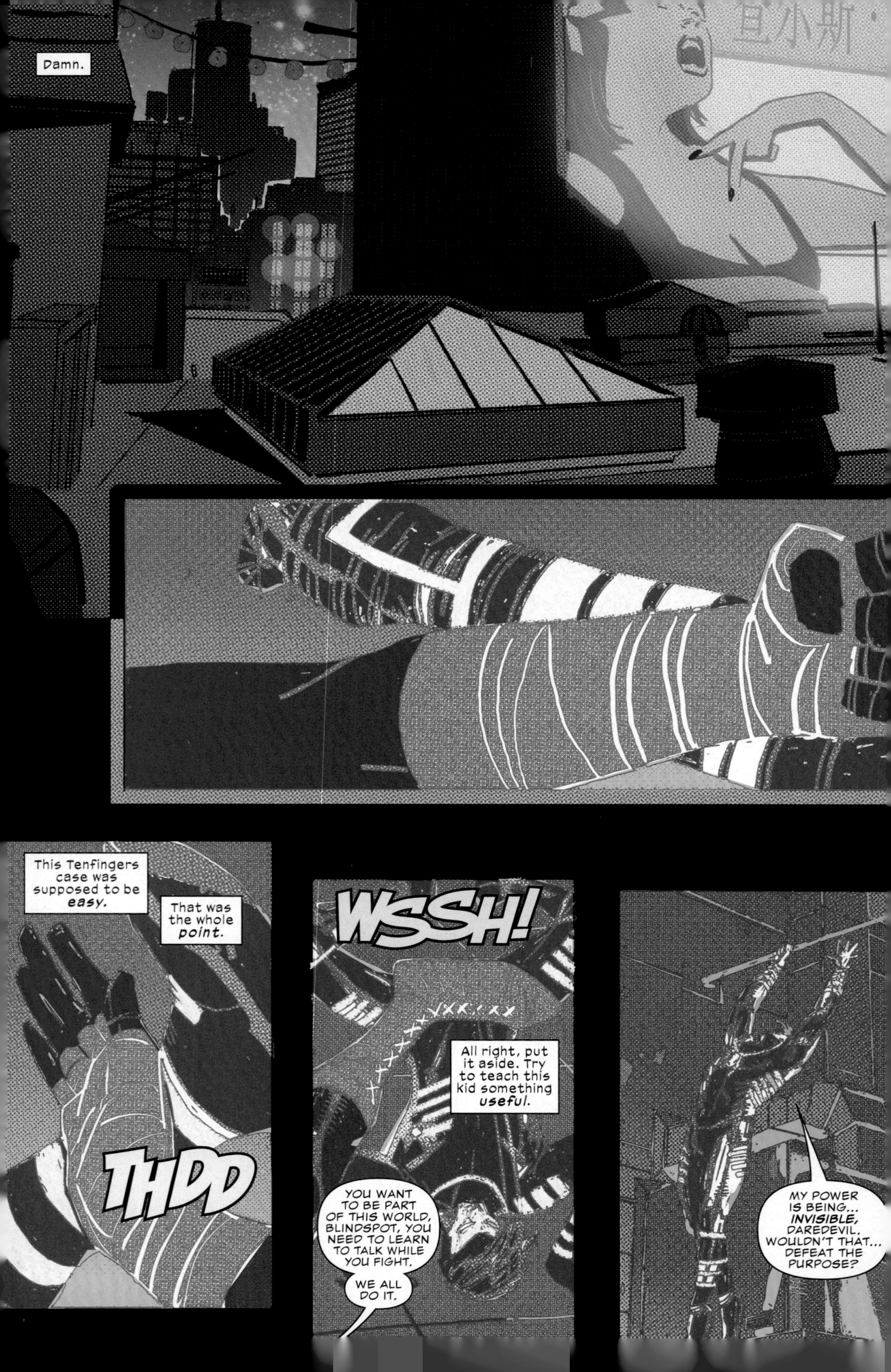
Damn.
This Tenfingers case was supposed to be *easy*.
That was the whole *point*.
THDD
WSSH!
All right, put it aside. Try to teach this kid something *useful*.
YOU WANT TO BE PART OF THIS WORLD, BLINDSPOT, YOU NEED TO LEARN TO TALK WHILE YOU FIGHT.
WE ALL DO IT.
MY POWER IS BEING... *INVISIBLE*, DAREDEVIL. WOULDN'T THAT... DEFEAT THE PURPOSE?

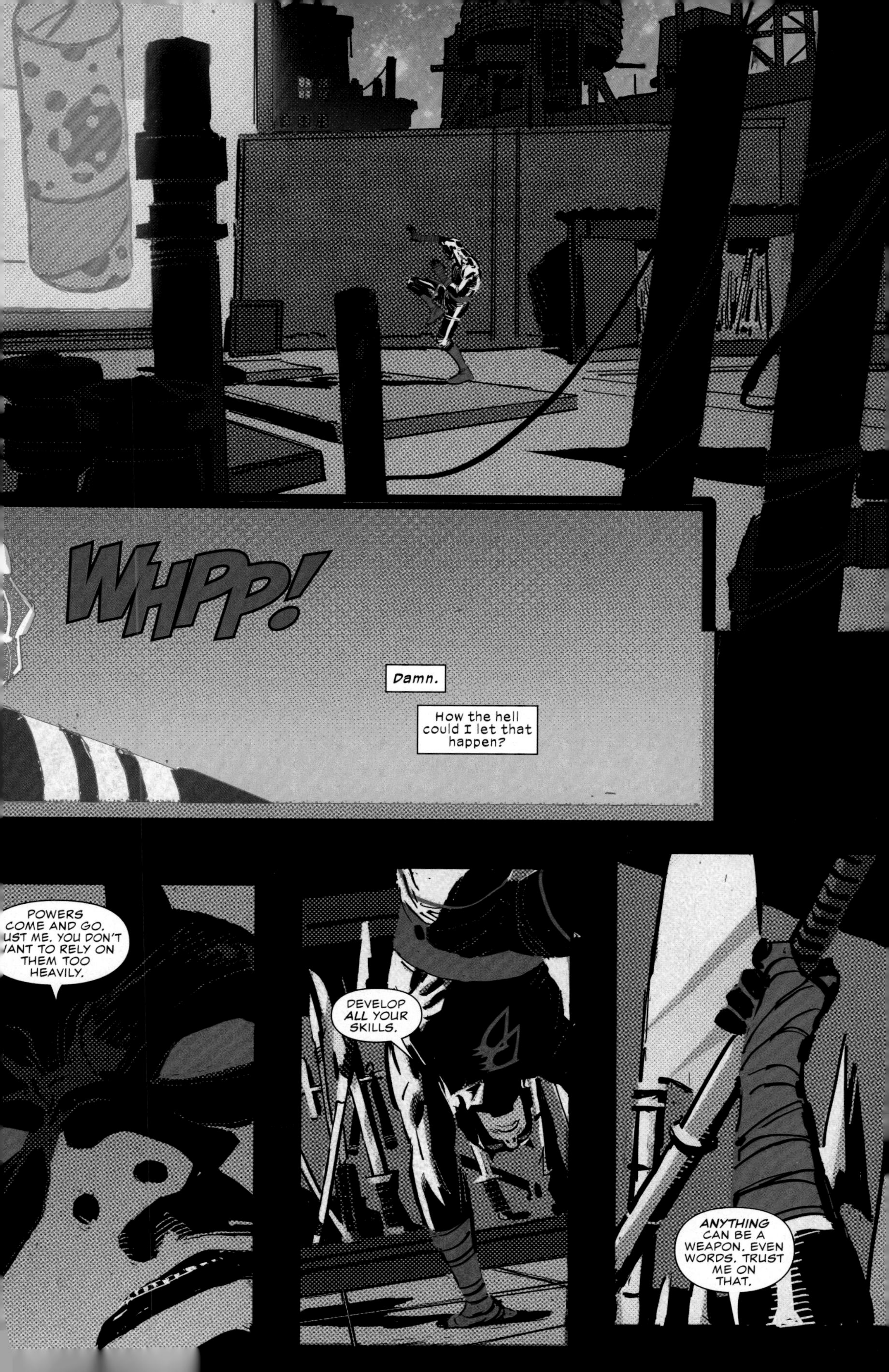
WHPP!
Damn.
How the hell could I let that happen?
POWERS COME AND GO. UST ME. YOU DON'T ANT TO RELY ON THEM TOO HEAVILY.
DEVELOP ALL YOUR SKILLS.
ANYTHING CAN BE A WEAPON. EVEN WORDS. TRUST ME ON THAT.

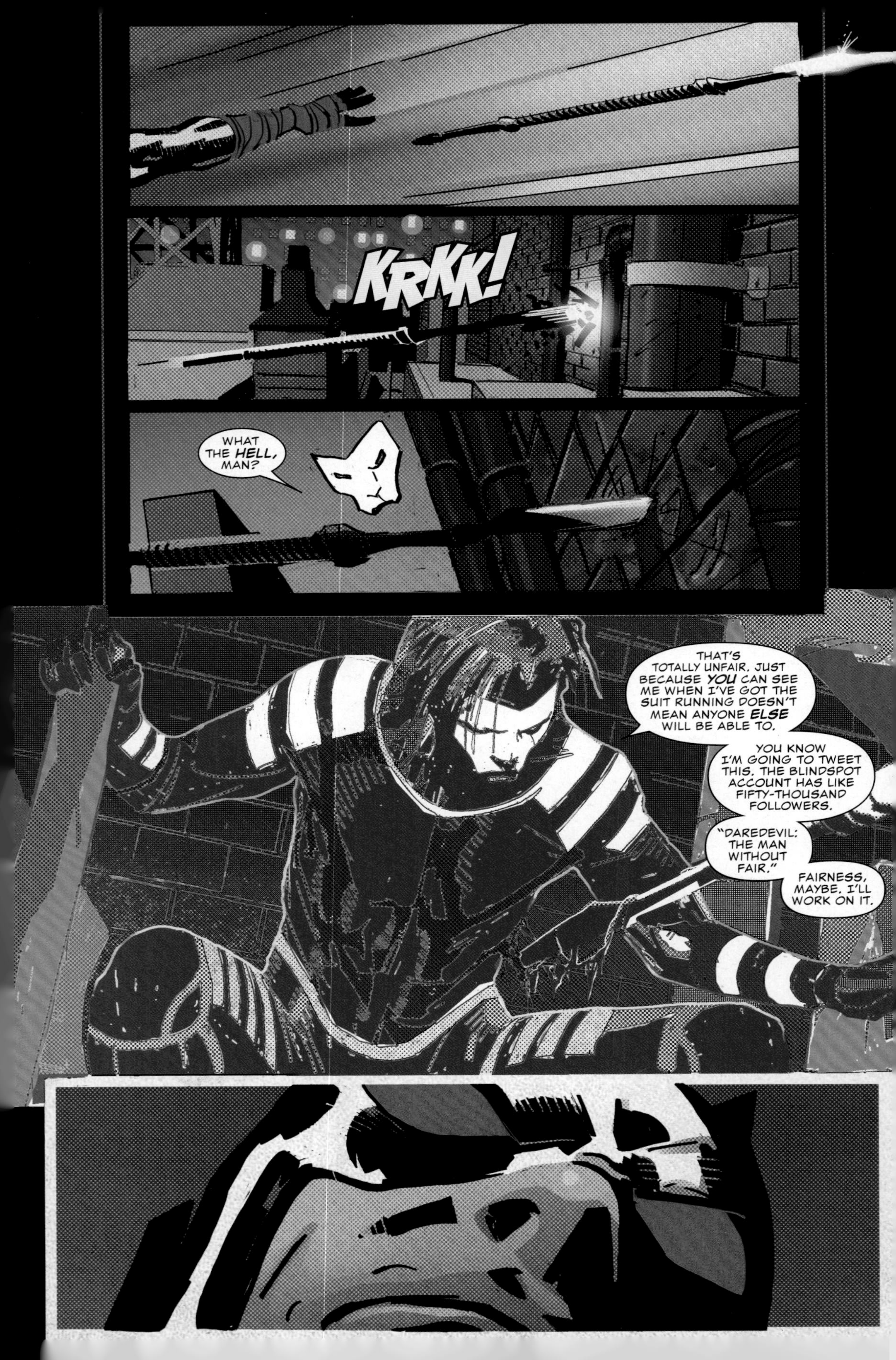
KRKK!
WHAT THE HELL, MAN?
THAT'S TOTALLY UNFAIR. JUST BECAUSE YOU CAN SEE ME WHEN I'VE GOT THE SUIT RUNNING DOESN'T MEAN ANYONE ELSE WILL BE ABLE TO.
YOU KNOW I'M GOING TO TWEET THIS. THE BLINDSPOT ACCOUNT HAS LIKE FIFTY-THOUSAND FOLLOWERS.
"DAREDEVIL: THE MAN WITHOUT FAIR."
FAIRNESS, MAYBE. I'LL WORK ON IT.

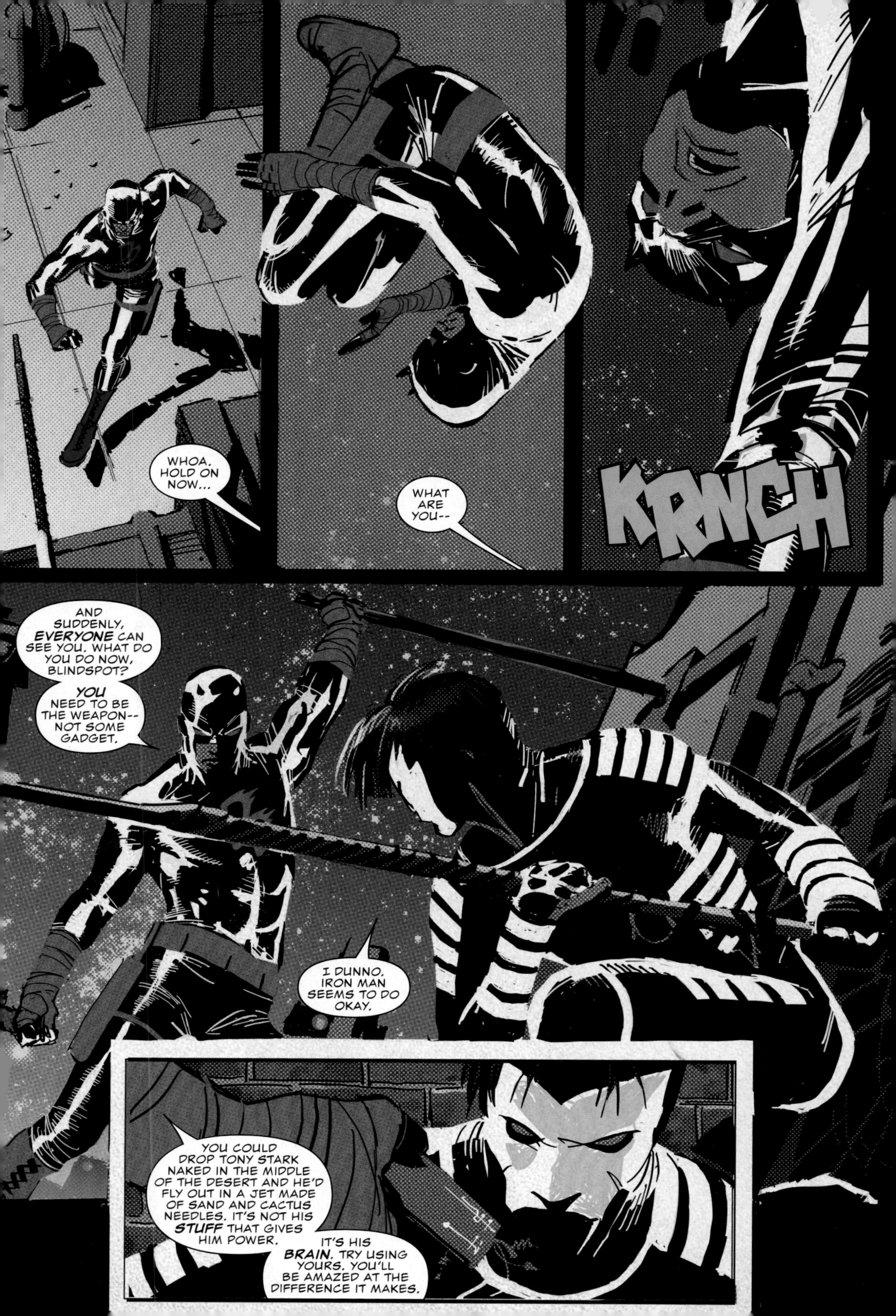

WHOA. HOLD ON NOW...
WHAT ARE YOU--
KRNCH
AND SUDDENLY, EVERYONE CAN SEE YOU. WHAT DO YOU DO NOW, BLINDSPOT?
YOU NEED TO BE THE WEAPON-- NOT SOME GADGET.
I DUNNO. IRON MAN SEEMS TO DO OKAY.
YOU COULD DROP TONY STARK NAKED IN THE MIDDLE OF THE DESERT AND HE'D FLY OUT IN A JET MADE OF SAND AND CACTUS NEEDLES. IT'S NOT HIS STUFF THAT GIVES HIM POWER.
IT'S HIS BRAIN. TRY USING YOURS. YOU'LL BE AMAZED AT THE DIFFERENCE IT MAKES.

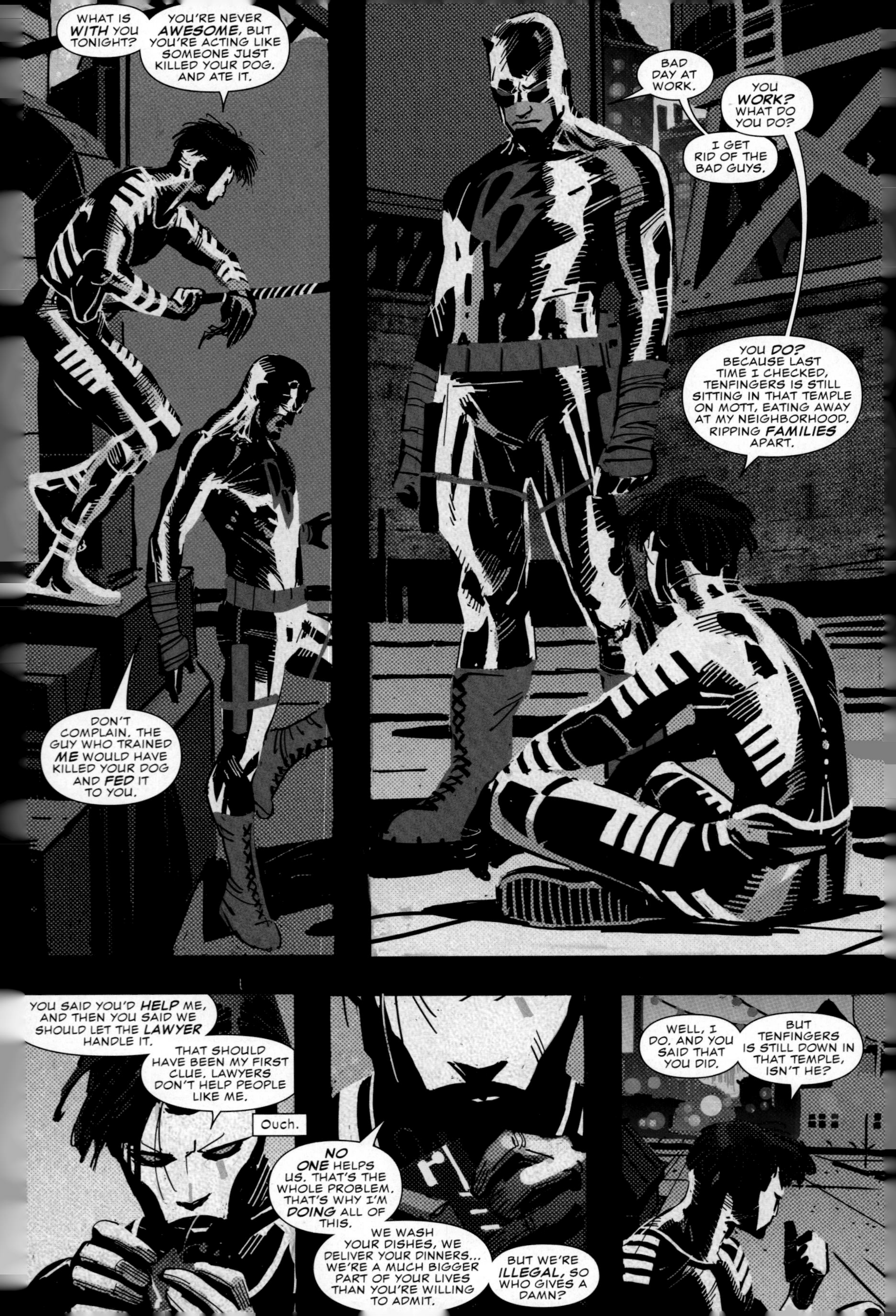
WHAT IS WITH YOU TONIGHT?
YOU'RE NEVER AWESOME, BUT YOU'RE ACTING LIKE SOMEONE JUST KILLED YOUR DOG. AND ATE IT.
DON'T COMPLAIN. THE GUY WHO TRAINED ME WOULD HAVE KILLED YOUR DOG AND FED IT TO YOU.
BAD DAY AT WORK.
YOU WORK? WHAT DO YOU DO?
I GET RID OF THE BAD GUYS.
YOU DO? BECAUSE LAST TIME I CHECKED, TENFINGERS IS STILL SITTING IN THAT TEMPLE ON MOTT, EATING AWAY AT MY NEIGHBORHOOD. RIPPING FAMILIES APART.
YOU SAID YOU'D HELP ME, AND THEN YOU SAID WE SHOULD LET THE LAWYER HANDLE IT.
THAT SHOULD HAVE BEEN MY FIRST CLUE. LAWYERS DON'T HELP PEOPLE LIKE ME.
Ouch.
NO ONE HELPS US. THAT'S THE WHOLE PROBLEM. THAT'S WHY I'M DOING ALL OF THIS.
WE WASH YOUR DISHES, WE DELIVER YOUR DINNERS... WE'RE A MUCH BIGGER PART OF YOUR LIVES THAN YOU'RE WILLING TO ADMIT.
BUT WE'RE ILLEGAL, SO WHO GIVES A DAMN?
WELL, I DO. AND YOU SAID THAT YOU DID.
BUT TENFINGERS IS STILL DOWN IN THAT TEMPLE, ISN'T HE?

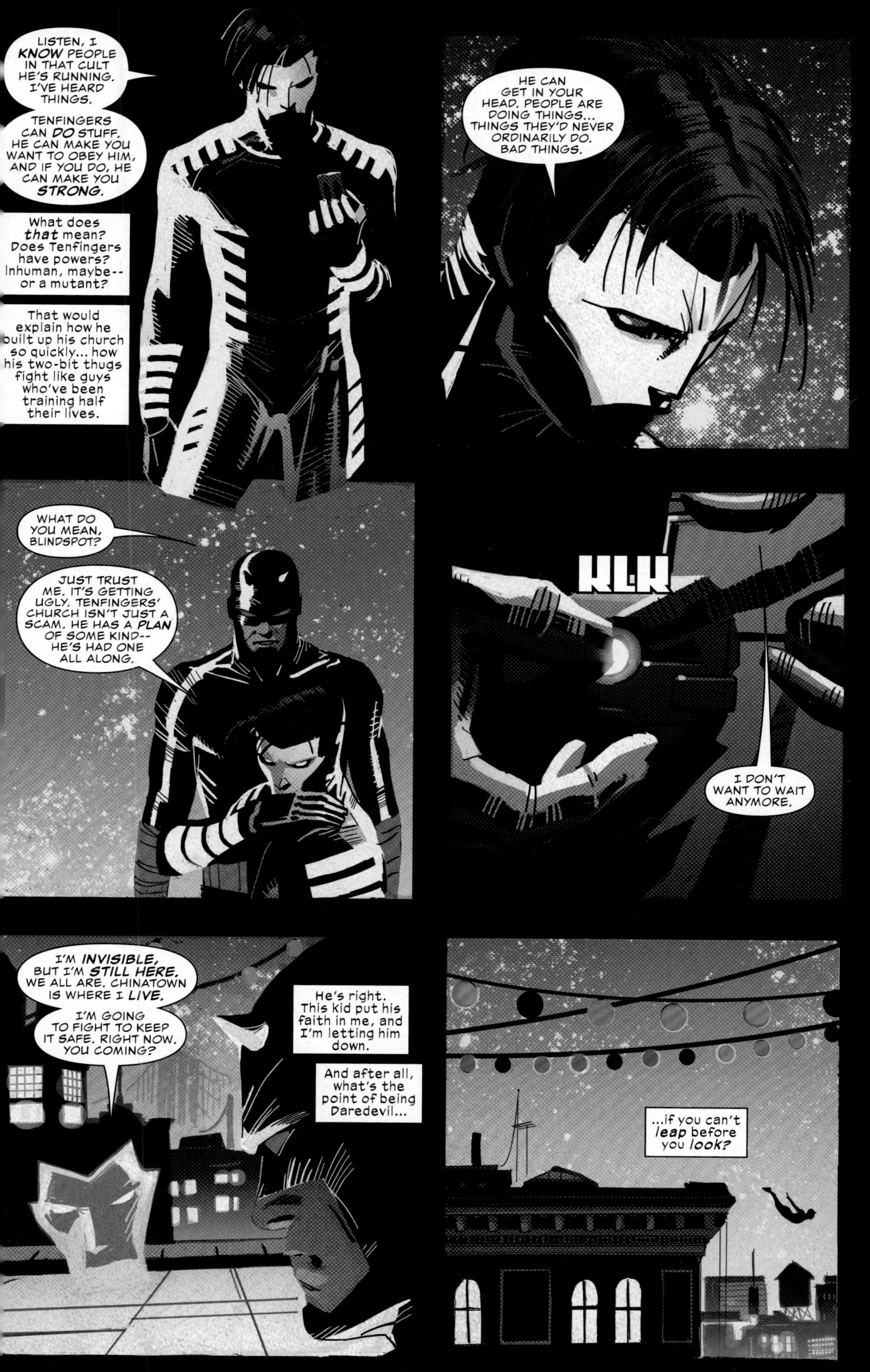
LISTEN, I KNOW PEOPLE IN THAT CULT HE'S RUNNING. I'VE HEARD THINGS.
TENFINGERS CAN DO STUFF. HE CAN MAKE YOU WANT TO OBEY HIM, AND IF YOU DO, HE CAN MAKE YOU STRONG.
What does that mean? Does Tenfingers have powers? Inhuman, maybe-- or a mutant?
That would explain how he built up his church so quickly... how his two-bit thugs fight like guys who've been training half their lives.
HE CAN GET IN YOUR HEAD. PEOPLE ARE DOING THINGS... THINGS THEY'D NEVER ORDINARILY DO. BAD THINGS.
WHAT DO YOU MEAN, BLINDSPOT?
JUST TRUST ME. IT'S GETTING UGLY. TENFINGERS' CHURCH ISN'T JUST A SCAM. HE HAS A PLAN OF SOME KIND-- HE'S HAD ONE ALL ALONG.
KLIK
I DON'T WANT TO WAIT ANYMORE.
I'M INVISIBLE, BUT I'M STILL HERE. WE ALL ARE. CHINATOWN IS WHERE I LIVE.
I'M GOING TO FIGHT TO KEEP IT SAFE. RIGHT NOW. YOU COMING?
He's right. This kid put his faith in me, and I'm letting him down.
And after all, what's the point of being Daredevil...
...if you can't leap before you look?

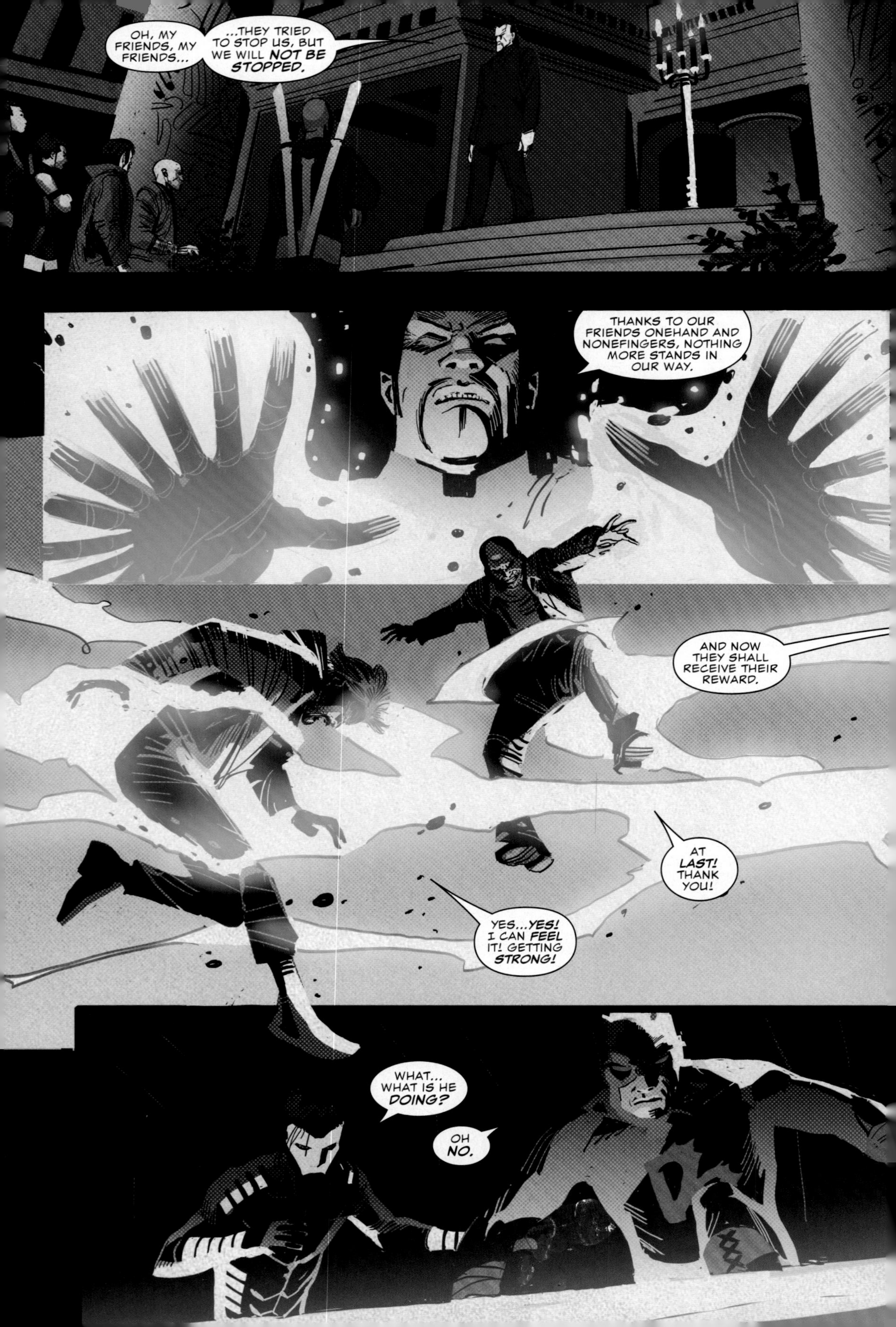
OH, MY FRIENDS, MY FRIENDS...
...THEY TRIED TO STOP US, BUT WE WILL NOT BE STOPPED.
THANKS TO OUR FRIENDS ONEHAND AND NONEFINGERS, NOTHING MORE STANDS IN OUR WAY.
AND NOW THEY SHALL RECEIVE THEIR REWARD.
AT LAST! THANK YOU!
YES...YES! I CAN FEEL IT! GETTING STRONG!
WHAT... WHAT IS HE DOING?
OH NO.

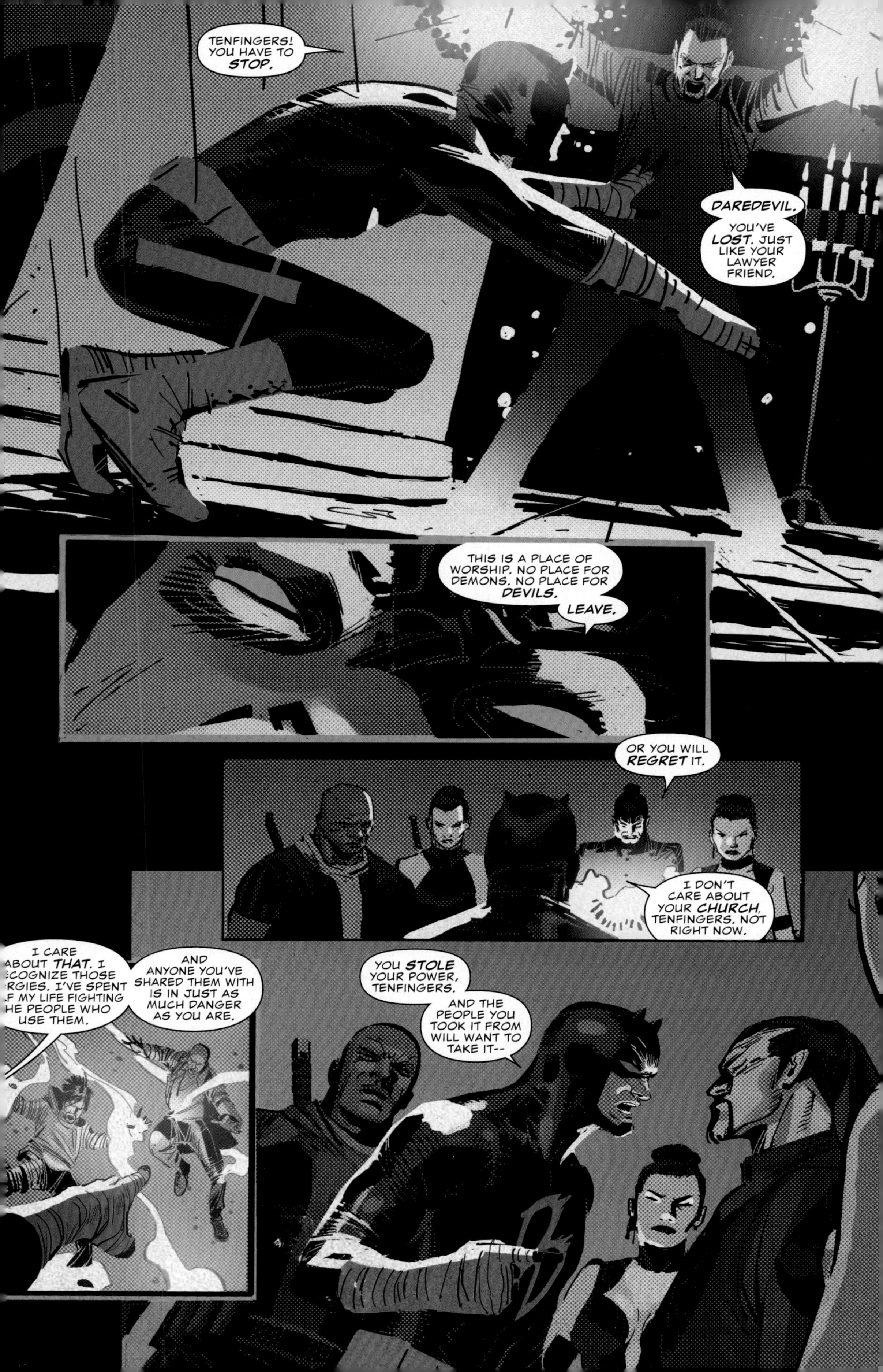
TENFINGERS! YOU HAVE TO STOP.
DAREDEVIL.
YOU'VE LOST. JUST LIKE YOUR LAWYER FRIEND.
THIS IS A PLACE OF WORSHIP. NO PLACE FOR DEMONS. NO PLACE FOR DEVILS.
LEAVE.
OR YOU WILL REGRET IT.
I DON'T CARE ABOUT YOUR CHURCH, TENFINGERS. NOT RIGHT NOW.
I CARE ABOUT THAT. I ECOGNIZE THOSE RGIES. I'VE SPENT F MY LIFE FIGHTING HE PEOPLE WHO USE THEM.
AND ANYONE YOU'VE SHARED THEM WITH IS IN JUST AS MUCH DANGER AS YOU ARE.
YOU STOLE YOUR POWER, TENFINGERS.
AND THE PEOPLE YOU TOOK IT FROM WILL WANT TO TAKE IT--

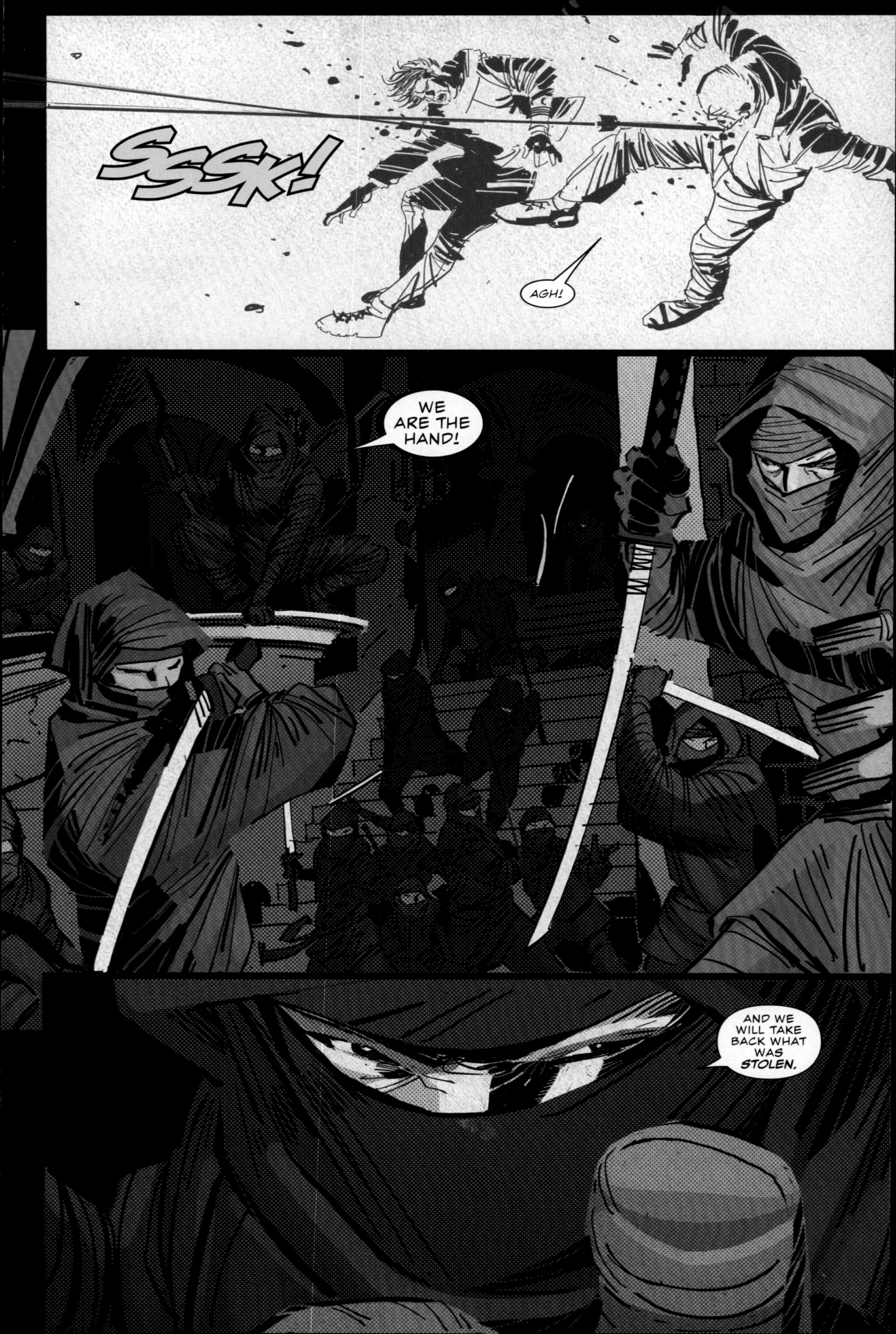
SSSK!
AGH!
WE ARE THE HAND!
AND WE WILL TAKE BACK WHAT WAS STOLEN.

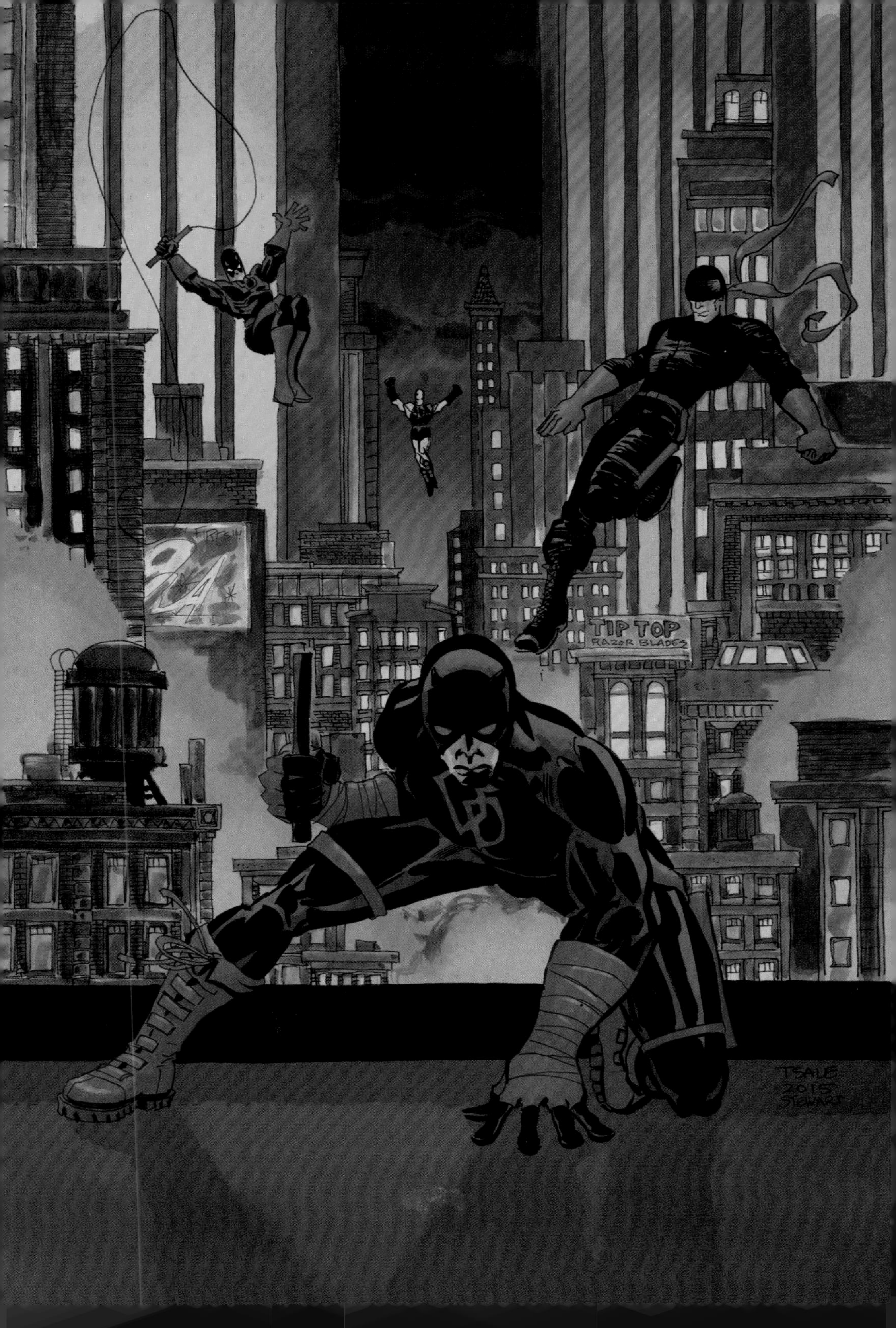
TIP TOP
RAZOR BLADES
TSALE
2015
STEWART

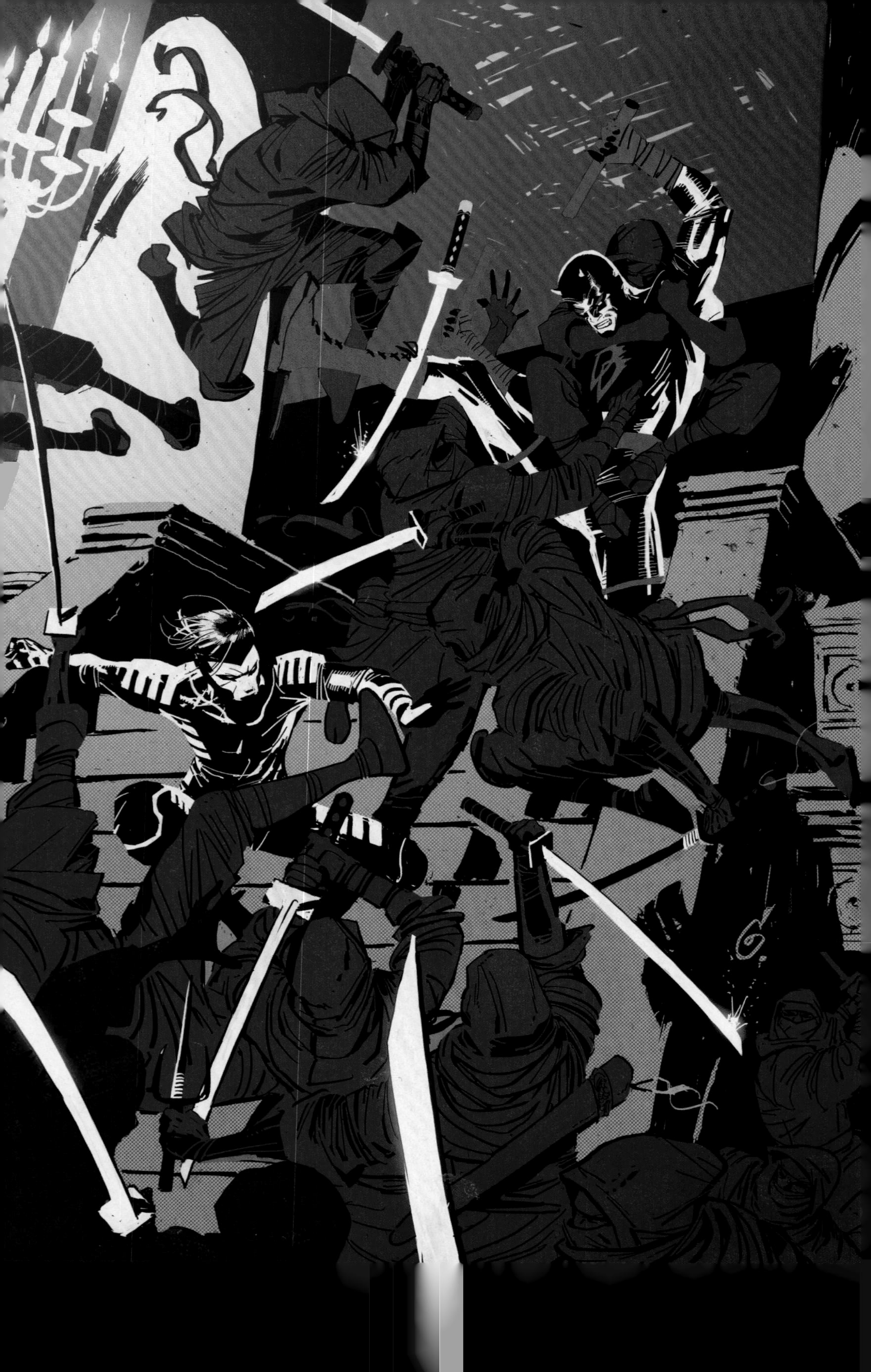

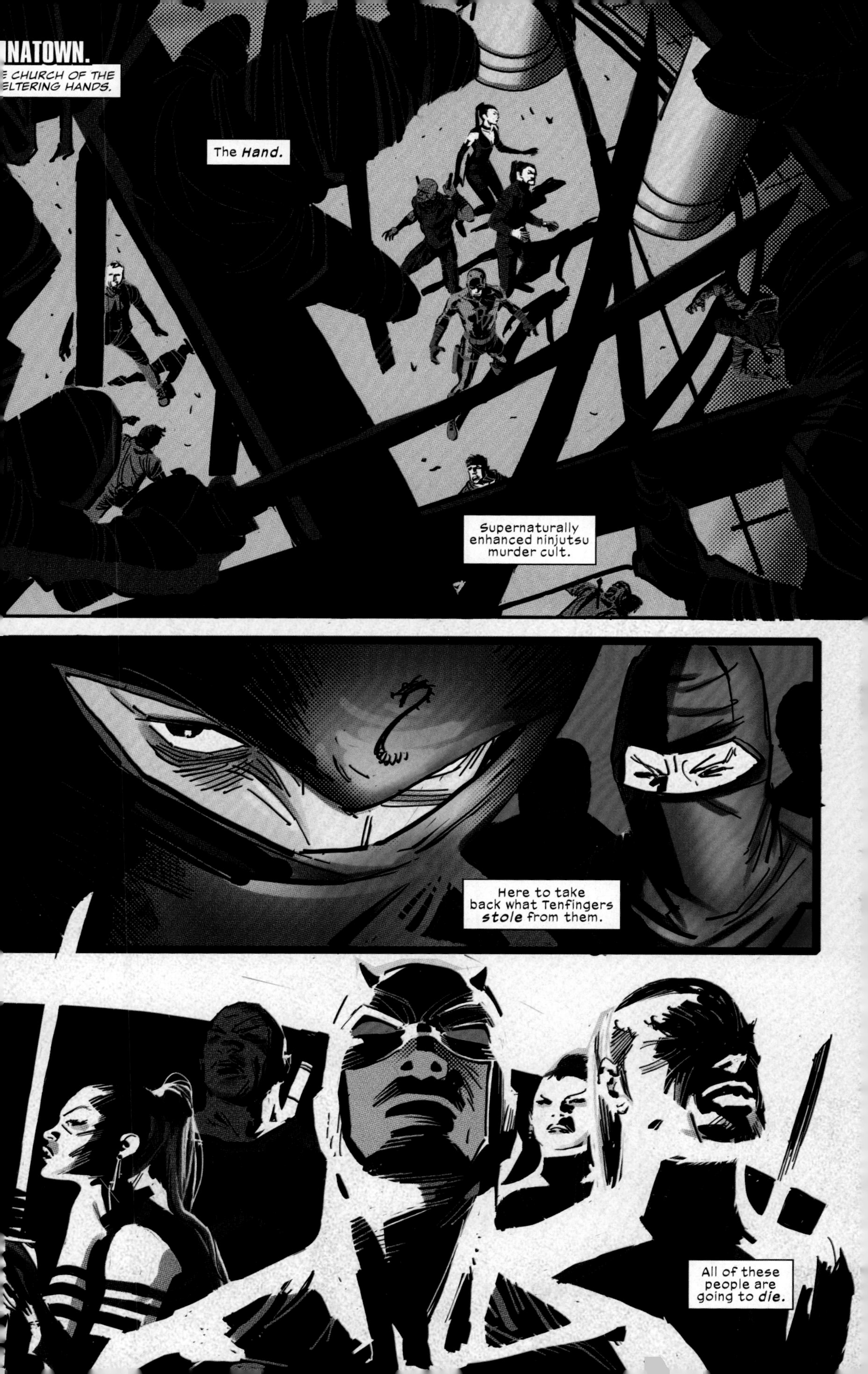

INATOWN.
E CHURCH OF THE
ELTERING HANDS.
The Hand.
Supernaturally enhanced ninjutsu murder cult.
Here to take back what Tenfingers stole from them.
All of these people are going to die.

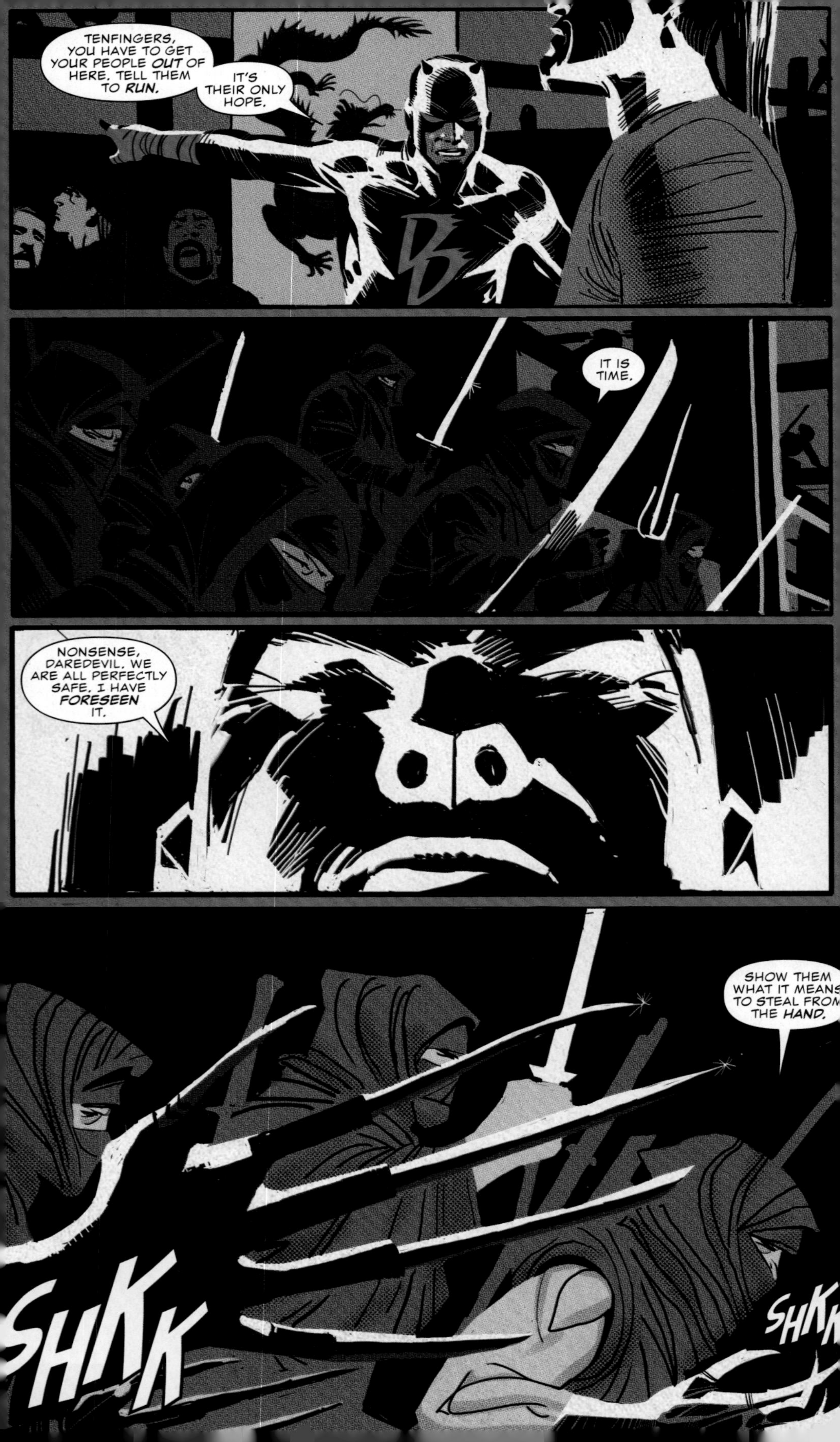
TENFINGERS, YOU HAVE TO GET YOUR PEOPLE OUT OF HERE. TELL THEM TO RUN.
IT'S THEIR ONLY HOPE.
IT IS TIME.
NONSENSE, DAREDEVIL. WE ARE ALL PERFECTLY SAFE. I HAVE FORESEEN IT.
SHOW THEM WHAT IT MEANS TO STEAL FROM THE HAND.
SHIKK
SHIKK

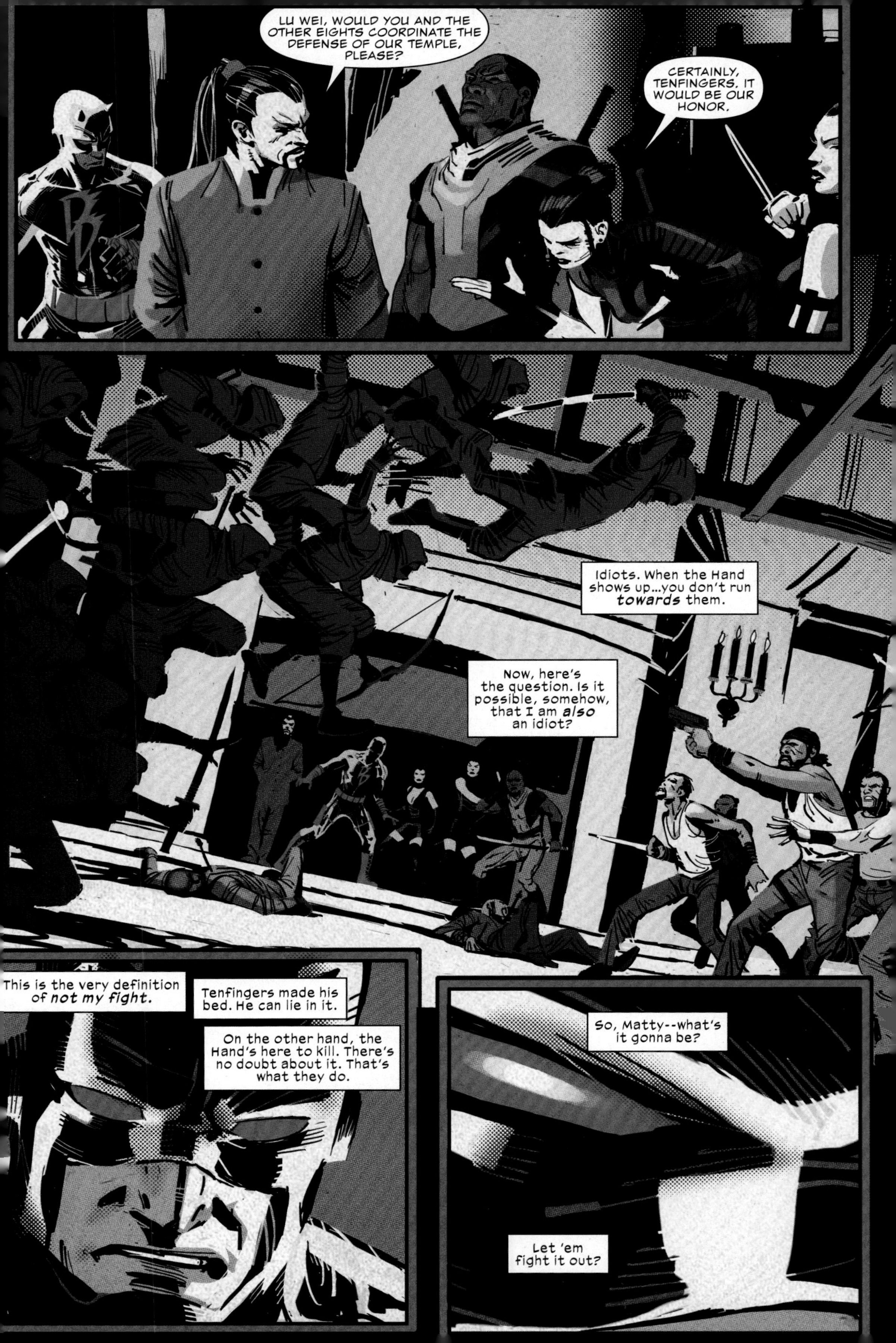
LU WEI, WOULD YOU AND THE OTHER EIGHTS COORDINATE THE DEFENSE OF OUR TEMPLE, PLEASE?
CERTAINLY, TENFINGERS. IT WOULD BE OUR HONOR.
Idiots. When the Hand shows up...you don't run *towards* them.
Now, here's the question. Is it possible, somehow, that I am *also* an idiot?
This is the very definition of *not my fight.*
Tenfingers made his bed. He can lie in it.
On the other hand, the Hand's here to kill. There's no doubt about it. That's what they do.
So, Matty--what's it gonna be?
Let 'em fight it out?

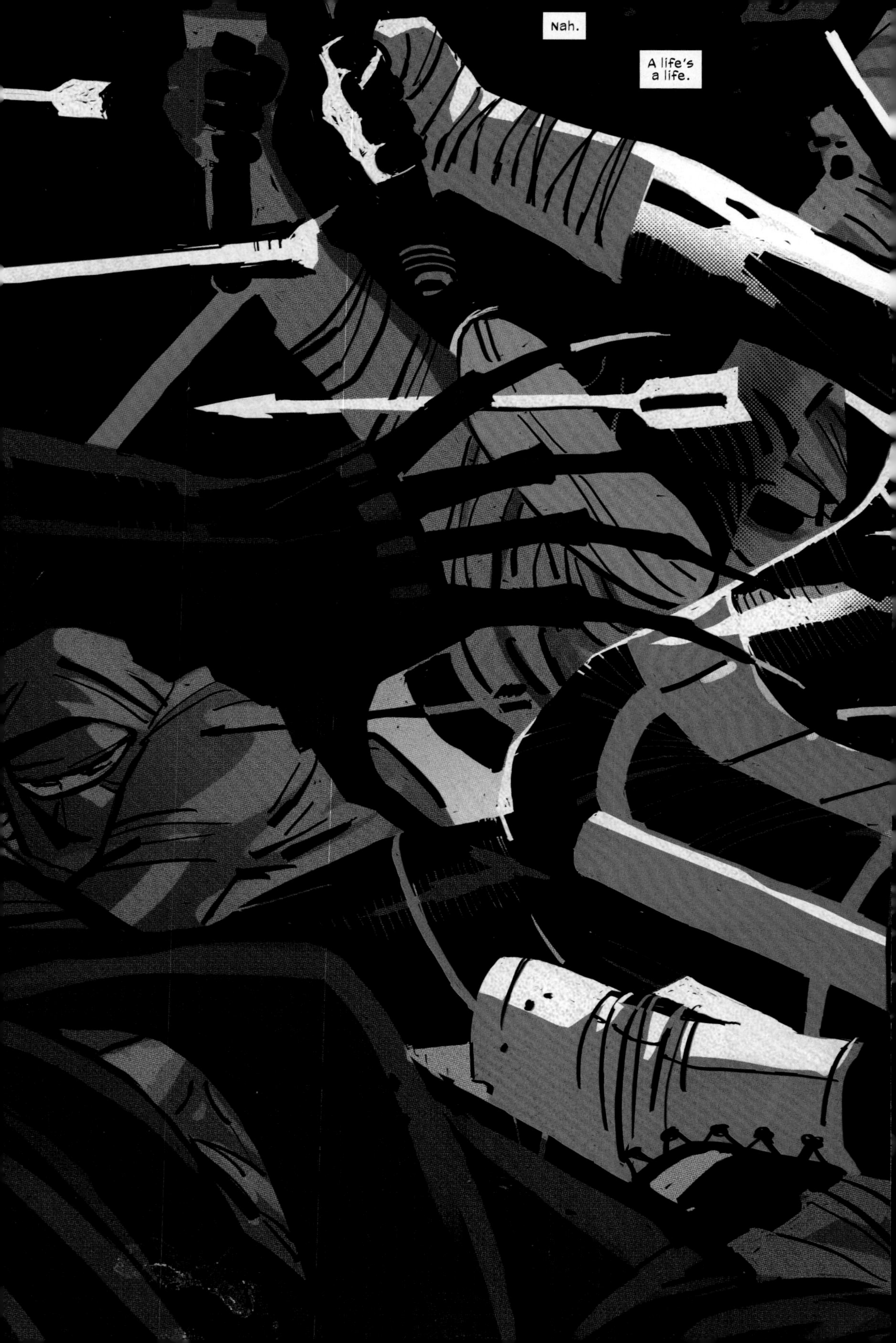
Nah.
A life's a life.

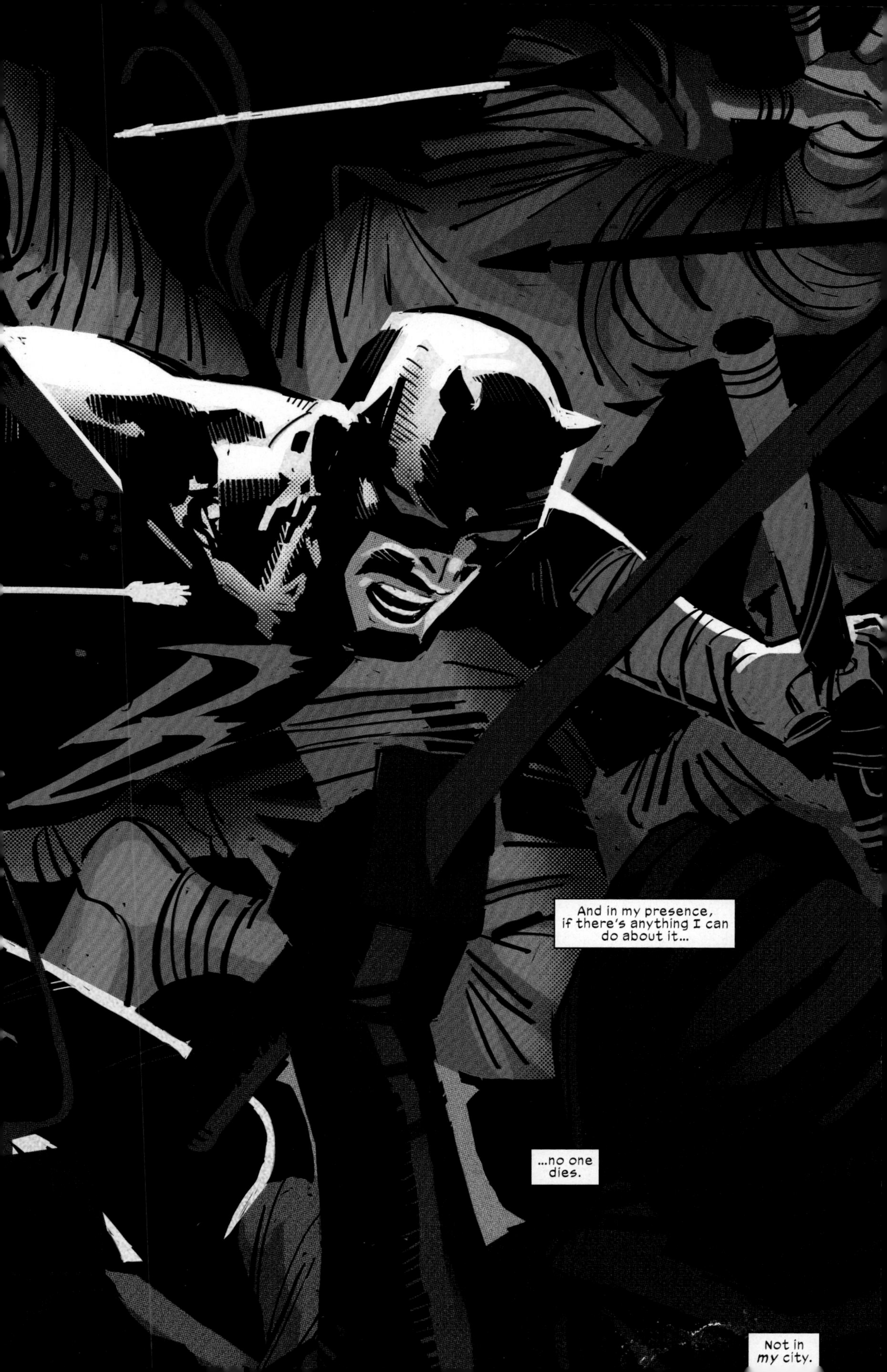
And in my presence, if there's anything I can do about it...
...no one dies.
Not in *my city*.

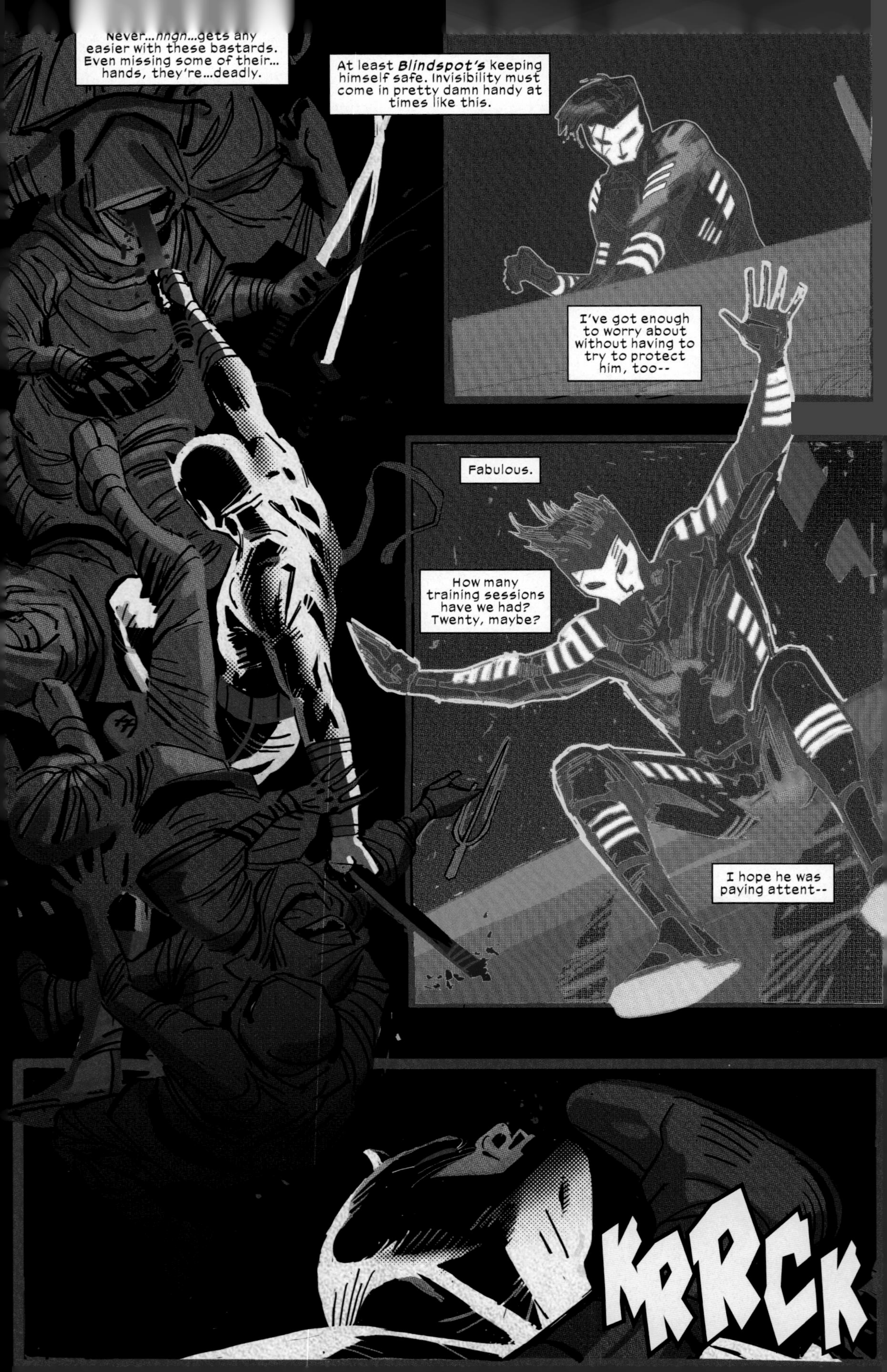
Never...*nngn*...gets any easier with these bastards. Even missing some of their... hands, they're...deadly.
At least *Blindspot's* keeping himself safe. Invisibility must come in pretty damn handy at times like this.
I've got enough to worry about without having to try to protect him, too--
Fabulous.
How many training sessions have we had? Twenty, maybe?
I hope he was paying attent--
KRRCK

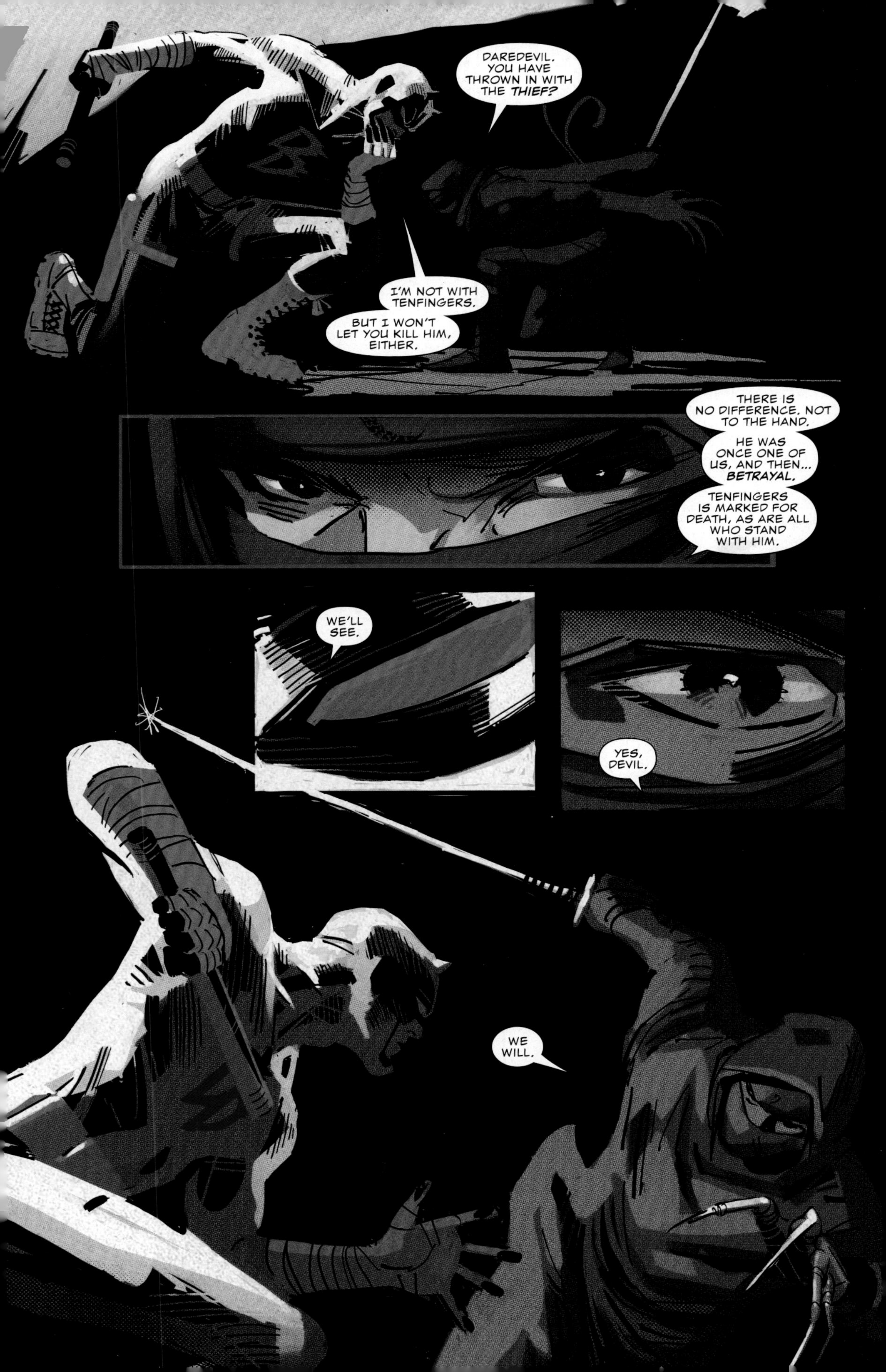
DAREDEVIL. YOU HAVE THROWN IN WITH THE *THIEF?*
I'M NOT WITH TENFINGERS.
BUT I WON'T LET YOU KILL HIM, EITHER.
THERE IS NO DIFFERENCE. NOT TO THE HAND.
HE WAS ONCE ONE OF US, AND THEN... *BETRAYAL.*
TENFINGERS IS MARKED FOR DEATH, AS ARE ALL WHO STAND WITH HIM.
WE'LL SEE.
YES, DEVIL.
WE WILL.

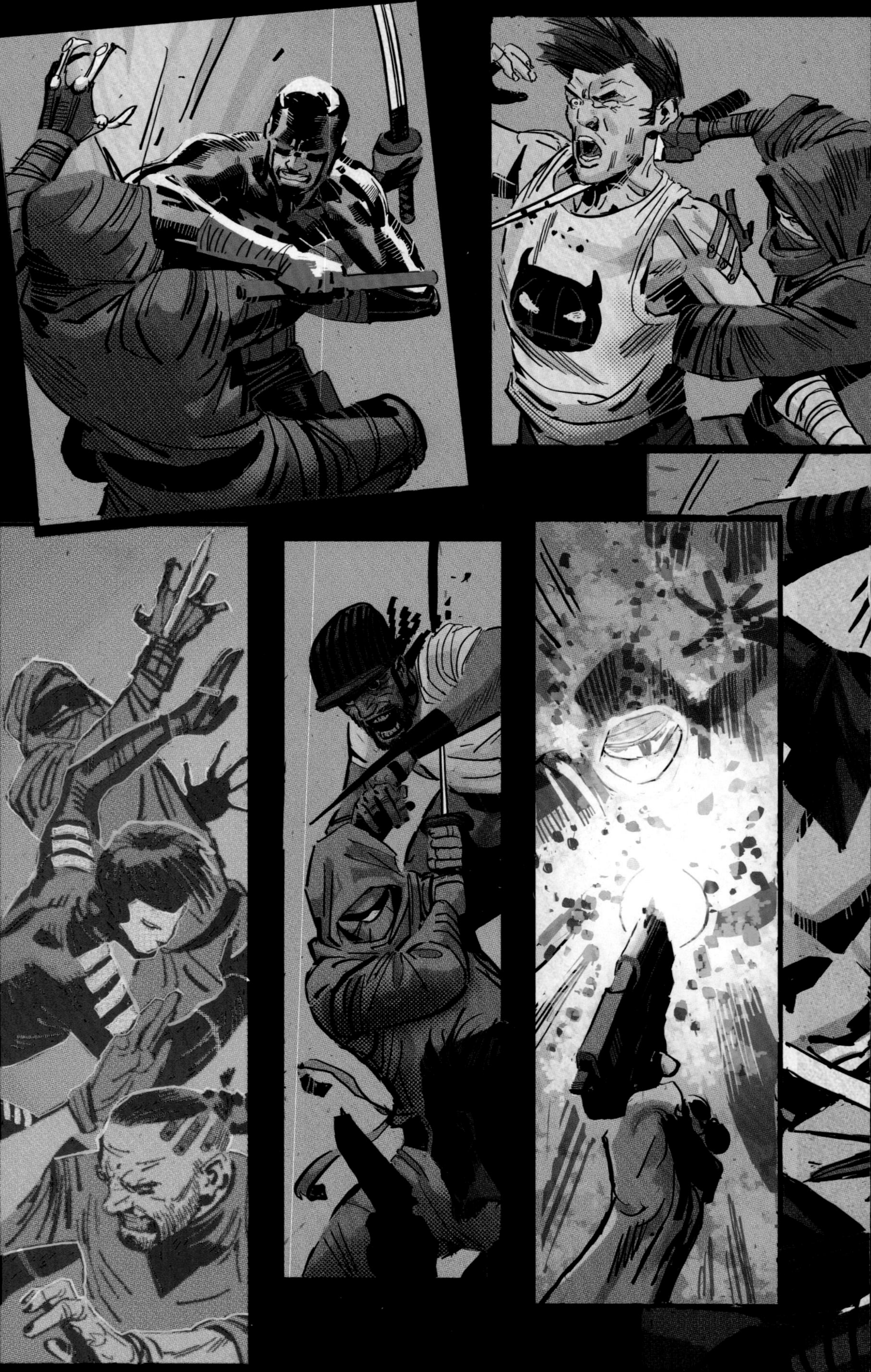

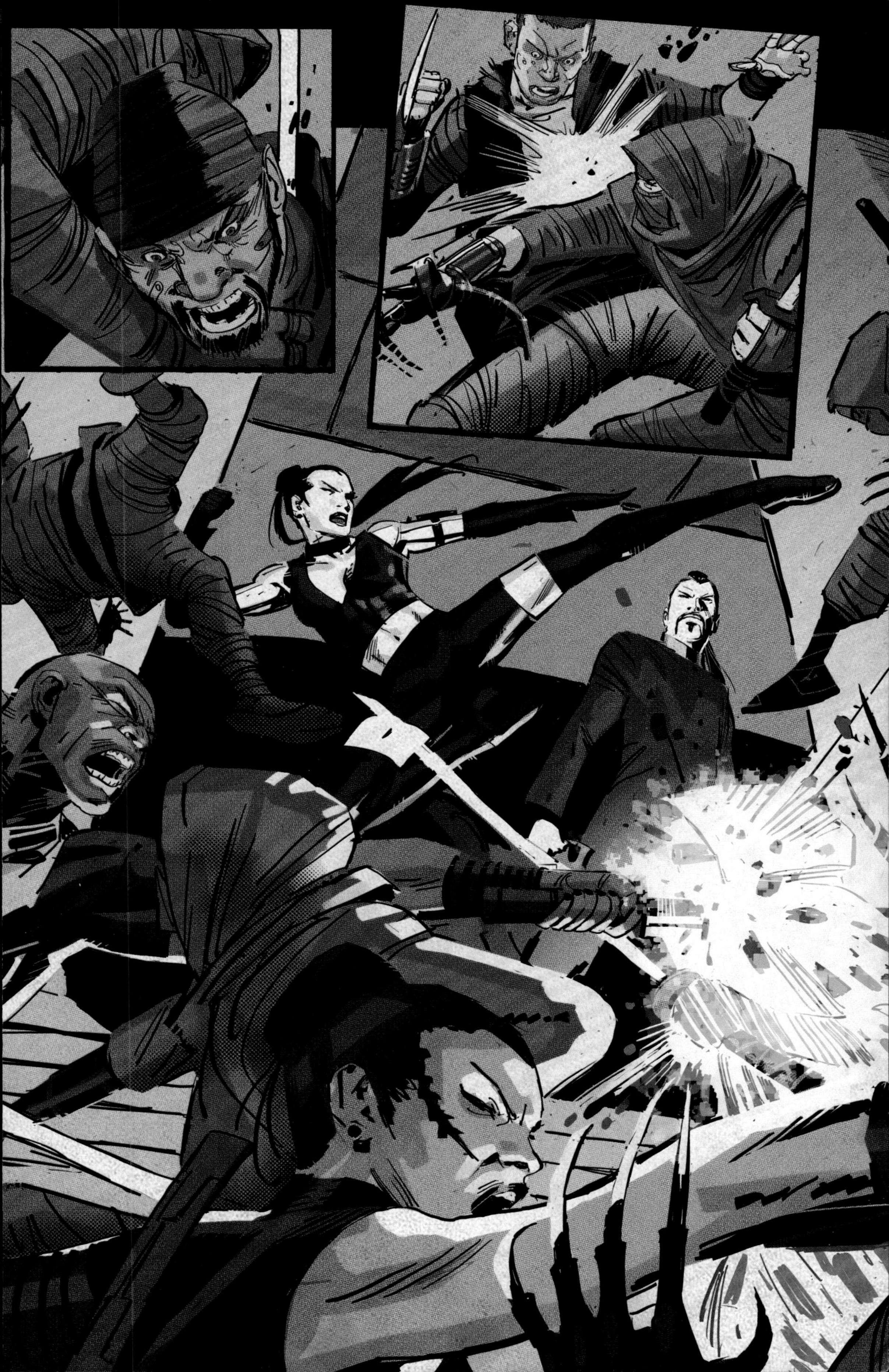

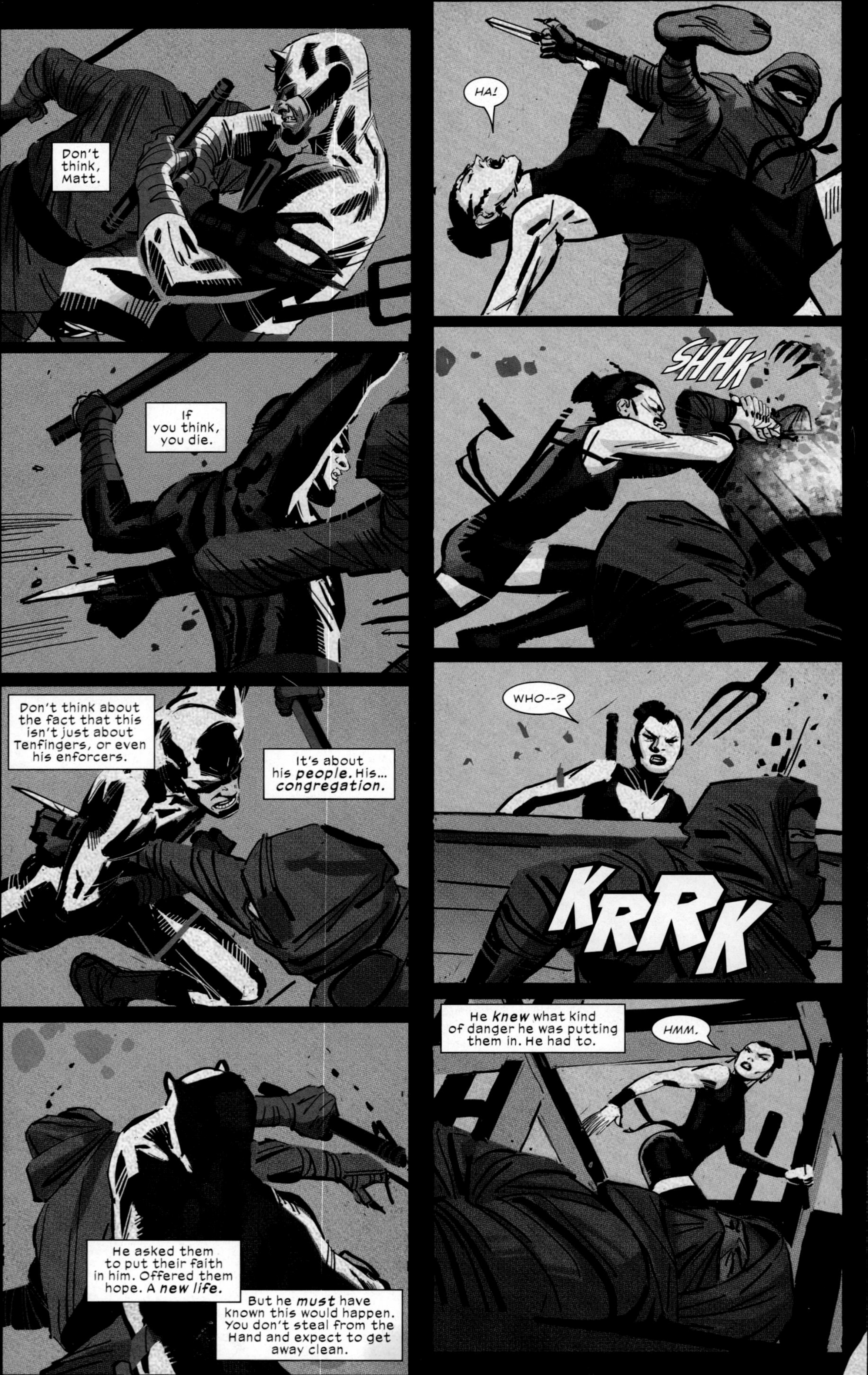
Don't think, Matt.
HA!
If you think, you die.
SHHK
Don't think about the fact that this isn't just about Tenfingers, or even his enforcers.
It's about his *people*. His... *congregation*.
WHO--?
KRRK
He asked them to put their faith in him. Offered them hope. A *new life*.
But he *must* have known this would happen. You don't steal from the Hand and expect to get away clean.
He *knew* what kind of danger he was putting them in. He had to.
HMM.

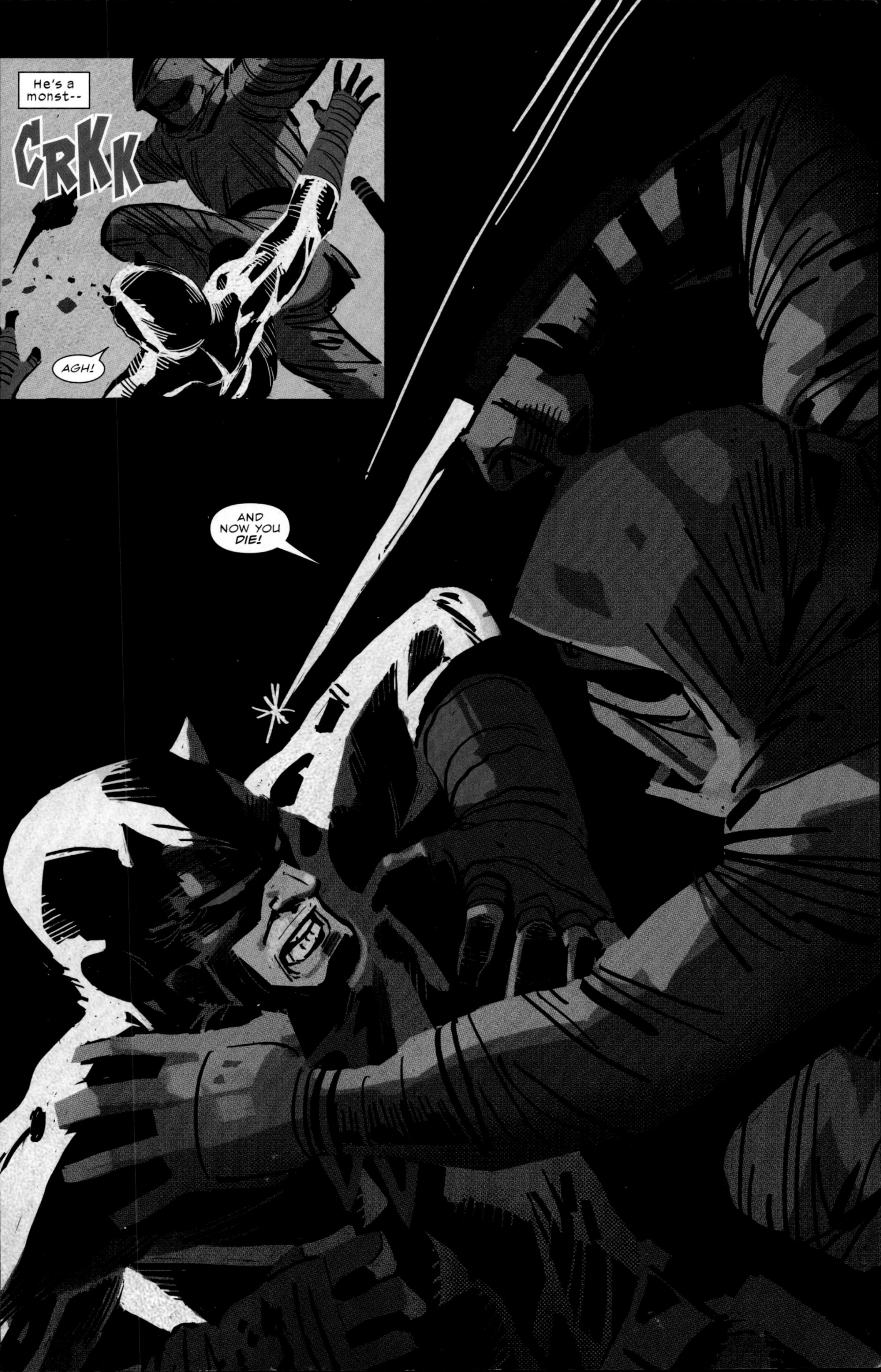
He's a monst--
CRKK
AGH!
AND NOW YOU DIE!

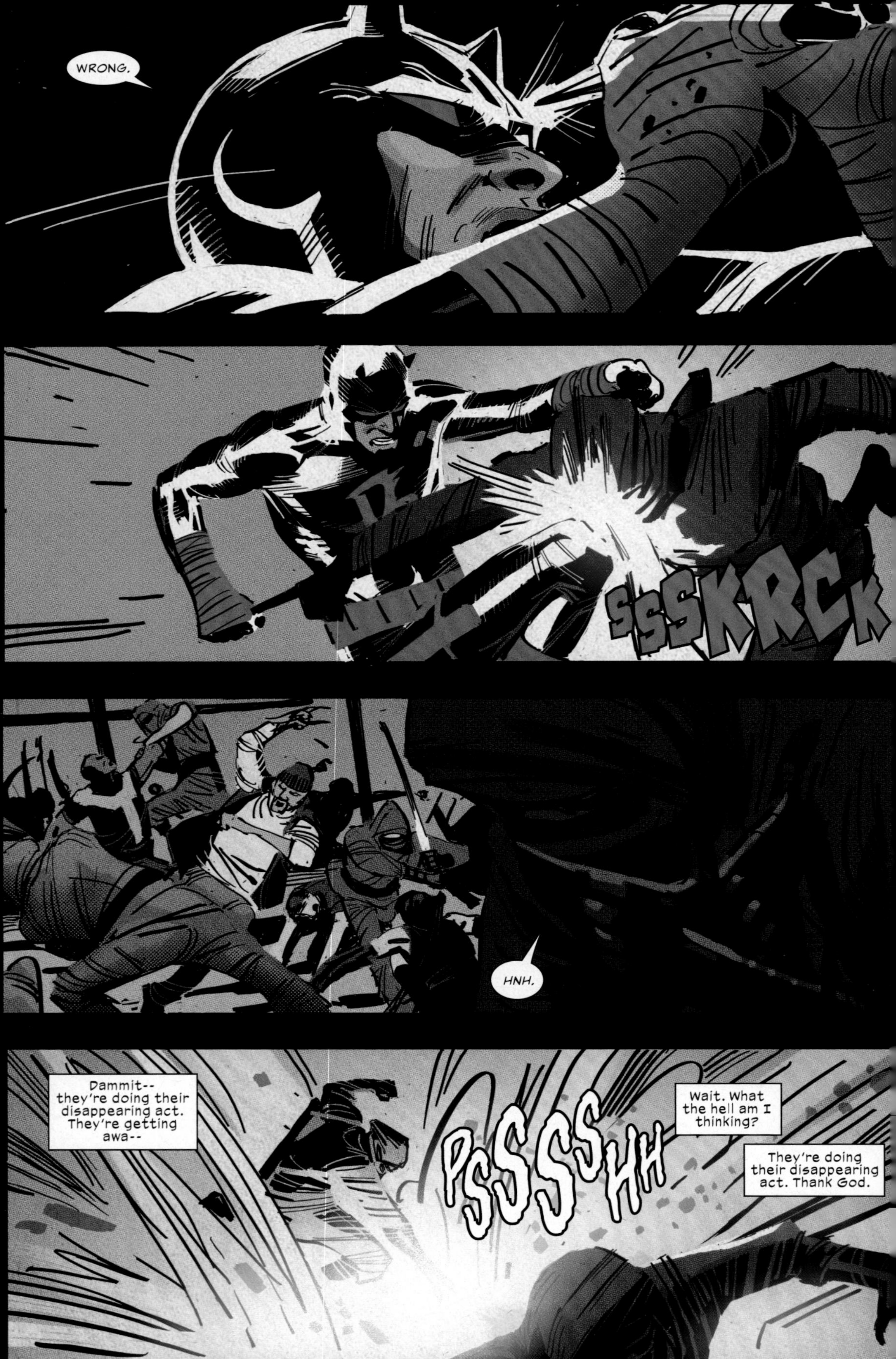
WRONG.
SSSKRCK
HNH.
Dammit-- they're doing their disappearing act. They're getting awa--
PSSSSSHH
Wait. What the hell am I thinking?
They're doing their disappearing act. Thank God.

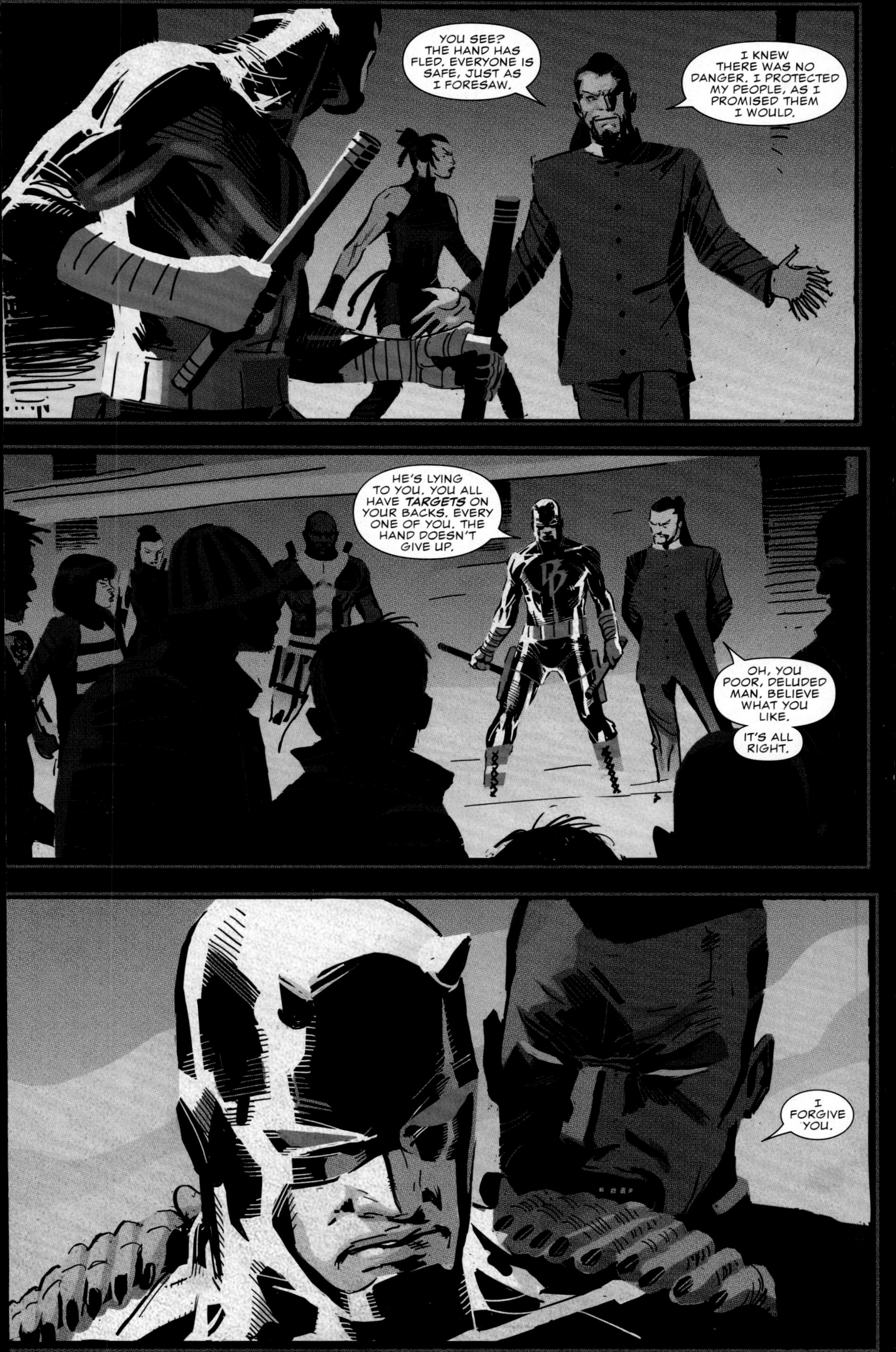
YOU SEE? THE HAND HAS FLED. EVERYONE IS SAFE, JUST AS I FORESAW.
I KNEW THERE WAS NO DANGER. I PROTECTED MY PEOPLE, AS I PROMISED THEM I WOULD.
HE'S LYING TO YOU. YOU ALL HAVE **TARGETS** ON YOUR BACKS. EVERY ONE OF YOU. THE HAND DOESN'T GIVE UP.
OH, YOU POOR, DELUDED MAN. BELIEVE WHAT YOU LIKE.
IT'S ALL RIGHT.
I FORGIVE YOU.

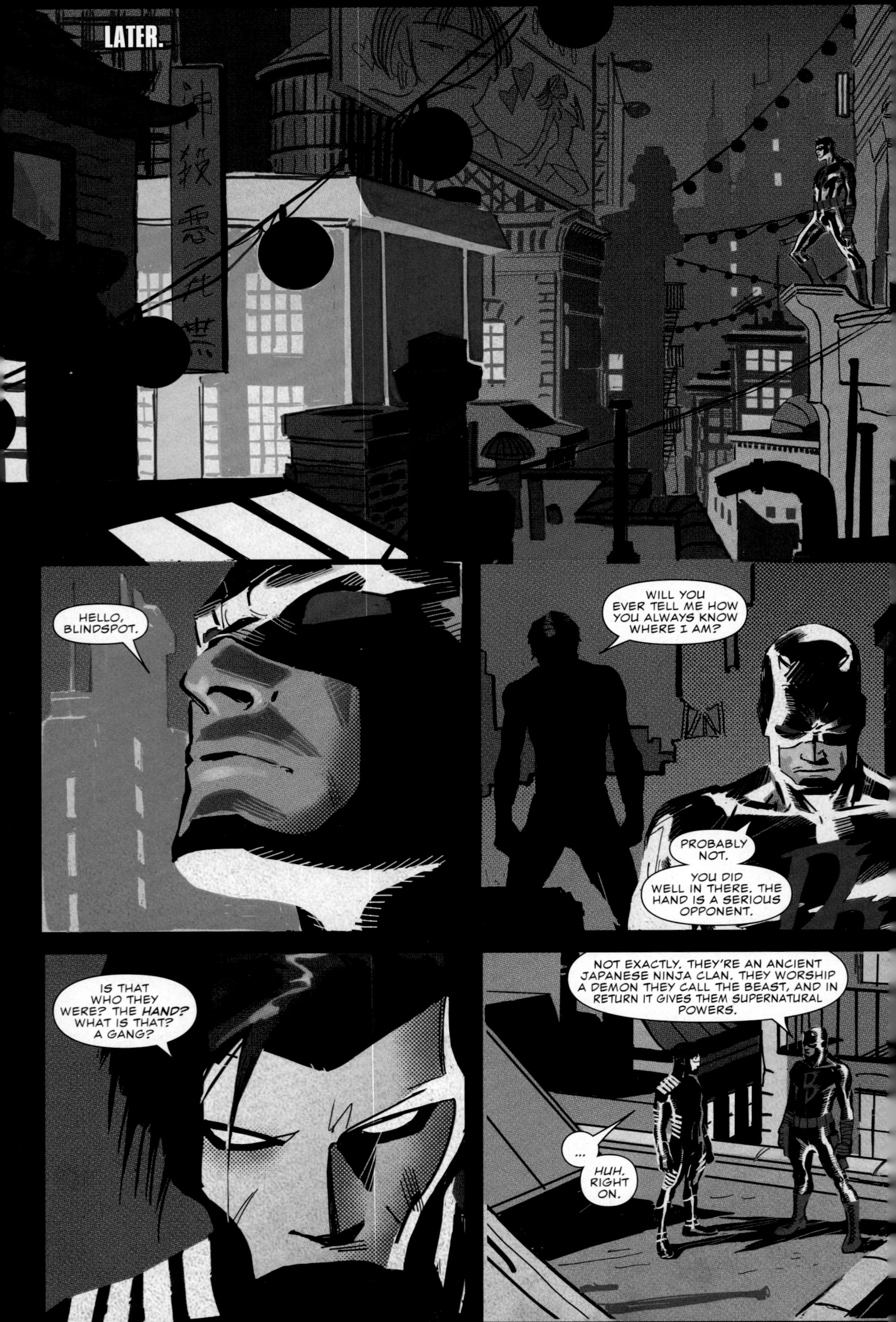
LATER.
HELLO, BLINDSPOT.
WILL YOU EVER TELL ME HOW YOU ALWAYS KNOW WHERE I AM?
PROBABLY NOT.
YOU DID WELL IN THERE. THE HAND IS A SERIOUS OPPONENT.
IS THAT WHO THEY WERE? THE *HAND?* WHAT IS THAT? A GANG?
NOT EXACTLY. THEY'RE AN ANCIENT JAPANESE NINJA CLAN. THEY WORSHIP A DEMON THEY CALL THE BEAST, AND IN RETURN IT GIVES THEM SUPERNATURAL POWERS.
... HUH. RIGHT ON.

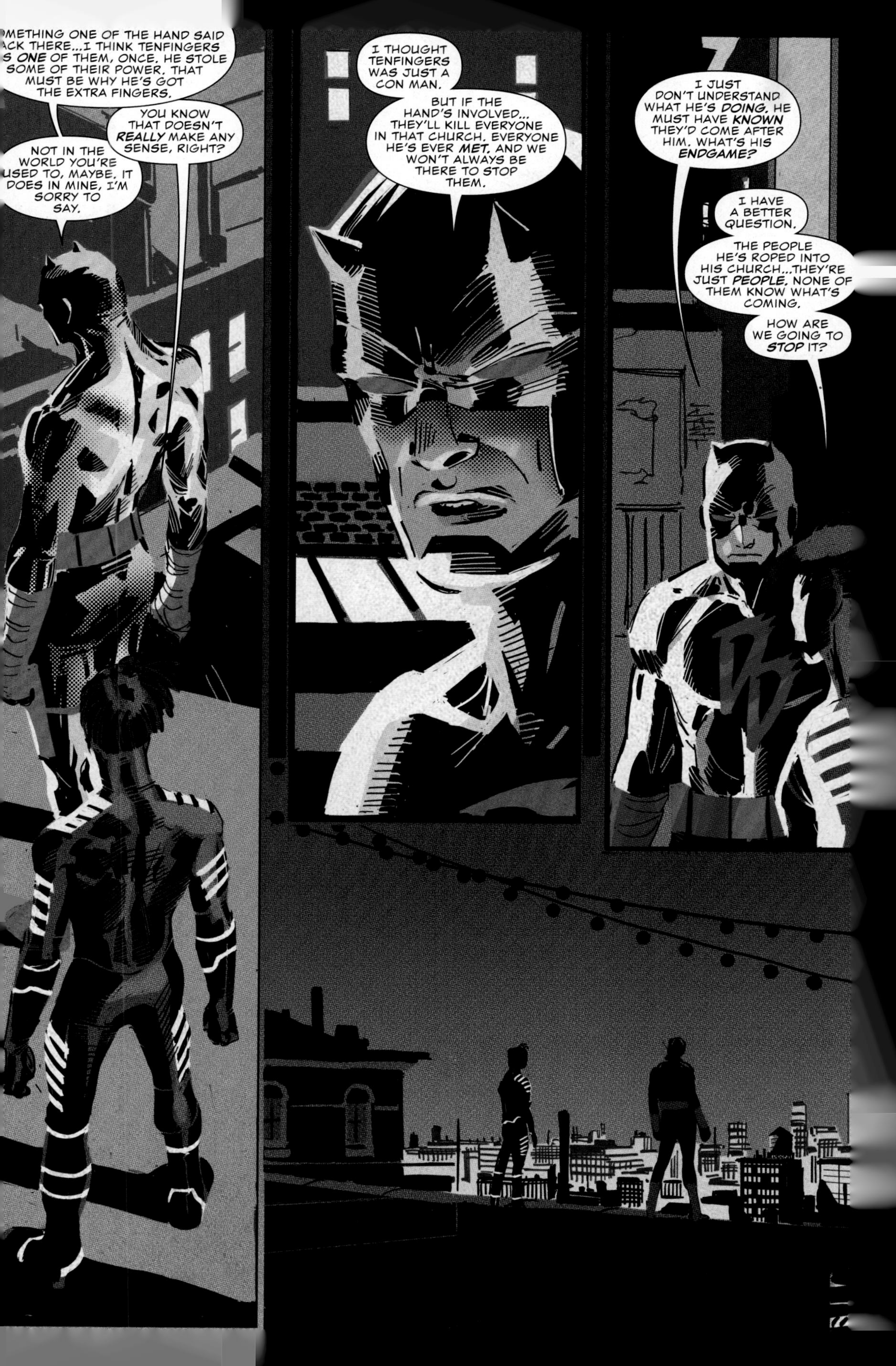

OMETHING ONE OF THE HAND SAID ACK THERE...I THINK TENFINGERS S ONE OF THEM, ONCE. HE STOLE SOME OF THEIR POWER. THAT MUST BE WHY HE'S GOT THE EXTRA FINGERS.
YOU KNOW THAT DOESN'T REALLY MAKE ANY SENSE, RIGHT?
NOT IN THE WORLD YOU'RE USED TO, MAYBE. IT DOES IN MINE, I'M SORRY TO SAY.
I THOUGHT TENFINGERS WAS JUST A CON MAN.
BUT IF THE HAND'S INVOLVED... THEY'LL KILL EVERYONE IN THAT CHURCH. EVERYONE HE'S EVER MET. AND WE WON'T ALWAYS BE THERE TO STOP THEM.
I JUST DON'T UNDERSTAND WHAT HE'S DOING. HE MUST HAVE KNOWN THEY'D COME AFTER HIM. WHAT'S HIS ENDGAME?
I HAVE A BETTER QUESTION.
THE PEOPLE HE'S ROPED INTO HIS CHURCH...THEY'RE JUST PEOPLE. NONE OF THEM KNOW WHAT'S COMING.
HOW ARE WE GOING TO STOP IT?

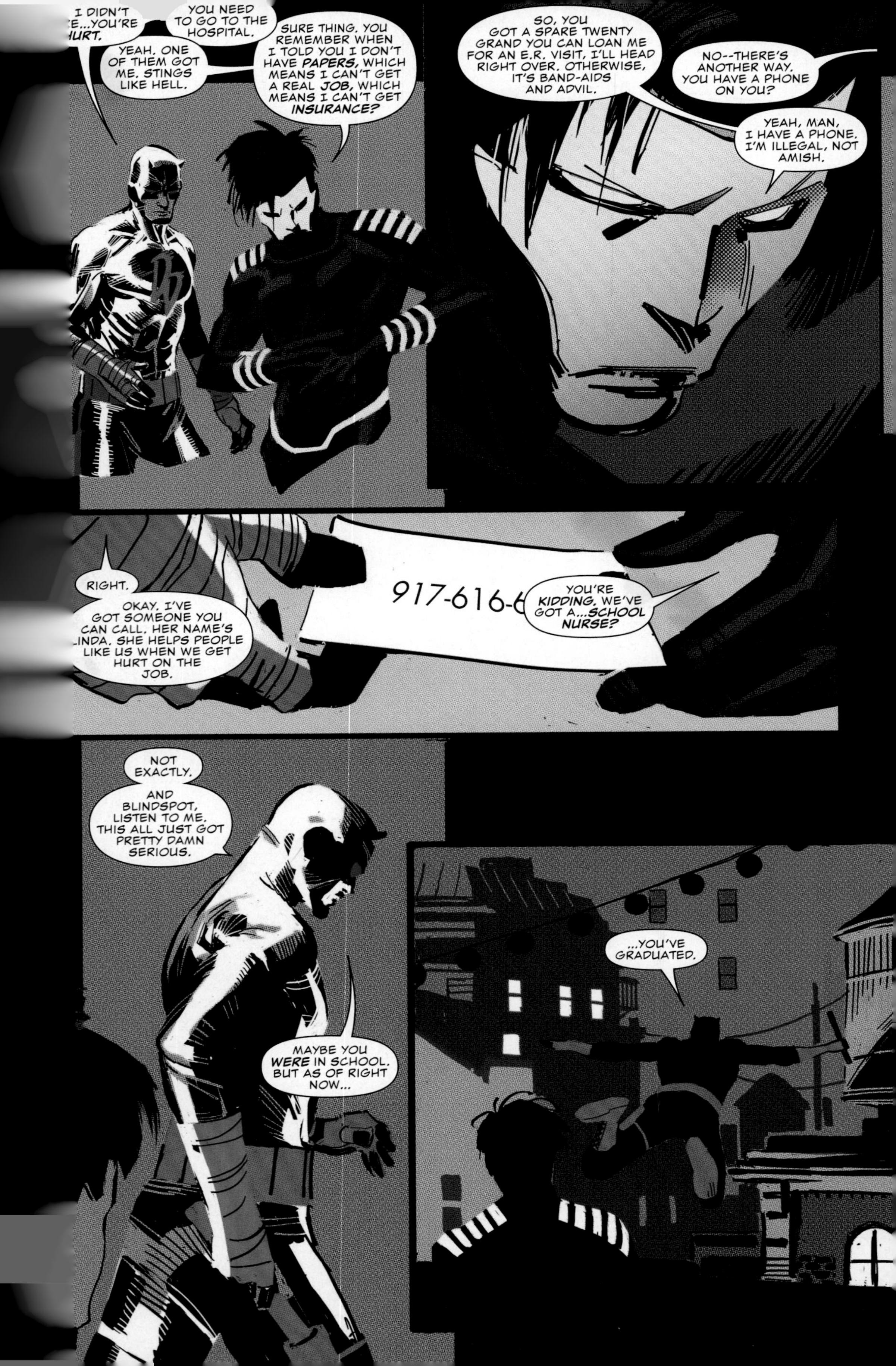
I DIDN'T ...E...YOU'RE HURT.
YOU NEED TO GO TO THE HOSPITAL.
YEAH. ONE OF THEM GOT ME. STINGS LIKE HELL.
SURE THING. YOU REMEMBER WHEN I TOLD YOU I DON'T HAVE PAPERS, WHICH MEANS I CAN'T GET A REAL JOB, WHICH MEANS I CAN'T GET INSURANCE?
SO, YOU GOT A SPARE TWENTY GRAND YOU CAN LOAN ME FOR AN E.R. VISIT, I'LL HEAD RIGHT OVER. OTHERWISE, IT'S BAND-AIDS AND ADVIL.
NO--THERE'S ANOTHER WAY. YOU HAVE A PHONE ON YOU?
YEAH, MAN, I HAVE A PHONE. I'M ILLEGAL, NOT AMISH.
RIGHT.
OKAY. I'VE GOT SOMEONE YOU CAN CALL. HER NAME'S LINDA. SHE HELPS PEOPLE LIKE US WHEN WE GET HURT ON THE JOB.
917-616-6
YOU'RE KIDDING. WE'VE GOT A...SCHOOL NURSE?
NOT EXACTLY.
AND BLINDSPOT, LISTEN TO ME. THIS ALL JUST GOT PRETTY DAMN SERIOUS.
MAYBE YOU WERE IN SCHOOL. BUT AS OF RIGHT NOW...
...YOU'VE GRADUATED.

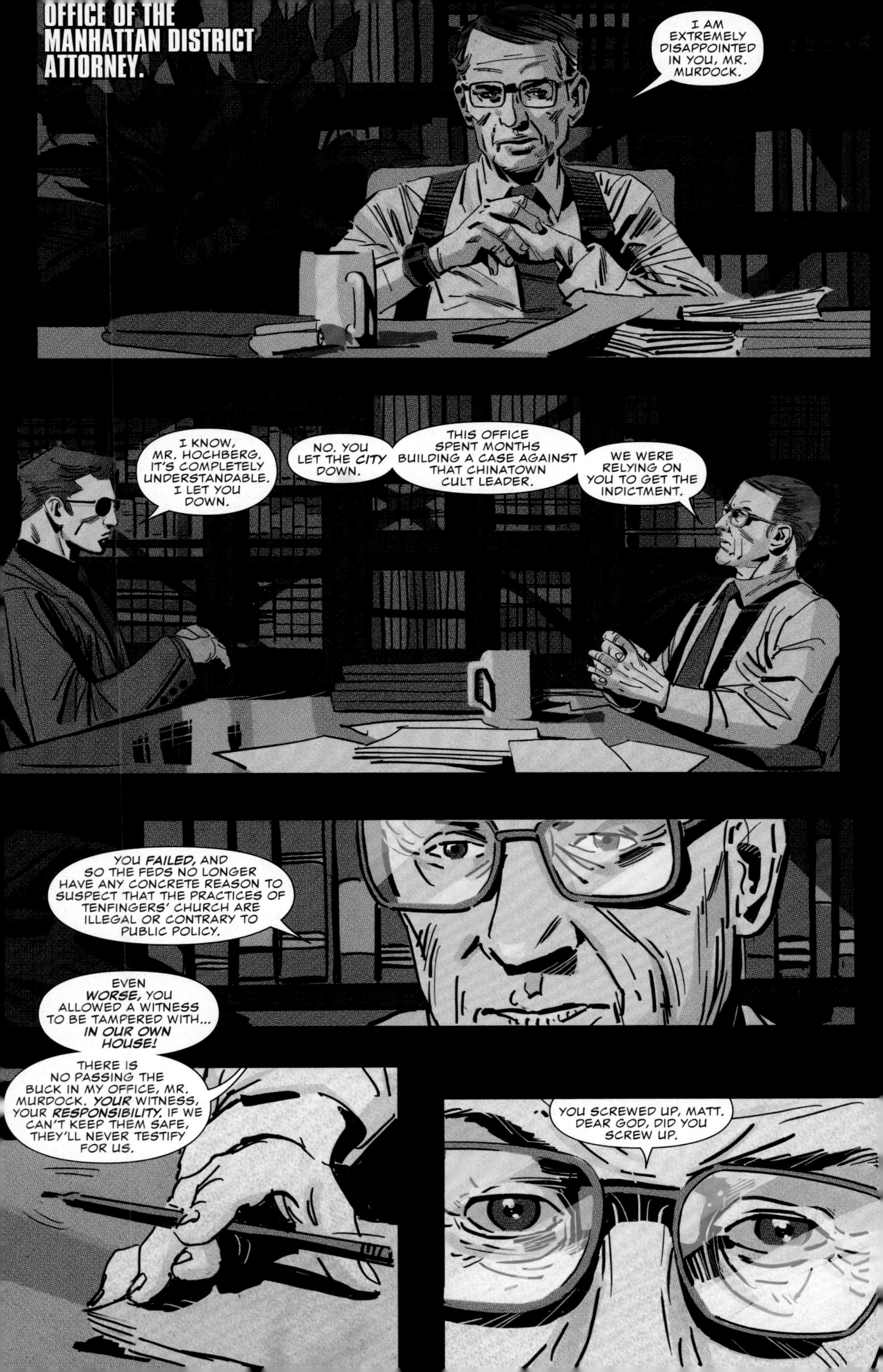
OFFICE OF THE MANHATTAN DISTRICT ATTORNEY.
I AM EXTREMELY DISAPPOINTED IN YOU, MR. MURDOCK.
I KNOW, MR. HOCHBERG. IT'S COMPLETELY UNDERSTANDABLE. I LET YOU DOWN.
NO. YOU LET THE CITY DOWN.
THIS OFFICE SPENT MONTHS BUILDING A CASE AGAINST THAT CHINATOWN CULT LEADER.
WE WERE RELYING ON YOU TO GET THE INDICTMENT.
YOU FAILED, AND SO THE FEDS NO LONGER HAVE ANY CONCRETE REASON TO SUSPECT THAT THE PRACTICES OF TENFINGERS' CHURCH ARE ILLEGAL OR CONTRARY TO PUBLIC POLICY.
EVEN WORSE, YOU ALLOWED A WITNESS TO BE TAMPERED WITH... IN OUR OWN HOUSE!
THERE IS NO PASSING THE BUCK IN MY OFFICE, MR. MURDOCK. YOUR WITNESS, YOUR RESPONSIBILITY. IF WE CAN'T KEEP THEM SAFE, THEY'LL NEVER TESTIFY FOR US.
YOU SCREWED UP, MATT. DEAR GOD, DID YOU SCREW UP.

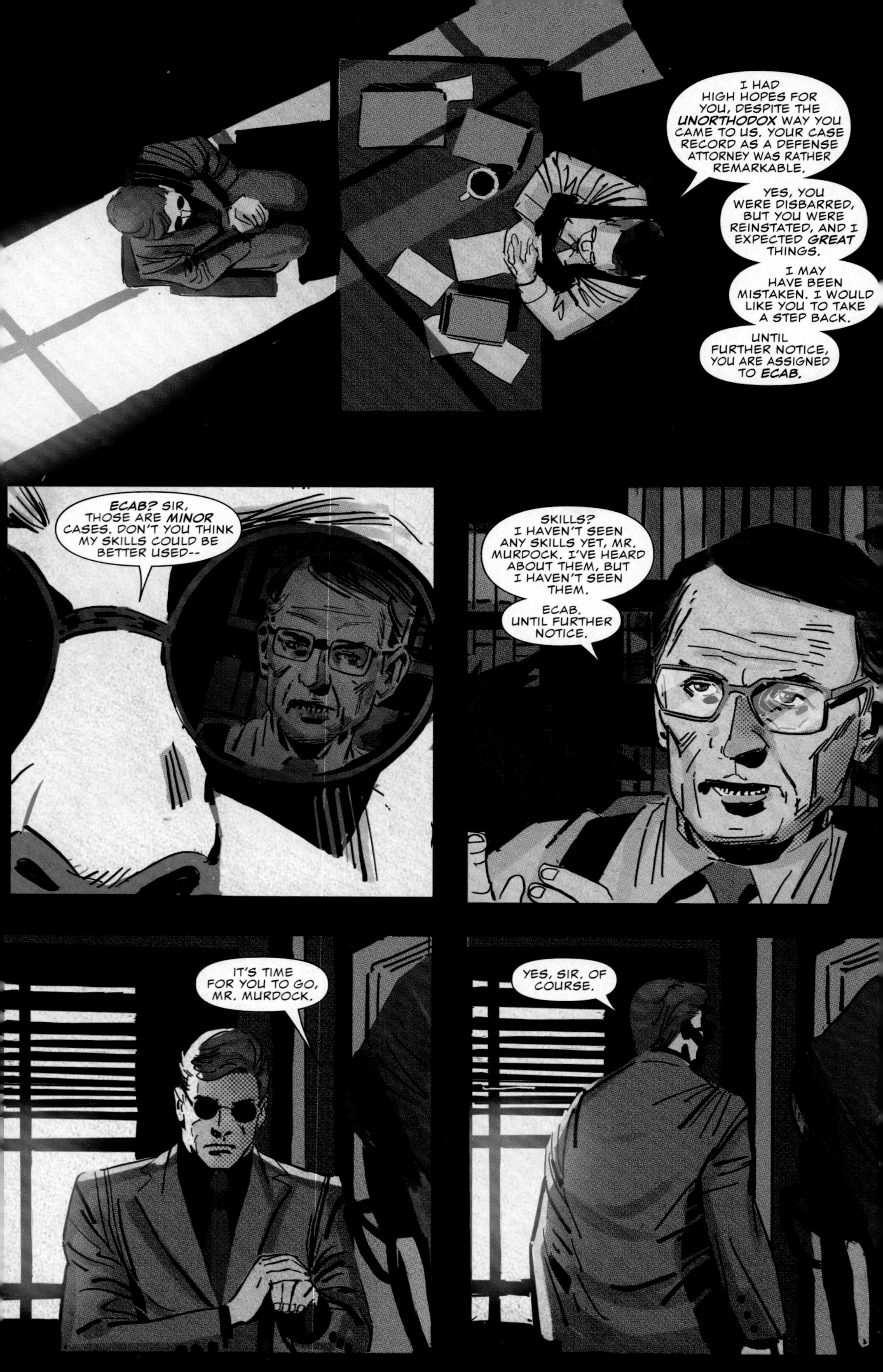
I HAD HIGH HOPES FOR YOU, DESPITE THE UNORTHODOX WAY YOU CAME TO US. YOUR CASE RECORD AS A DEFENSE ATTORNEY WAS RATHER REMARKABLE.
YES, YOU WERE DISBARRED, BUT YOU WERE REINSTATED, AND I EXPECTED GREAT THINGS.
I MAY HAVE BEEN MISTAKEN. I WOULD LIKE YOU TO TAKE A STEP BACK.
UNTIL FURTHER NOTICE, YOU ARE ASSIGNED TO ECAB.
ECAB? SIR, THOSE ARE MINOR CASES. DON'T YOU THINK MY SKILLS COULD BE BETTER USED--
SKILLS? I HAVEN'T SEEN ANY SKILLS YET, MR. MURDOCK. I'VE HEARD ABOUT THEM, BUT I HAVEN'T SEEN THEM.
ECAB. UNTIL FURTHER NOTICE.
IT'S TIME FOR YOU TO GO, MR. MURDOCK.
YES, SIR. OF COURSE.

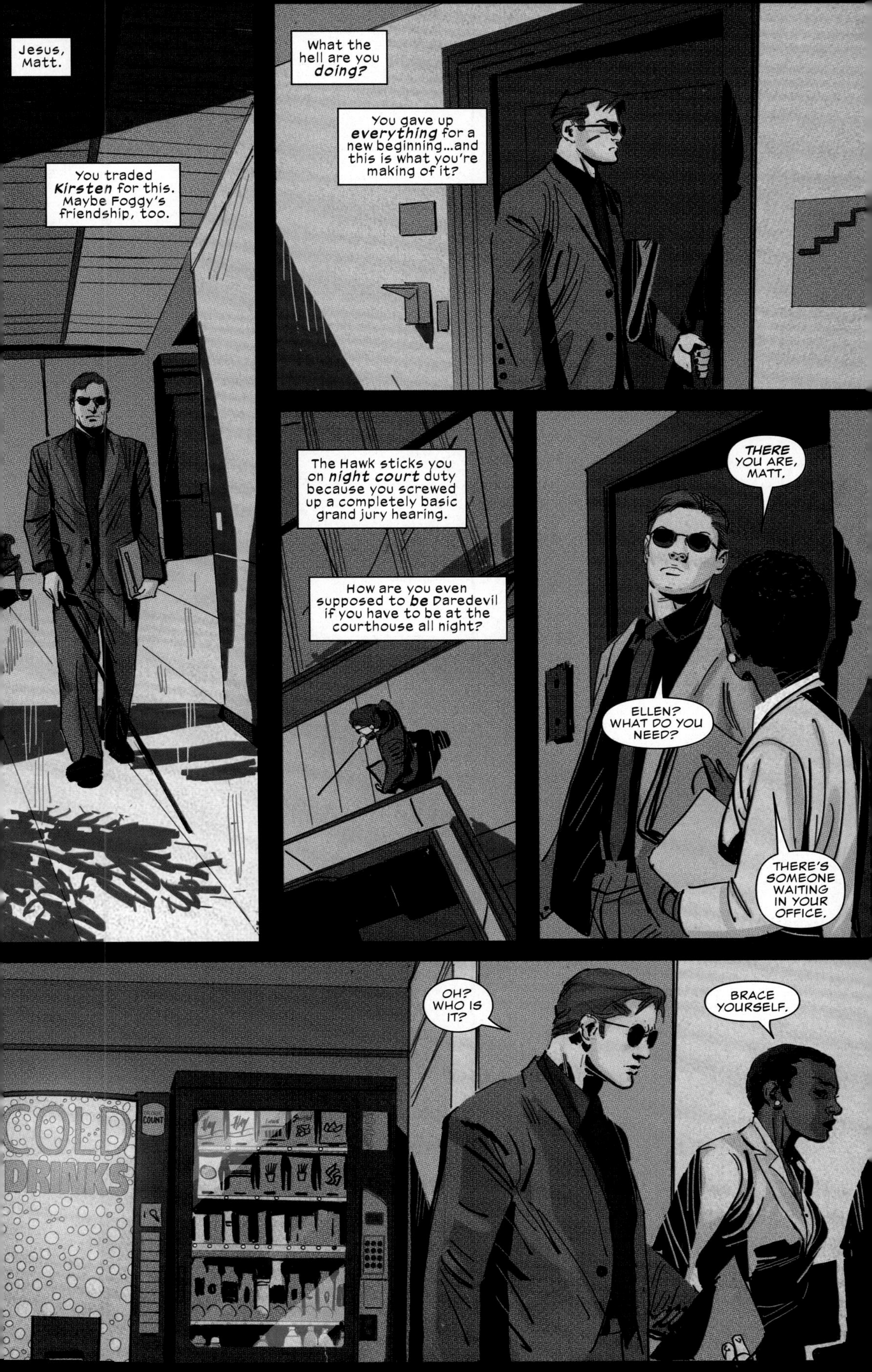
Jesus, Matt.
You traded *Kirsten* for this. Maybe Foggy's friendship, too.
What the hell are you *doing?*
You gave up *everything* for a new beginning...and this is what you're making of it?
The Hawk sticks you on *night court* duty because you screwed up a completely basic grand jury hearing.
How are you even supposed to *be* Daredevil if you have to be at the courthouse all night?
THERE YOU ARE, MATT.
ELLEN? WHAT DO YOU NEED?
THERE'S SOMEONE WAITING IN YOUR OFFICE.
COLD DRINKS
OH? WHO IS IT?
BRACE YOURSELF.

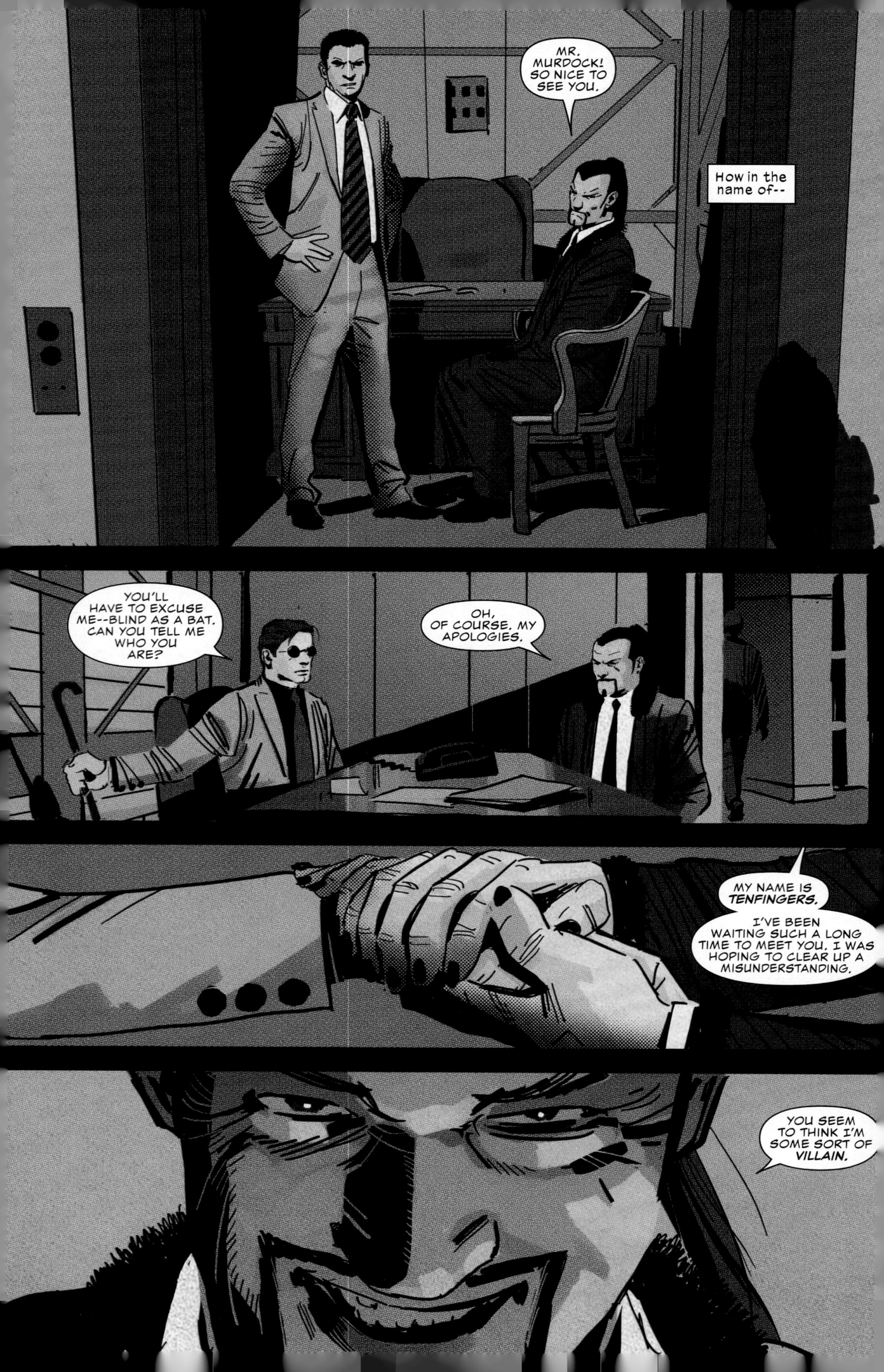

MR. MURDOCK! SO NICE TO SEE YOU.
How in the name of--
YOU'LL HAVE TO EXCUSE ME--BLIND AS A BAT. CAN YOU TELL ME WHO YOU ARE?
OH, OF COURSE. MY APOLOGIES.
MY NAME IS TENFINGERS.
I'VE BEEN WAITING SUCH A LONG TIME TO MEET YOU. I WAS HOPING TO CLEAR UP A MISUNDERSTANDING.
YOU SEEM TO THINK I'M SOME SORT OF VILLAIN.

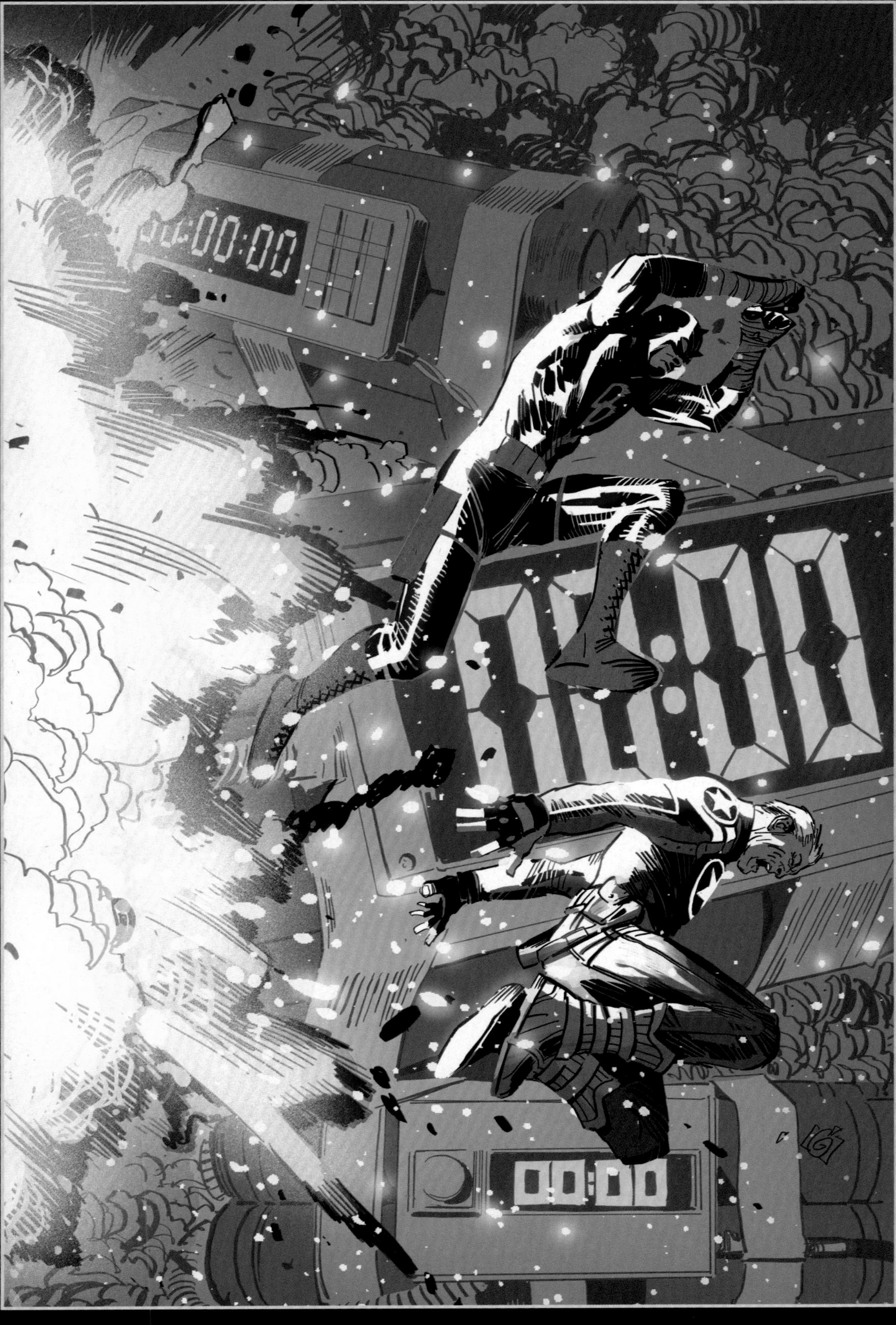
00:00
00:00

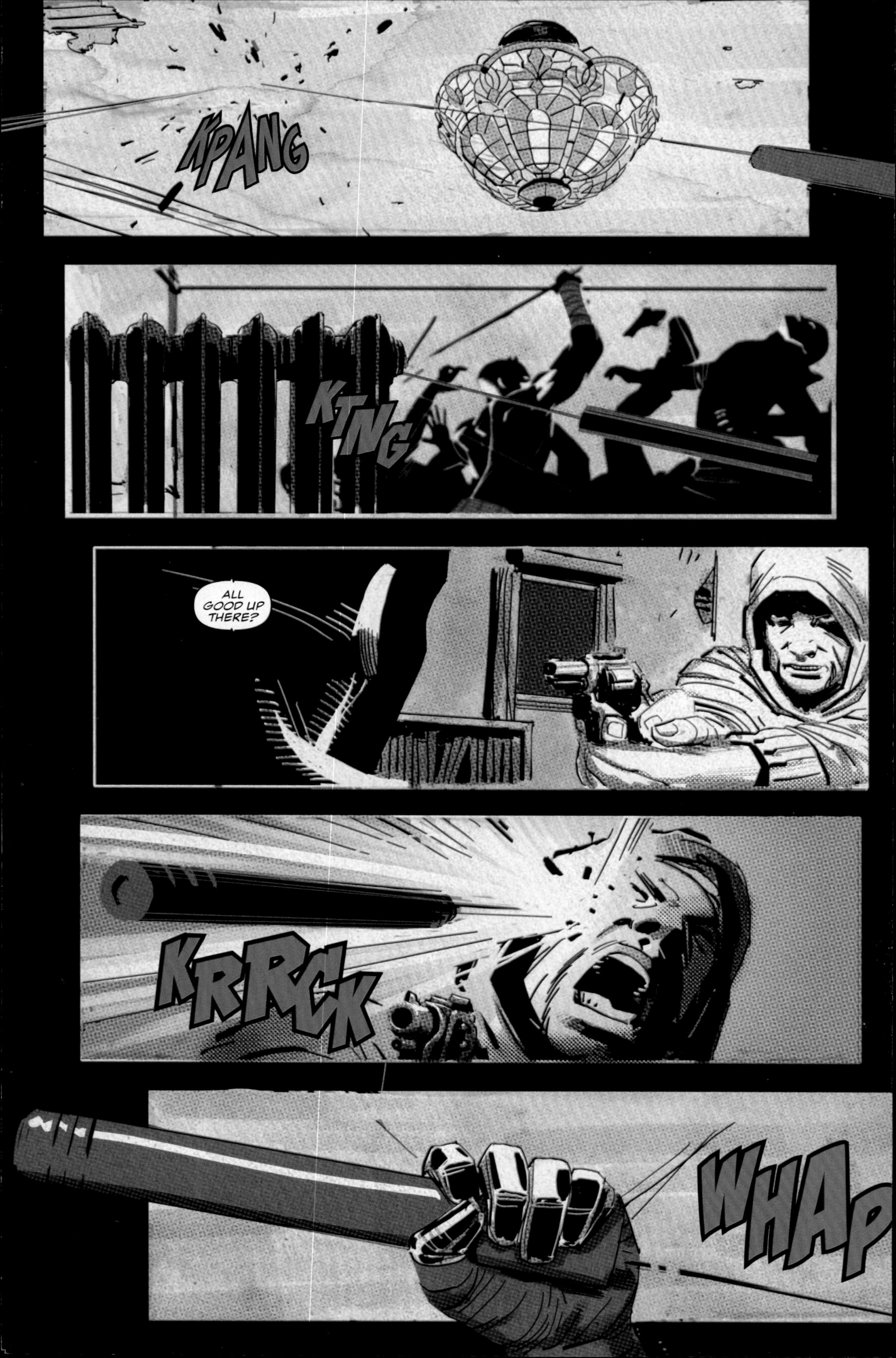
KPANG
KTNG
ALL GOOD UP THERE?
KRRCK
WHAP

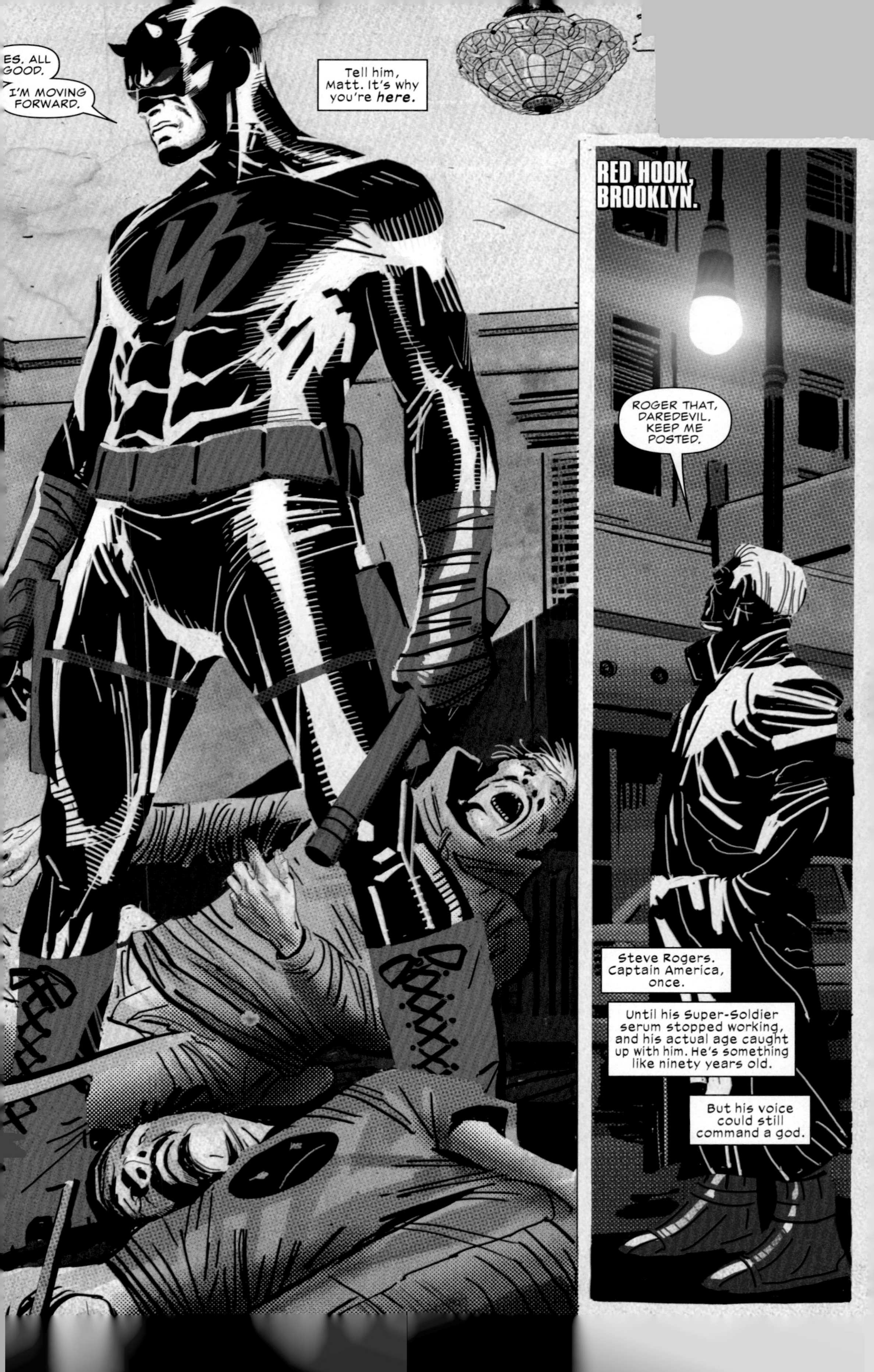

ES. ALL GOOD.
I'M MOVING FORWARD.
Tell him, Matt. It's why you're *here*.
RED HOOK, BROOKLYN.
ROGER THAT, DAREDEVIL. KEEP ME POSTED.
Steve Rogers. Captain America, once.
Until his Super-Soldier serum stopped working, and his actual age caught up with him. He's something like ninety years old.
But his voice could still command a god.

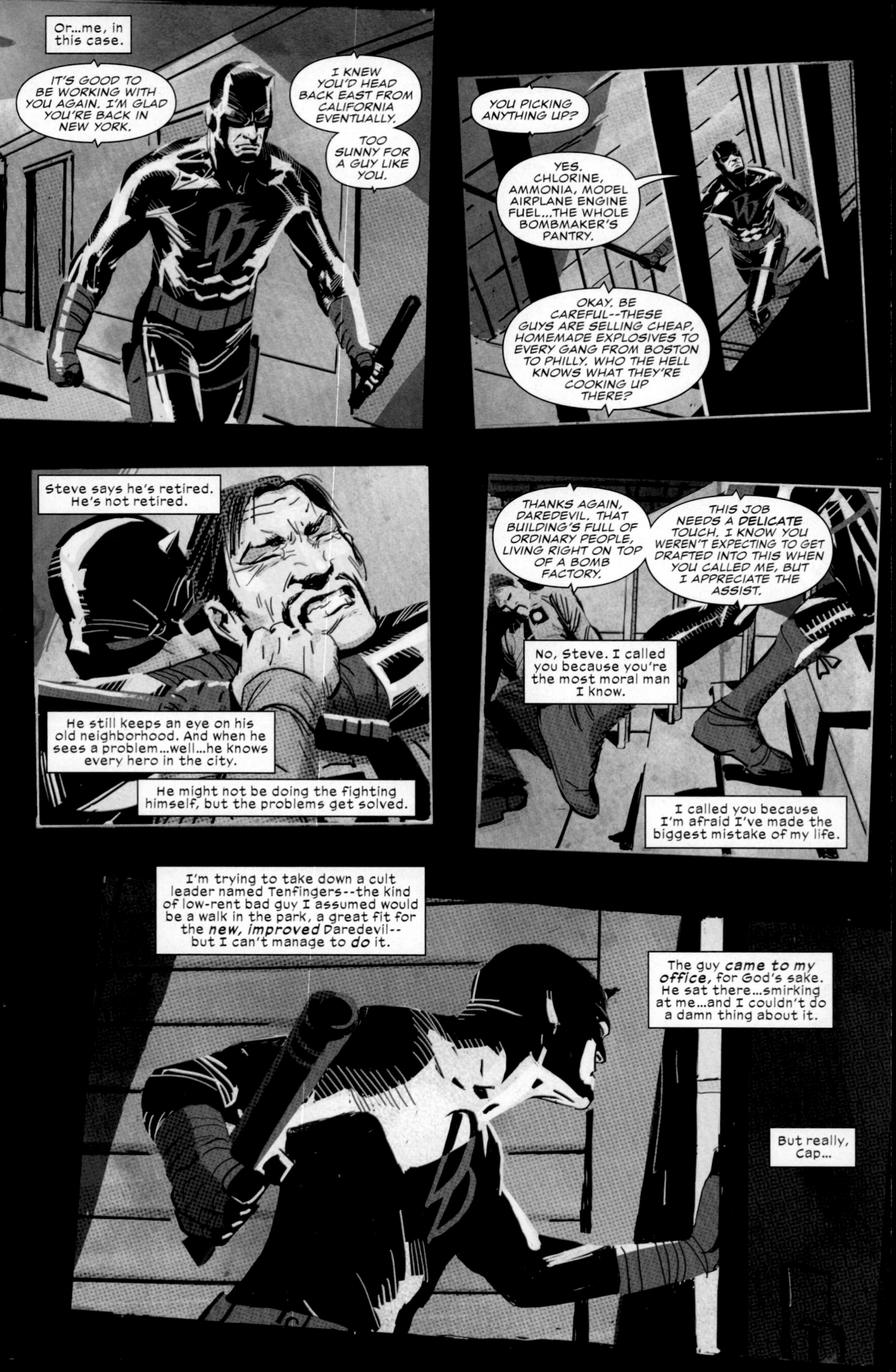

Or...me, in this case.
IT'S GOOD TO BE WORKING WITH YOU AGAIN. I'M GLAD YOU'RE BACK IN NEW YORK.
I KNEW YOU'D HEAD BACK EAST FROM CALIFORNIA EVENTUALLY.
TOO SUNNY FOR A GUY LIKE YOU.
YOU PICKING ANYTHING UP?
YES. CHLORINE, AMMONIA, MODEL AIRPLANE ENGINE FUEL...THE WHOLE BOMBMAKER'S PANTRY.
OKAY. BE CAREFUL--THESE GUYS ARE SELLING CHEAP, HOMEMADE EXPLOSIVES TO EVERY GANG FROM BOSTON TO PHILLY. WHO THE HELL KNOWS WHAT THEY'RE COOKING UP THERE?
Steve says he's retired. He's not retired.
He still keeps an eye on his old neighborhood. And when he sees a problem...well...he knows every hero in the city.
He might not be doing the fighting himself, but the problems get solved.
THANKS AGAIN, DAREDEVIL. THAT BUILDING'S FULL OF ORDINARY PEOPLE, LIVING RIGHT ON TOP OF A BOMB FACTORY.
THIS JOB NEEDS A **DELICATE** TOUCH. I KNOW YOU WEREN'T EXPECTING TO GET DRAFTED INTO THIS WHEN YOU CALLED ME, BUT I APPRECIATE THE ASSIST.
No, Steve. I called you because you're the most moral man I know.
I called you because I'm afraid I've made the biggest mistake of my life.
I'm trying to take down a cult leader named Tenfingers--the kind of low-rent bad guy I assumed would be a walk in the park, a great fit for the *new, improved* Daredevil--but I can't manage to *do* it.
The guy *came to my office,* for God's sake. He sat there...smirking at me...and I couldn't do a damn thing about it.
But really, Cap...

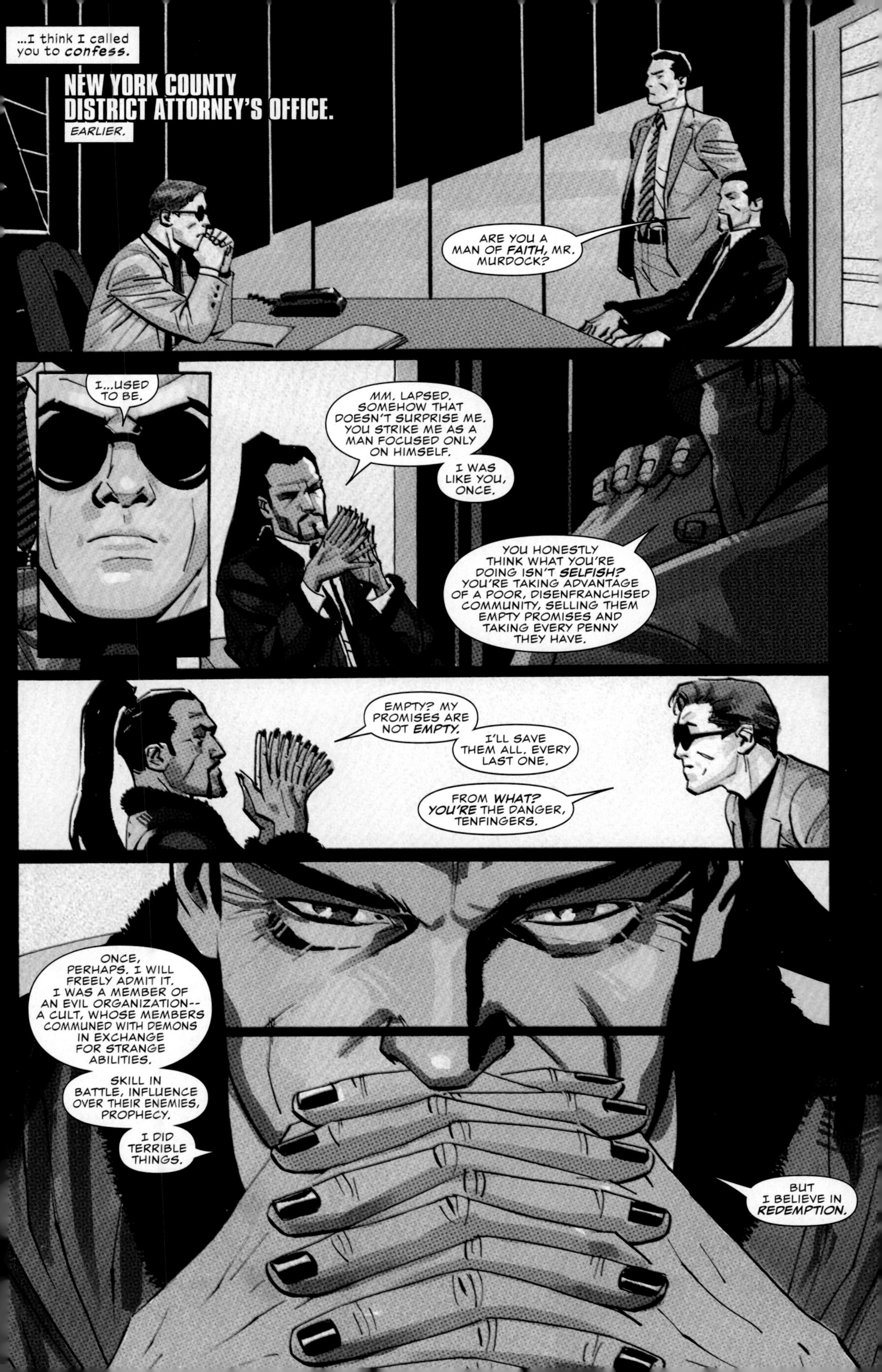

...I think I called you to *confess.*
NEW YORK COUNTY DISTRICT ATTORNEY'S OFFICE.
EARLIER.
ARE YOU A MAN OF *FAITH*, MR. MURDOCK?
I...USED TO BE.
MM. LAPSED. SOMEHOW THAT DOESN'T SURPRISE ME. YOU STRIKE ME AS A MAN FOCUSED ONLY ON HIMSELF.
I WAS LIKE YOU, ONCE.
YOU HONESTLY THINK WHAT YOU'RE DOING ISN'T *SELFISH?* YOU'RE TAKING ADVANTAGE OF A POOR, DISENFRANCHISED COMMUNITY, SELLING THEM EMPTY PROMISES AND TAKING EVERY PENNY THEY HAVE.
EMPTY? MY PROMISES ARE NOT *EMPTY.*
I'LL SAVE THEM ALL. EVERY LAST ONE.
FROM *WHAT? YOU'RE* THE DANGER, TENFINGERS.
ONCE, PERHAPS. I WILL FREELY ADMIT IT. I WAS A MEMBER OF AN EVIL ORGANIZATION-- A CULT, WHOSE MEMBERS COMMUNED WITH DEMONS IN EXCHANGE FOR STRANGE ABILITIES.
SKILL IN BATTLE, INFLUENCE OVER THEIR ENEMIES, PROPHECY.
I DID TERRIBLE THINGS.
BUT I BELIEVE IN *REDEMPTION.*

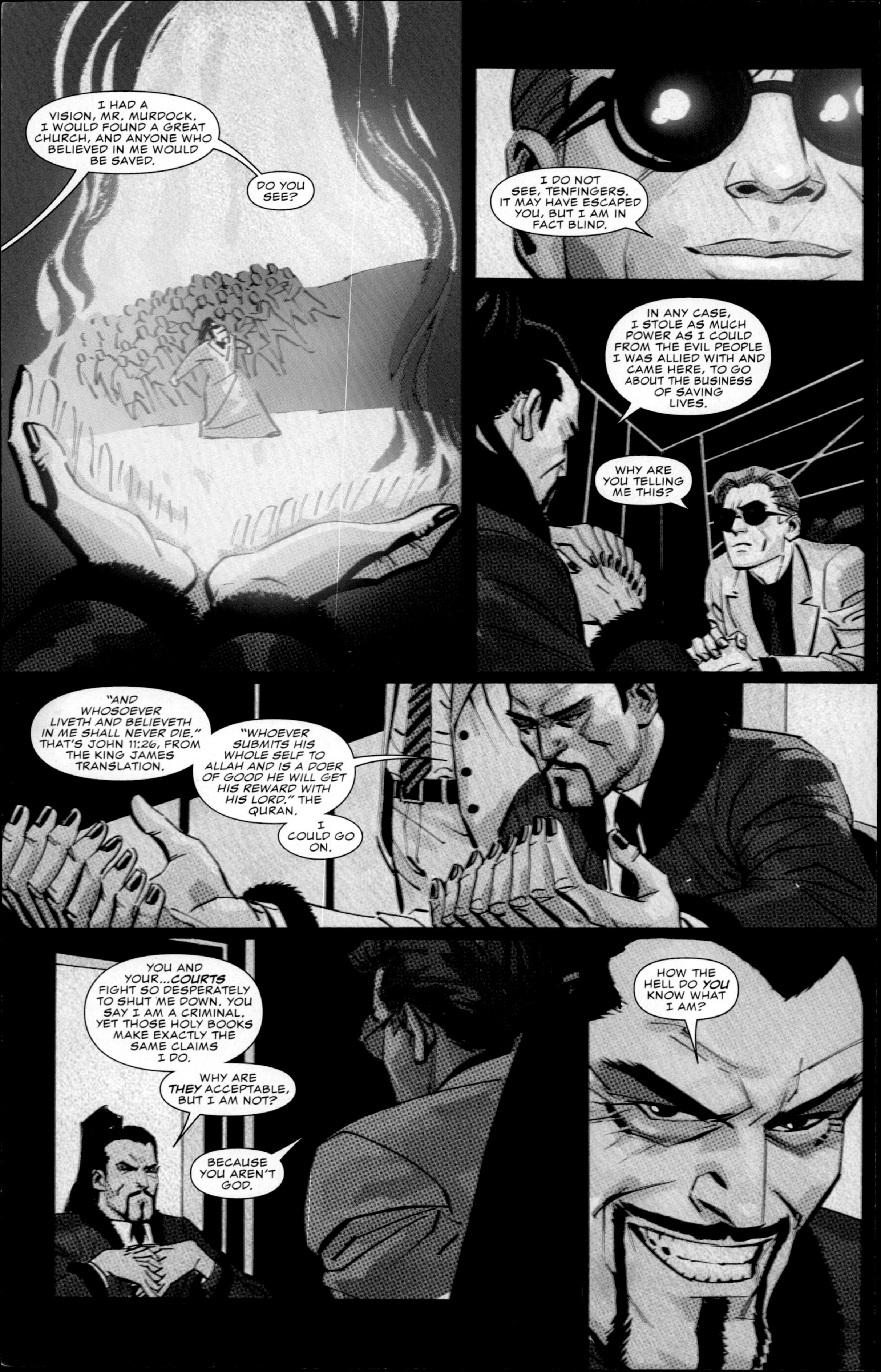
I HAD A VISION, MR. MURDOCK. I WOULD FOUND A GREAT CHURCH, AND ANYONE WHO BELIEVED IN ME WOULD BE SAVED.
DO YOU SEE?
I DO NOT SEE, TENFINGERS. IT MAY HAVE ESCAPED YOU, BUT I AM IN FACT BLIND.
IN ANY CASE, I STOLE AS MUCH POWER AS I COULD FROM THE EVIL PEOPLE I WAS ALLIED WITH AND CAME HERE, TO GO ABOUT THE BUSINESS OF SAVING LIVES.
WHY ARE YOU TELLING ME THIS?
"AND WHOSOEVER LIVETH AND BELIEVETH IN ME SHALL NEVER DIE." THAT'S JOHN 11:26, FROM THE KING JAMES TRANSLATION.
"WHOEVER SUBMITS HIS WHOLE SELF TO ALLAH AND IS A DOER OF GOOD HE WILL GET HIS REWARD WITH HIS LORD." THE QURAN.
I COULD GO ON.
YOU AND YOUR...COURTS FIGHT SO DESPERATELY TO SHUT ME DOWN. YOU SAY I AM A CRIMINAL. YET THOSE HOLY BOOKS MAKE EXACTLY THE SAME CLAIMS I DO.
WHY ARE THEY ACCEPTABLE, BUT I AM NOT?
BECAUSE YOU AREN'T GOD.
HOW THE HELL DO YOU KNOW WHAT I AM?

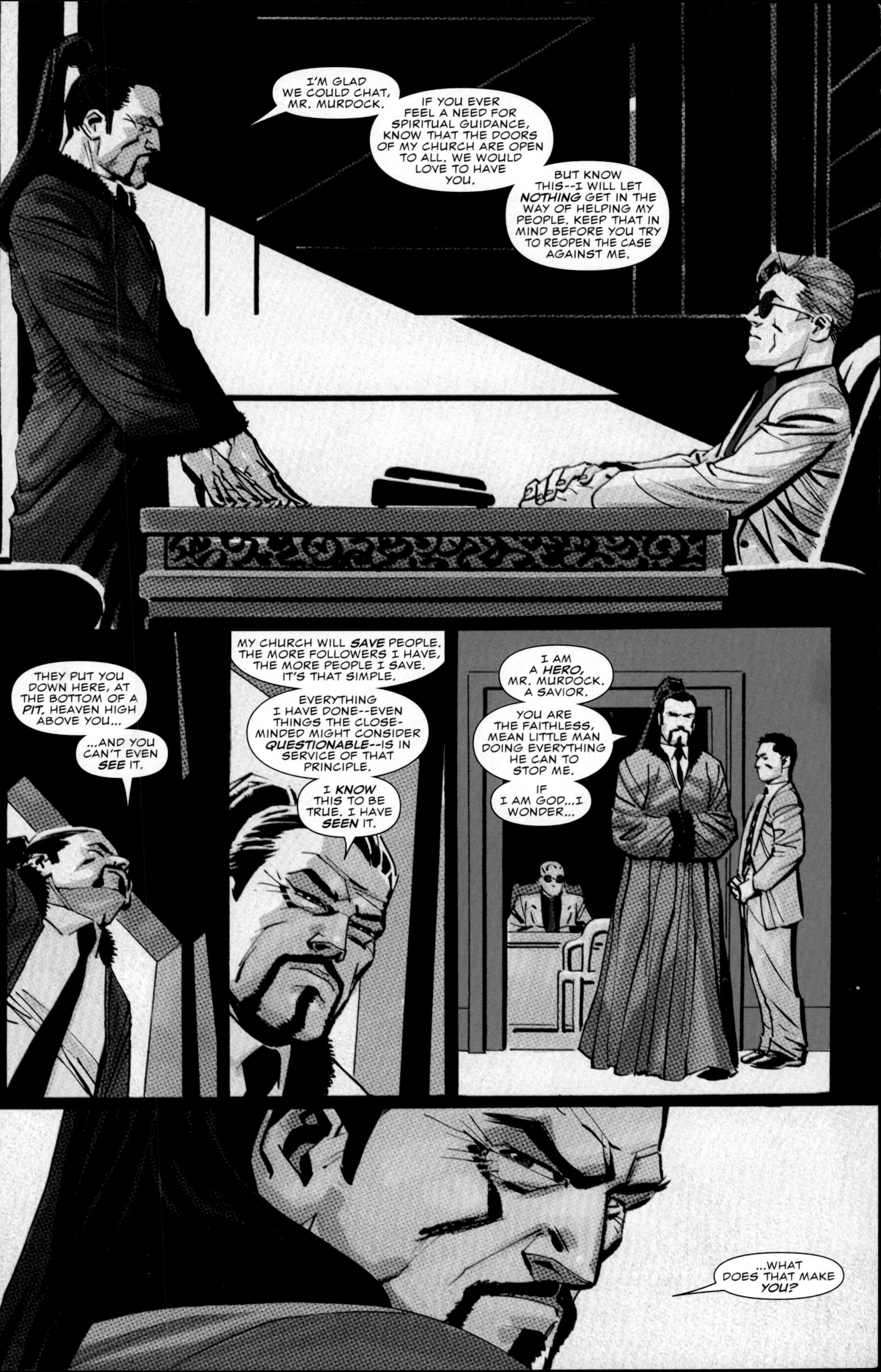
I'M GLAD WE COULD CHAT, MR. MURDOCK.
IF YOU EVER FEEL A NEED FOR SPIRITUAL GUIDANCE, KNOW THAT THE DOORS OF MY CHURCH ARE OPEN TO ALL. WE WOULD LOVE TO HAVE YOU.
BUT KNOW THIS--I WILL LET NOTHING GET IN THE WAY OF HELPING MY PEOPLE. KEEP THAT IN MIND BEFORE YOU TRY TO REOPEN THE CASE AGAINST ME.
THEY PUT YOU DOWN HERE, AT THE BOTTOM OF A PIT, HEAVEN HIGH ABOVE YOU...
...AND YOU CAN'T EVEN SEE IT.
MY CHURCH WILL SAVE PEOPLE. THE MORE FOLLOWERS I HAVE, THE MORE PEOPLE I SAVE. IT'S THAT SIMPLE.
EVERYTHING I HAVE DONE--EVEN THINGS THE CLOSE-MINDED MIGHT CONSIDER QUESTIONABLE--IS IN SERVICE OF THAT PRINCIPLE.
I KNOW THIS TO BE TRUE. I HAVE SEEN IT.
I AM A HERO, MR. MURDOCK. A SAVIOR.
YOU ARE THE FAITHLESS, MEAN LITTLE MAN DOING EVERYTHING HE CAN TO STOP ME.
IF I AM GOD...I WONDER...
...WHAT DOES THAT MAKE YOU?

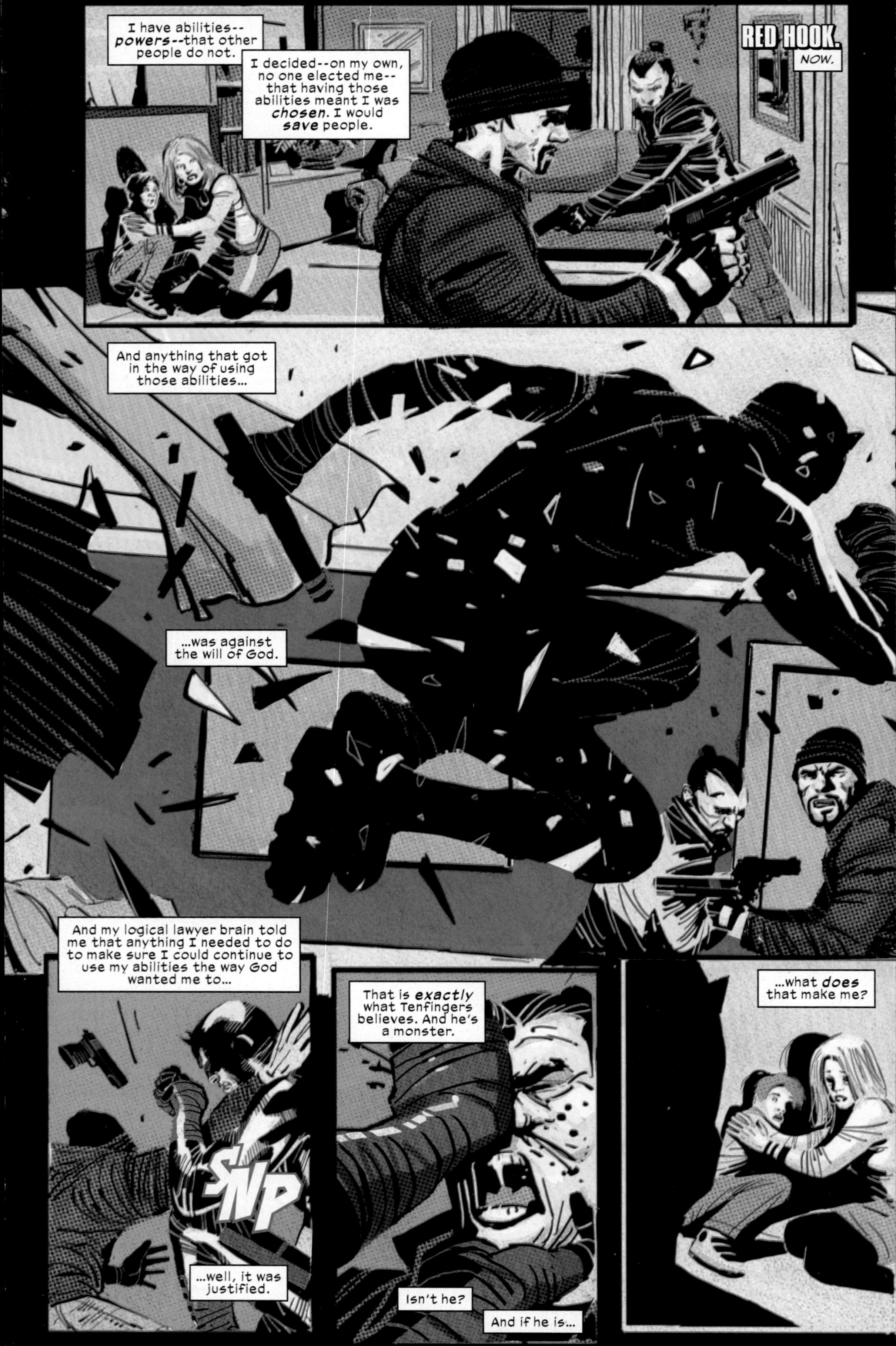
I have abilities--
powers--that other
people do not.
I decided--on my own,
no one elected me--
that having those
abilities meant I was
chosen. I would
save people.
RED HOOK.
NOW.
And anything that got
in the way of using
those abilities...
...was against
the will of God.
And my logical lawyer brain told
me that anything I needed to do
to make sure I could continue to
use my abilities the way God
wanted me to...
SNP
...well, it was
justified.
That is *exactly*
what Tenfingers
believes. And he's
a monster.
Isn't he?
And if he is...
...what *does*
that make me?

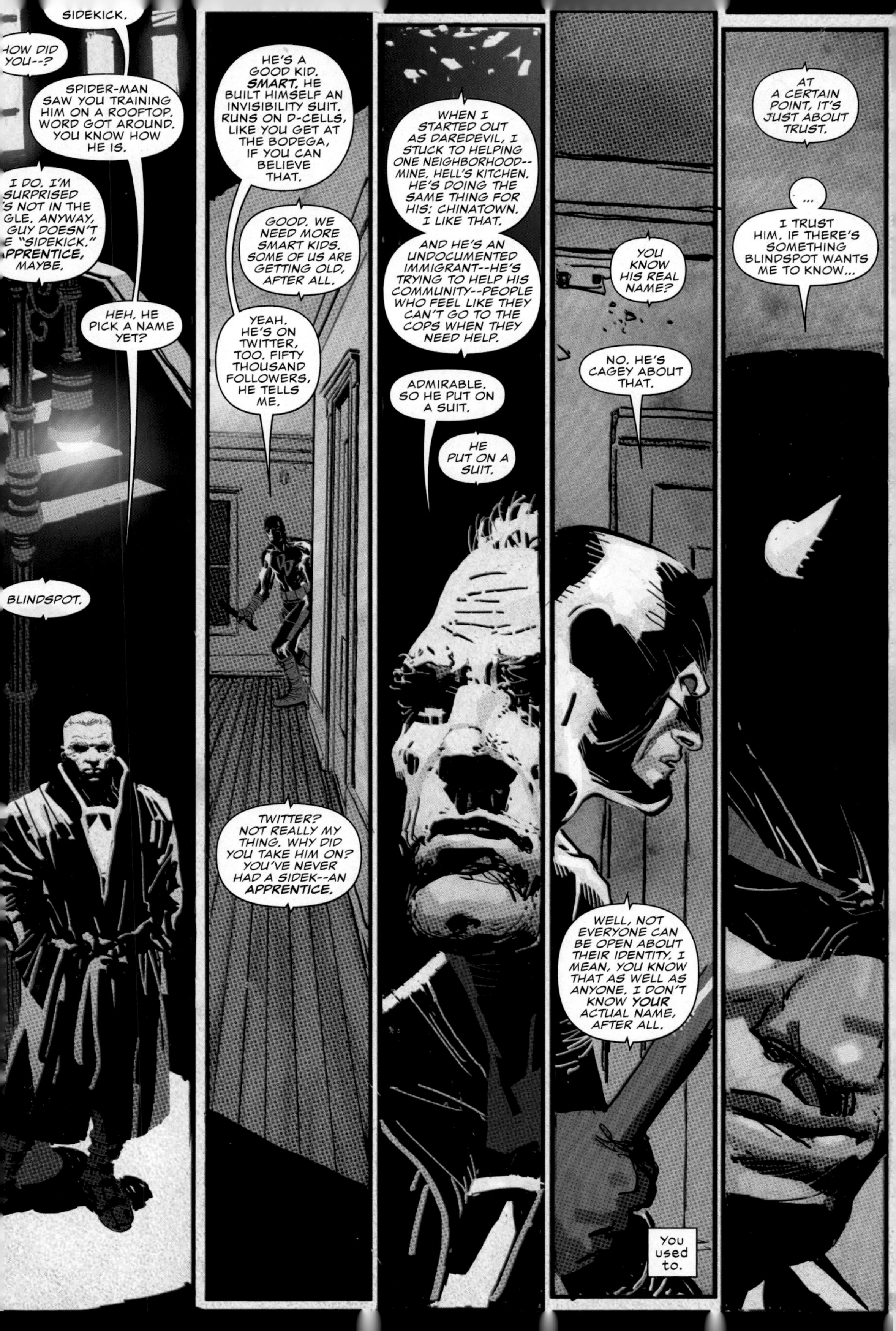
SIDEKICK.
HOW DID YOU--?
SPIDER-MAN SAW YOU TRAINING HIM ON A ROOFTOP. WORD GOT AROUND. YOU KNOW HOW HE IS.
I DO. I'M SURPRISED 'S NOT IN THE GLE. ANYWAY, GUY DOESN'T E "SIDEKICK." PPRENTICE, MAYBE.
HEH. HE PICK A NAME YET?
BLINDSPOT.
HE'S A GOOD KID. **SMART.** HE BUILT HIMSELF AN INVISIBILITY SUIT. RUNS ON D-CELLS, LIKE YOU GET AT THE BODEGA, IF YOU CAN BELIEVE THAT.
GOOD. WE NEED MORE SMART KIDS. SOME OF US ARE GETTING OLD, AFTER ALL.
YEAH. HE'S ON TWITTER, TOO. FIFTY THOUSAND FOLLOWERS, HE TELLS ME.
TWITTER? NOT REALLY MY THING. WHY DID YOU TAKE HIM ON? YOU'VE NEVER HAD A SIDEK--AN **APPRENTICE.**
WHEN I STARTED OUT AS DAREDEVIL, I STUCK TO HELPING ONE NEIGHBORHOOD--MINE. HELL'S KITCHEN. HE'S DOING THE SAME THING FOR HIS: CHINATOWN. I LIKE THAT.
AND HE'S AN UNDOCUMENTED IMMIGRANT--HE'S TRYING TO HELP HIS COMMUNITY--PEOPLE WHO FEEL LIKE THEY CAN'T GO TO THE COPS WHEN THEY NEED HELP.
ADMIRABLE. SO HE PUT ON A SUIT.
HE PUT ON A SUIT.
YOU KNOW HIS REAL NAME?
NO. HE'S CAGEY ABOUT THAT.
WELL, NOT EVERYONE CAN BE OPEN ABOUT THEIR IDENTITY. I MEAN, YOU KNOW THAT AS WELL AS ANYONE. I DON'T KNOW **YOUR** ACTUAL NAME, AFTER ALL.
You used to.
AT A CERTAIN POINT, IT'S JUST ABOUT TRUST.
...
I TRUST HIM. IF THERE'S SOMETHING BLINDSPOT WANTS ME TO KNOW...

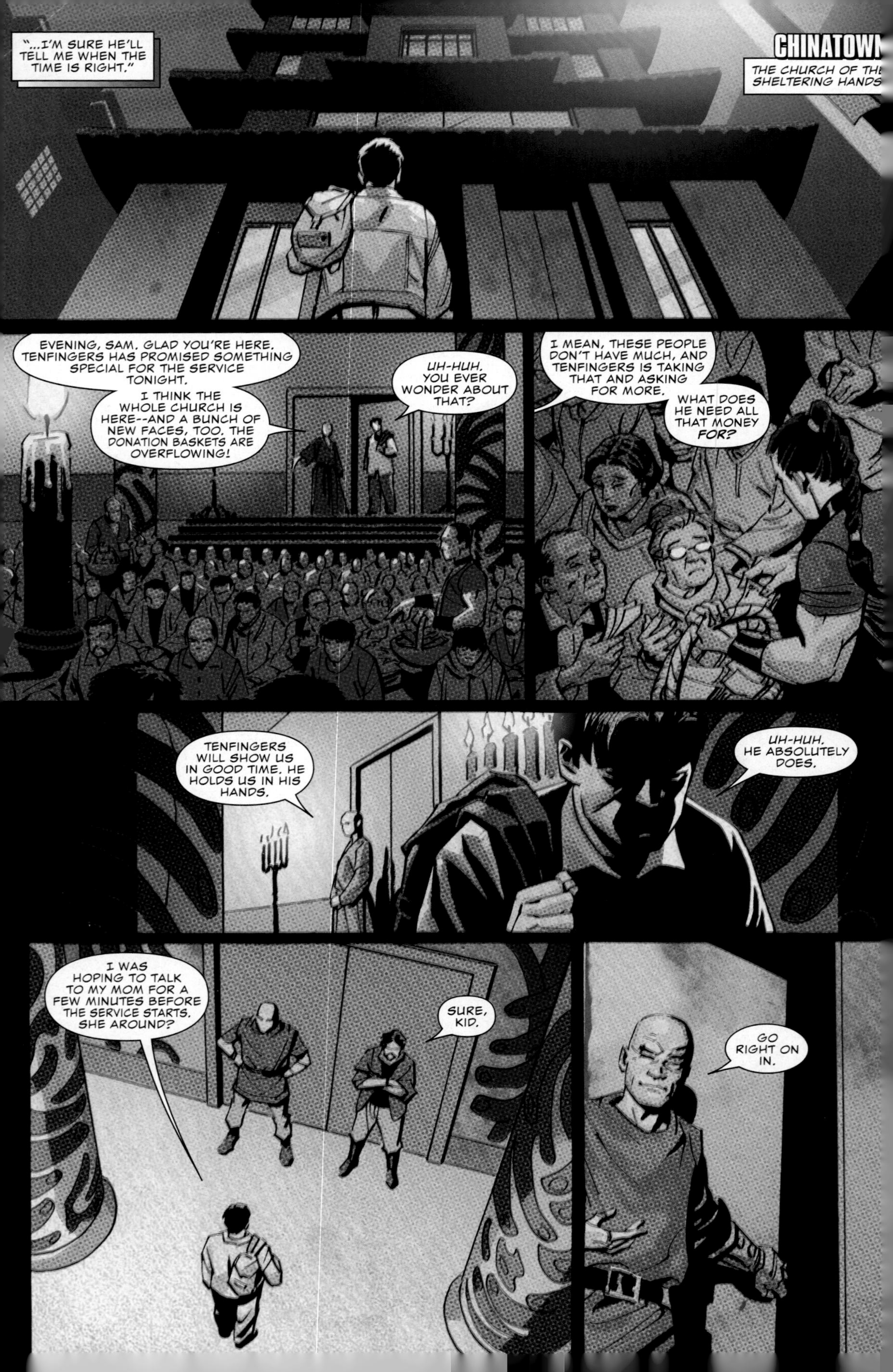
"...I'M SURE HE'LL TELL ME WHEN THE TIME IS RIGHT."
CHINATOWN
THE CHURCH OF THE SHELTERING HANDS
EVENING, SAM. GLAD YOU'RE HERE. TENFINGERS HAS PROMISED SOMETHING SPECIAL FOR THE SERVICE TONIGHT.
I THINK THE WHOLE CHURCH IS HERE--AND A BUNCH OF NEW FACES, TOO. THE DONATION BASKETS ARE OVERFLOWING!
UH-HUH. YOU EVER WONDER ABOUT THAT?
I MEAN, THESE PEOPLE DON'T HAVE MUCH, AND TENFINGERS IS TAKING THAT AND ASKING FOR MORE.
WHAT DOES HE NEED ALL THAT MONEY FOR?
TENFINGERS WILL SHOW US IN GOOD TIME. HE HOLDS US IN HIS HANDS.
UH-HUH. HE ABSOLUTELY DOES.
I WAS HOPING TO TALK TO MY MOM FOR A FEW MINUTES BEFORE THE SERVICE STARTS. SHE AROUND?
SURE, KID.
GO RIGHT ON IN.

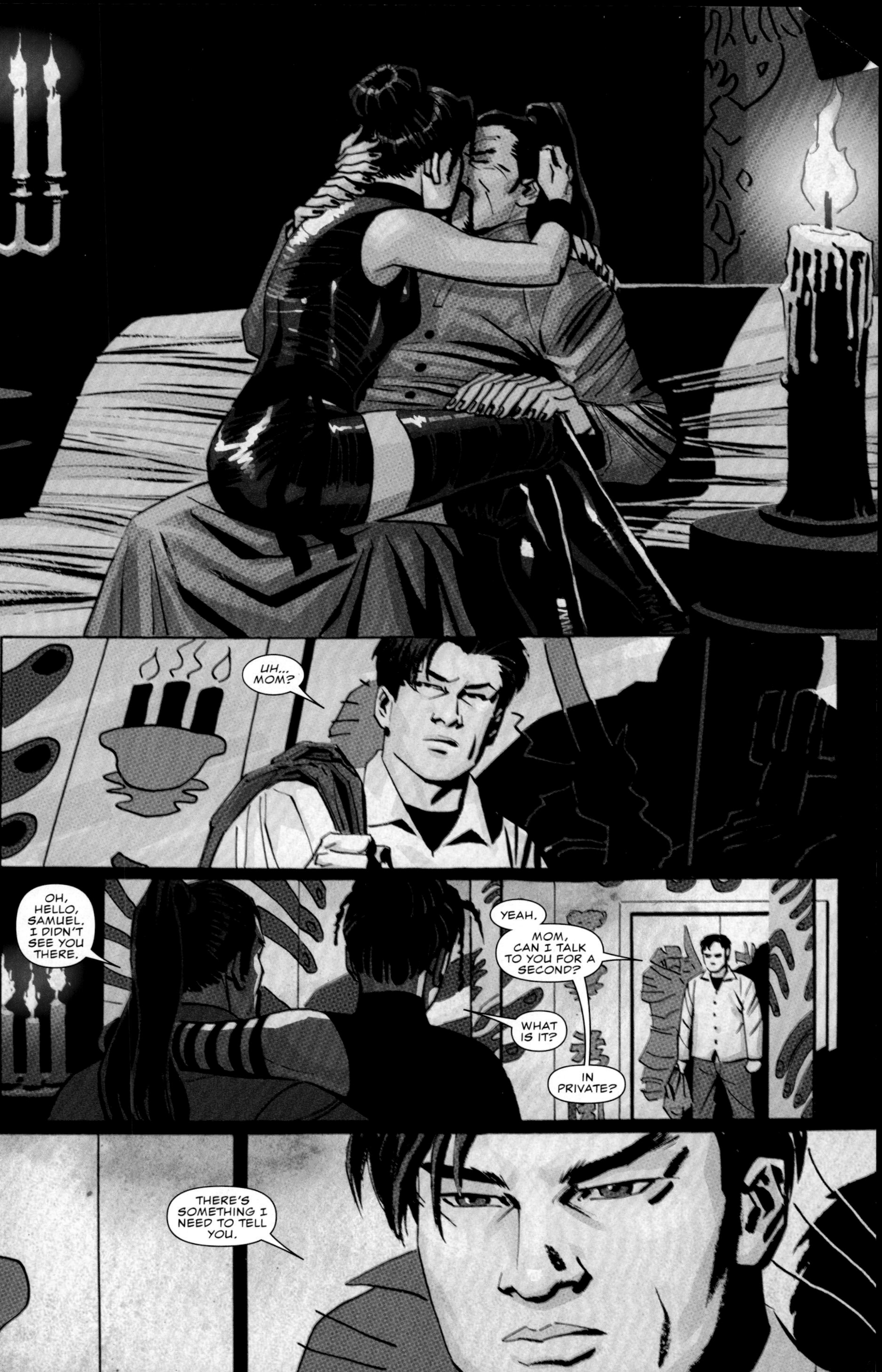
UH... MOM?
OH, HELLO, SAMUEL. I DIDN'T SEE YOU THERE.
YEAH.
MOM, CAN I TALK TO YOU FOR A SECOND?
WHAT IS IT?
IN PRIVATE?
THERE'S SOMETHING I NEED TO TELL YOU.

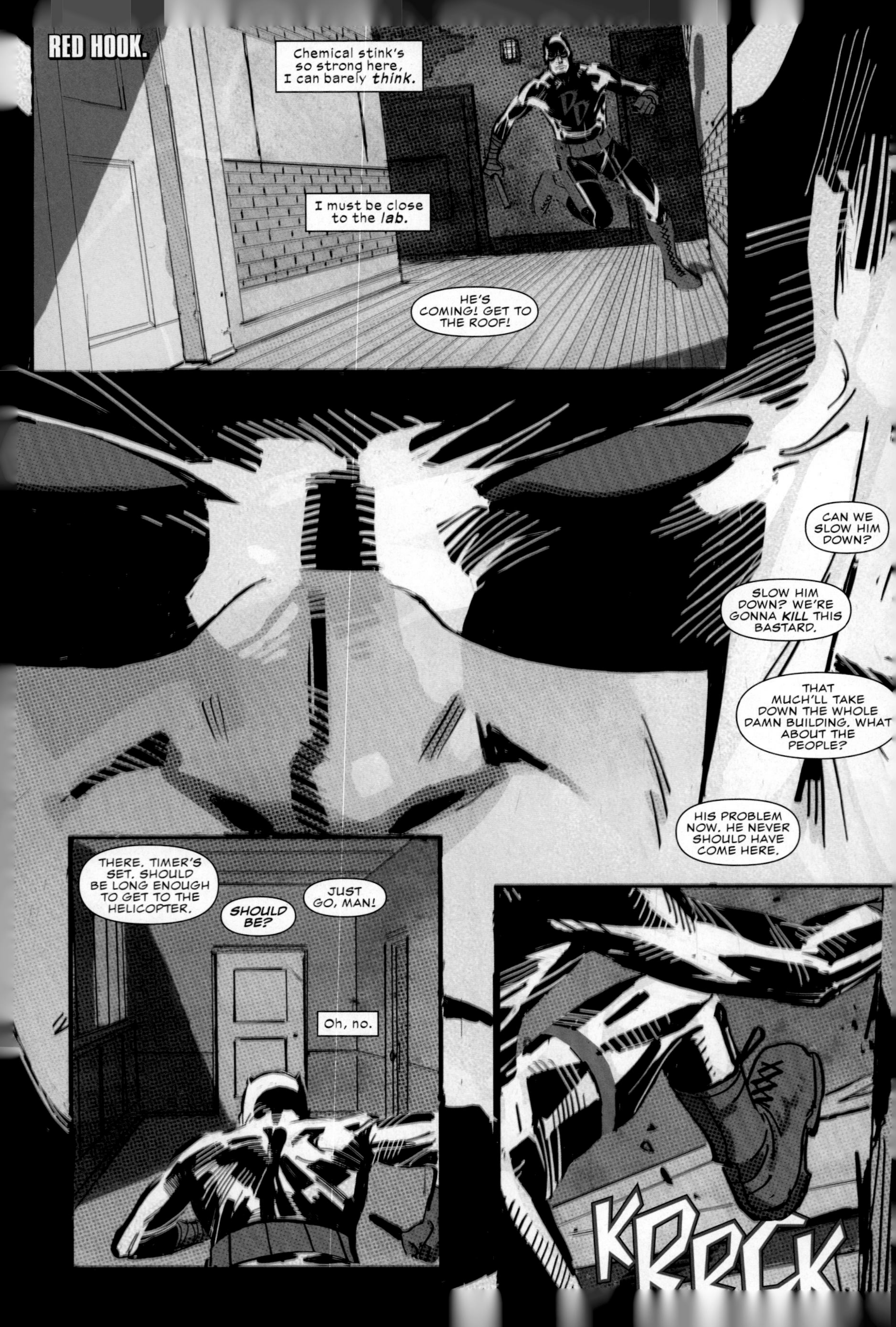
RED HOOK.
Chemical stink's so strong here, I can barely think.
I must be close to the lab.
HE'S COMING! GET TO THE ROOF!
CAN WE SLOW HIM DOWN?
SLOW HIM DOWN? WE'RE GONNA KILL THIS BASTARD.
THAT MUCH'LL TAKE DOWN THE WHOLE DAMN BUILDING. WHAT ABOUT THE PEOPLE?
HIS PROBLEM NOW. HE NEVER SHOULD HAVE COME HERE.
THERE. TIMER'S SET. SHOULD BE LONG ENOUGH TO GET TO THE HELICOPTER.
SHOULD BE?
JUST GO, MAN!
Oh, no.
KRRCK

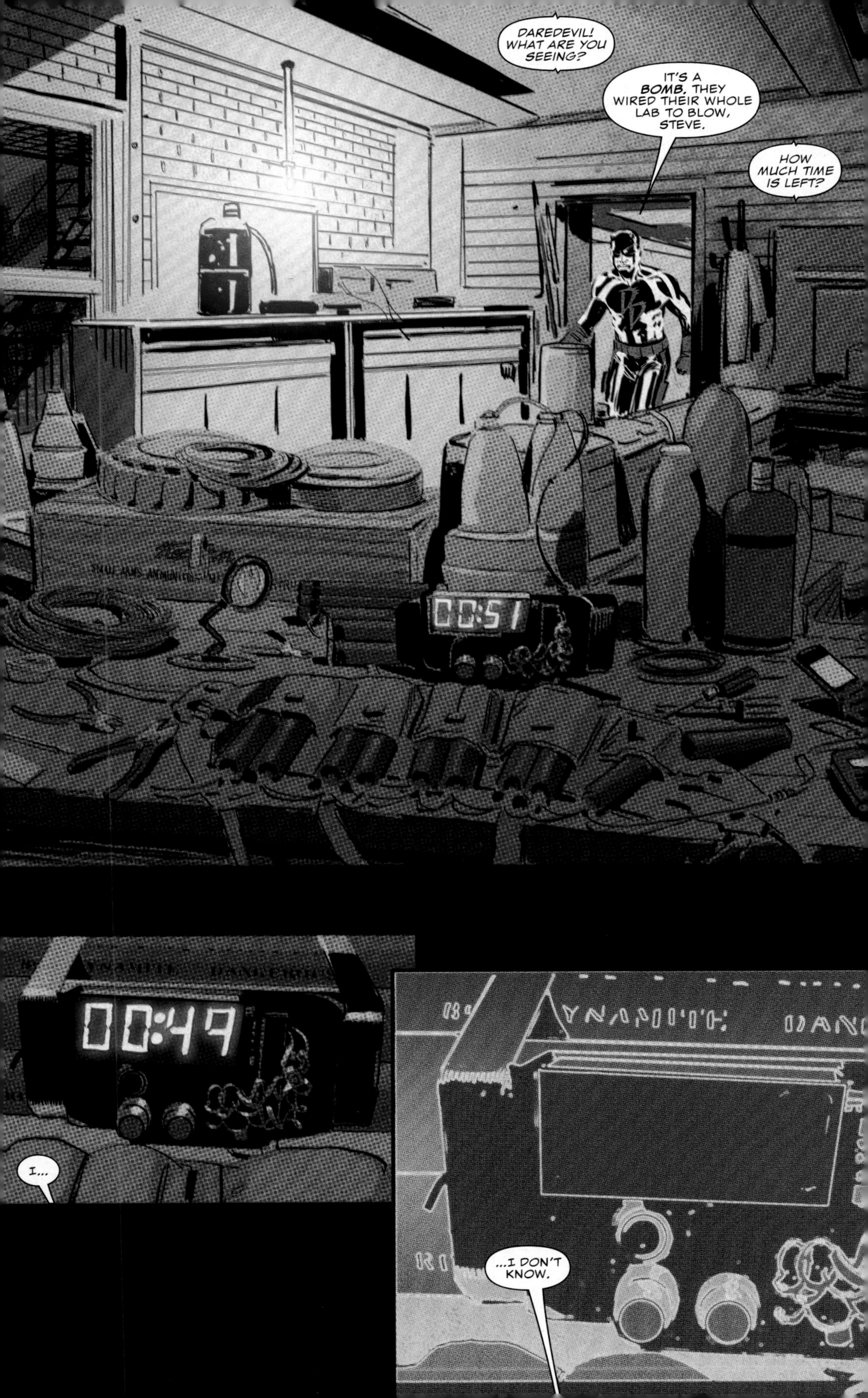
DAREDEVIL! WHAT ARE YOU SEEING?
IT'S A **BOMB.** THEY WIRED THEIR WHOLE LAB TO BLOW, STEVE.
HOW MUCH TIME IS LEFT?
00:51
00:49
I...
...I DON'T KNOW.

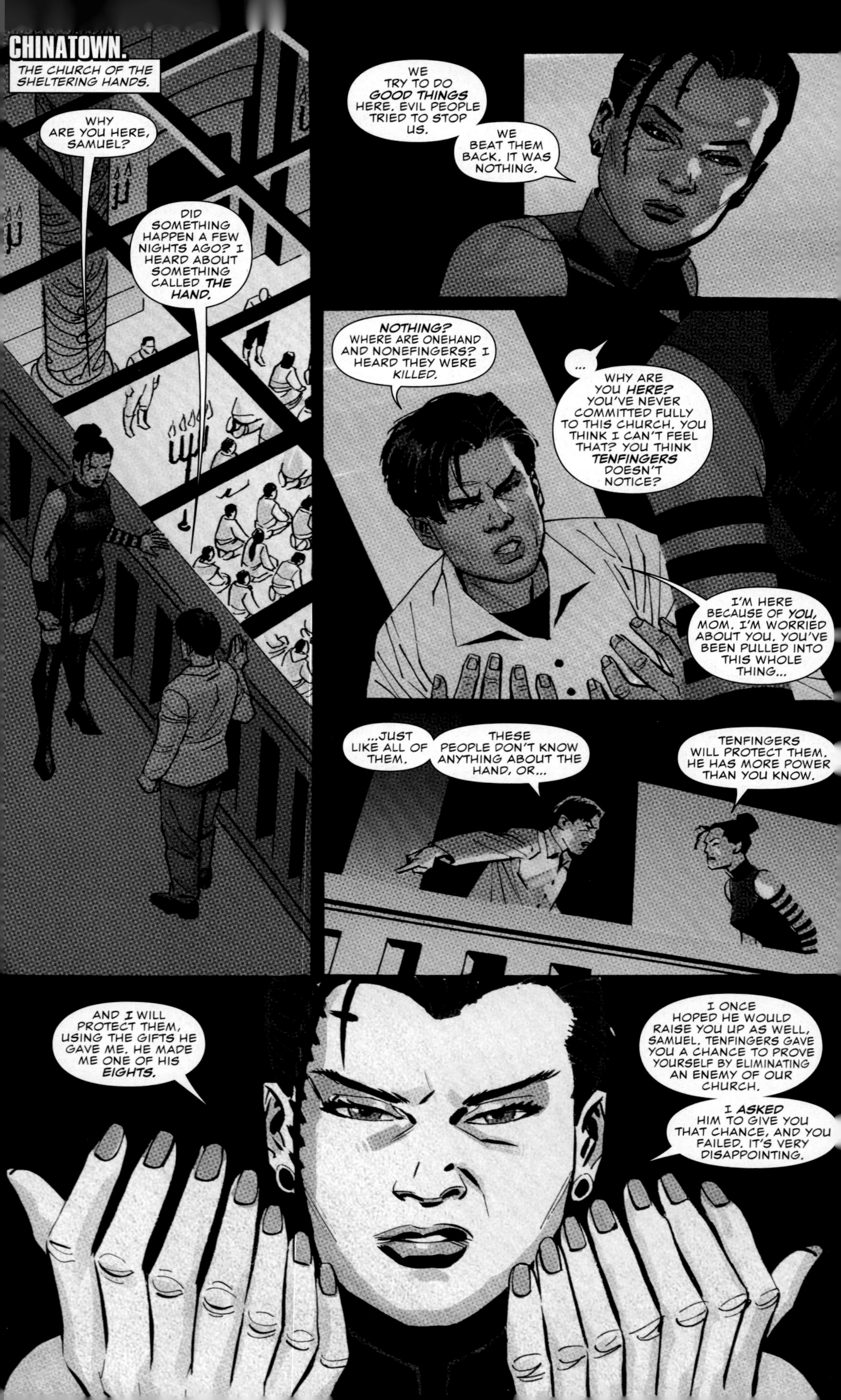

CHINATOWN.
THE CHURCH OF THE SHELTERING HANDS.
WHY ARE YOU HERE, SAMUEL?
DID SOMETHING HAPPEN A FEW NIGHTS AGO? I HEARD ABOUT SOMETHING CALLED THE HAND.
WE TRY TO DO GOOD THINGS HERE. EVIL PEOPLE TRIED TO STOP US.
WE BEAT THEM BACK. IT WAS NOTHING.
NOTHING? WHERE ARE ONEHAND AND NONEFINGERS? I HEARD THEY WERE KILLED.
...
WHY ARE YOU HERE? YOU'VE NEVER COMMITTED FULLY TO THIS CHURCH. YOU THINK I CAN'T FEEL THAT? YOU THINK TENFINGERS DOESN'T NOTICE?
I'M HERE BECAUSE OF YOU, MOM. I'M WORRIED ABOUT YOU. YOU'VE BEEN PULLED INTO THIS WHOLE THING...
...JUST LIKE ALL OF THEM.
THESE PEOPLE DON'T KNOW ANYTHING ABOUT THE HAND, OR...
TENFINGERS WILL PROTECT THEM. HE HAS MORE POWER THAN YOU KNOW.
AND I WILL PROTECT THEM, USING THE GIFTS HE GAVE ME. HE MADE ME ONE OF HIS EIGHTS.
I ONCE HOPED HE WOULD RAISE YOU UP AS WELL, SAMUEL. TENFINGERS GAVE YOU A CHANCE TO PROVE YOURSELF BY ELIMINATING AN ENEMY OF OUR CHURCH.
I ASKED HIM TO GIVE YOU THAT CHANCE, AND YOU FAILED. IT'S VERY DISAPPOINTING.

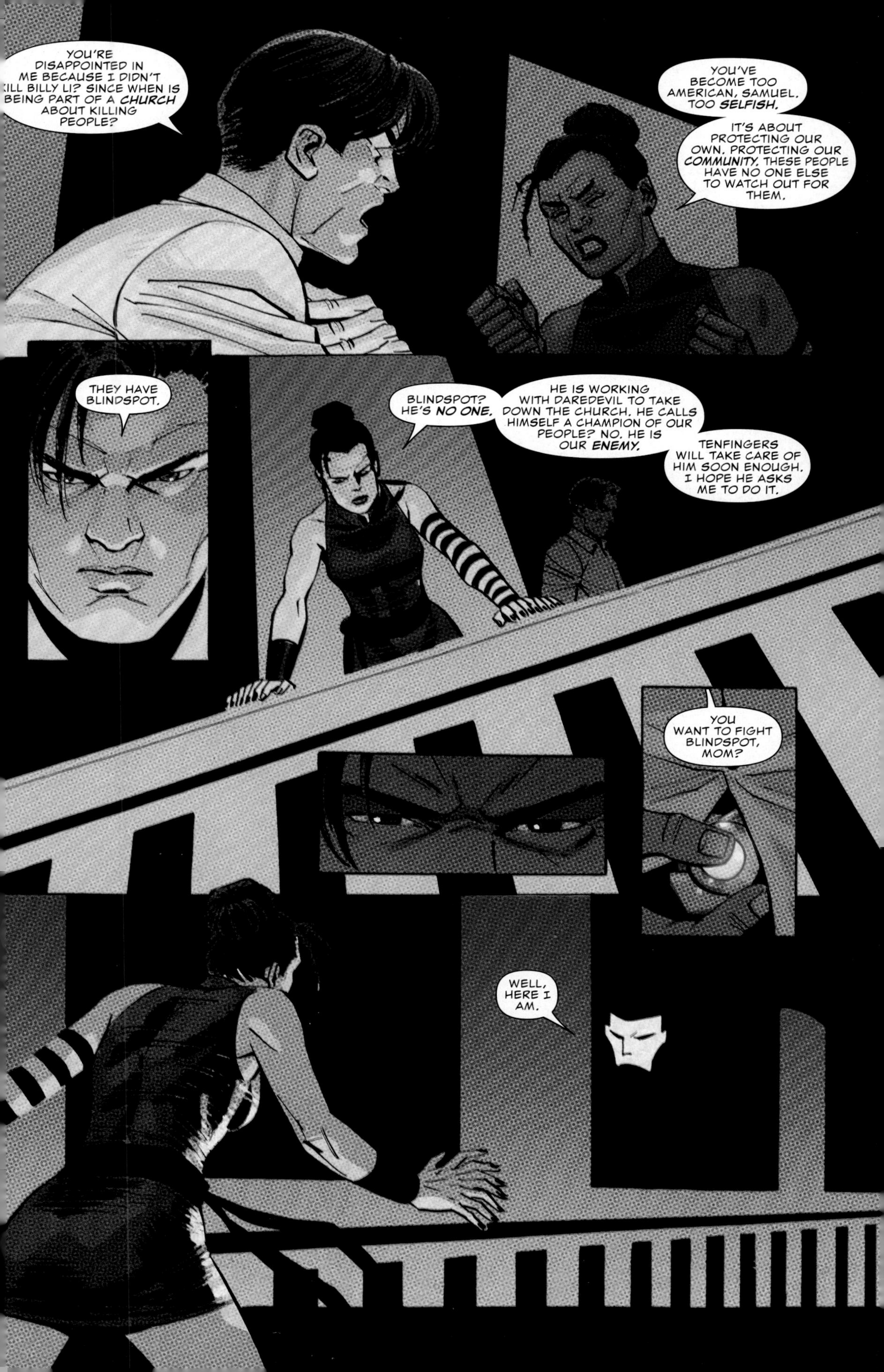
YOU'RE DISAPPOINTED IN ME BECAUSE I DIDN'T KILL BILLY LI? SINCE WHEN IS BEING PART OF A CHURCH ABOUT KILLING PEOPLE?
YOU'VE BECOME TOO AMERICAN, SAMUEL. TOO SELFISH.
IT'S ABOUT PROTECTING OUR OWN. PROTECTING OUR COMMUNITY. THESE PEOPLE HAVE NO ONE ELSE TO WATCH OUT FOR THEM.
THEY HAVE BLINDSPOT.
BLINDSPOT? HE'S NO ONE.
HE IS WORKING WITH DAREDEVIL TO TAKE DOWN THE CHURCH. HE CALLS HIMSELF A CHAMPION OF OUR PEOPLE? NO. HE IS OUR ENEMY.
TENFINGERS WILL TAKE CARE OF HIM SOON ENOUGH. I HOPE HE ASKS ME TO DO IT.
YOU WANT TO FIGHT BLINDSPOT, MOM?
WELL, HERE I AM.

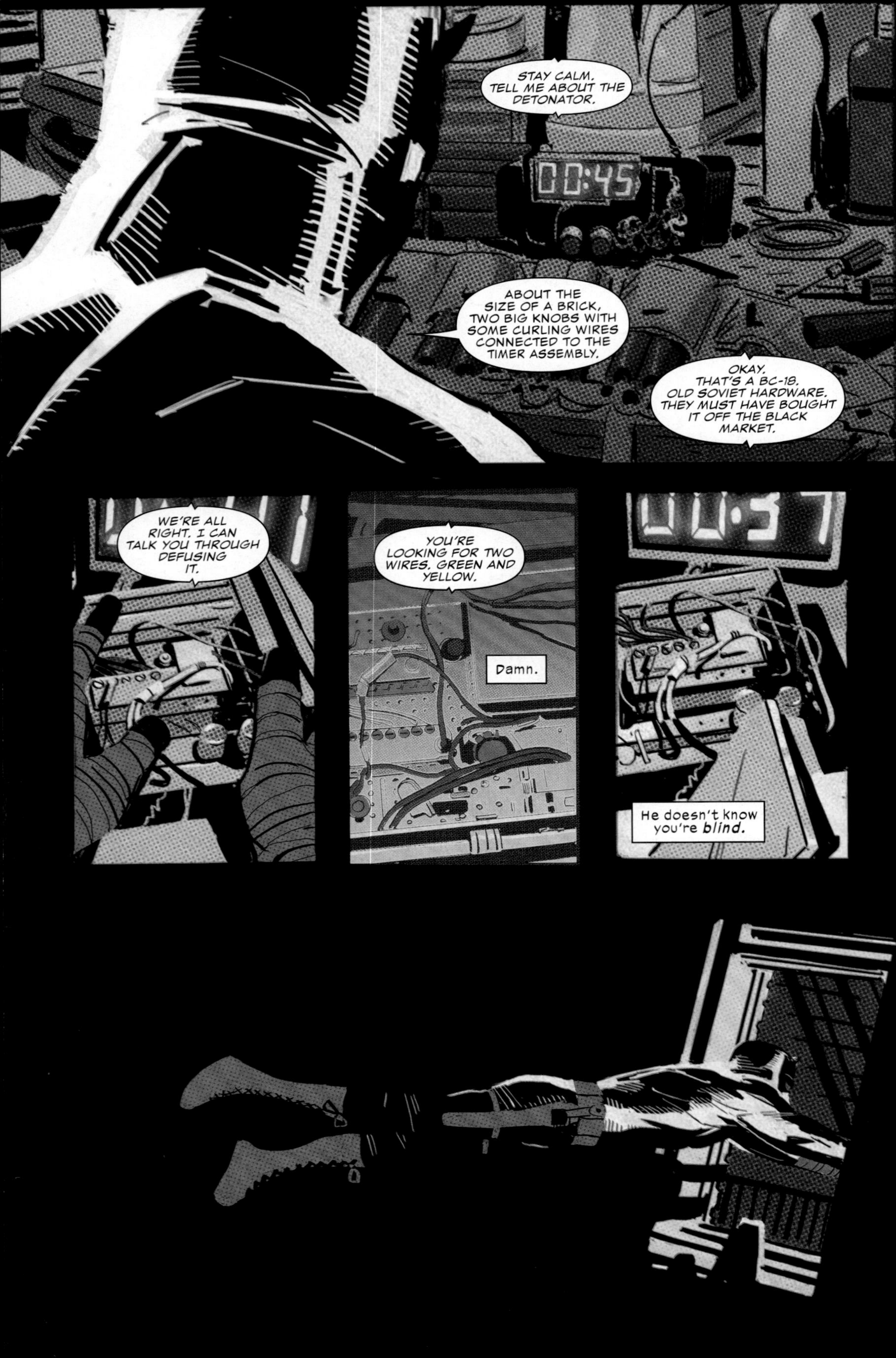
STAY CALM. TELL ME ABOUT THE DETONATOR.
00:45
ABOUT THE SIZE OF A BRICK, TWO BIG KNOBS WITH SOME CURLING WIRES CONNECTED TO THE TIMER ASSEMBLY.
OKAY. THAT'S A BC-18. OLD SOVIET HARDWARE. THEY MUST HAVE BOUGHT IT OFF THE BLACK MARKET.
WE'RE ALL RIGHT. I CAN TALK YOU THROUGH DEFUSING IT.
YOU'RE LOOKING FOR TWO WIRES. GREEN AND YELLOW.
Damn.
00:37
He doesn't know you're *blind.*

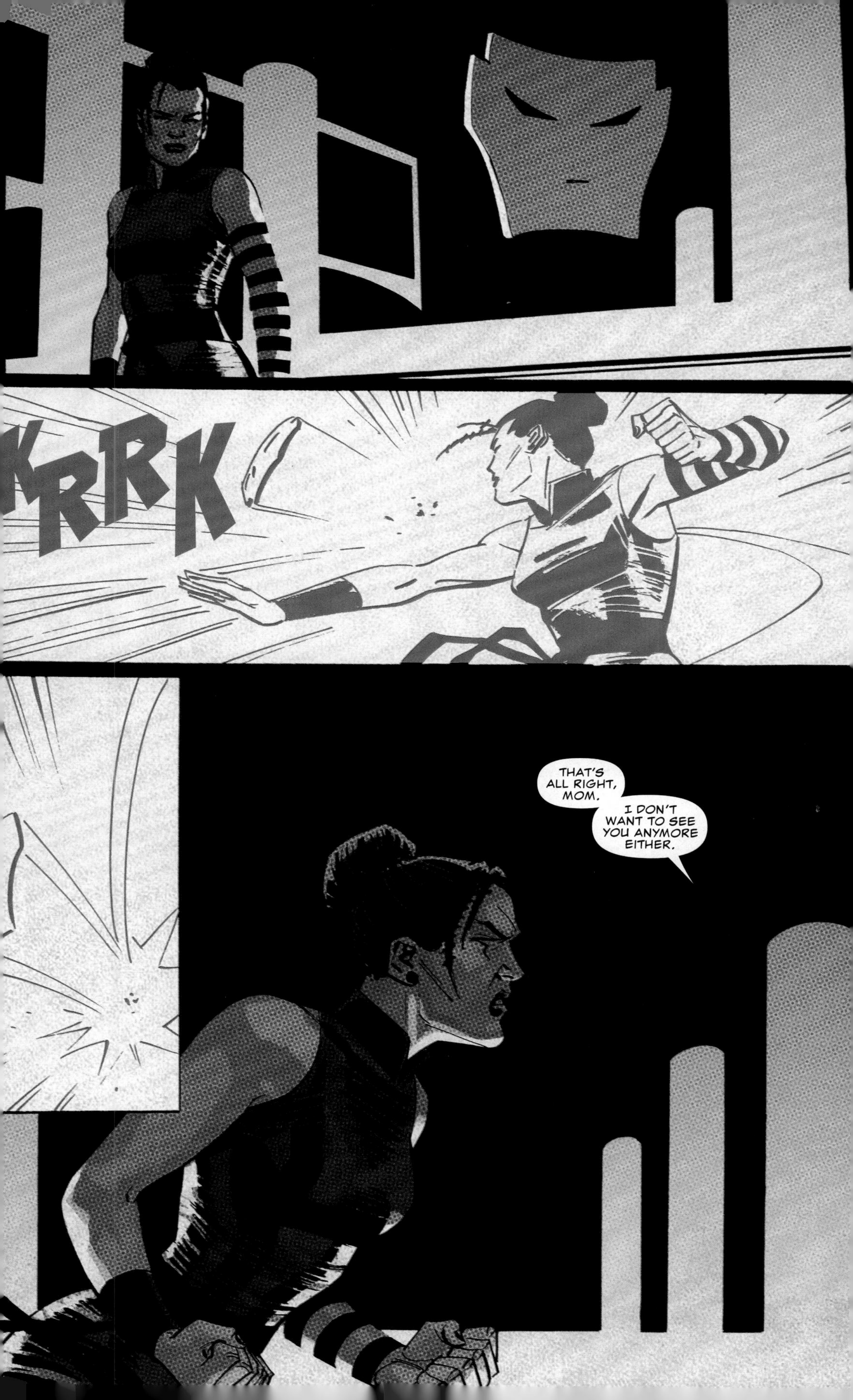
KRRK
THAT'S ALL RIGHT, MOM.
I DON'T WANT TO SEE YOU ANYMORE EITHER.

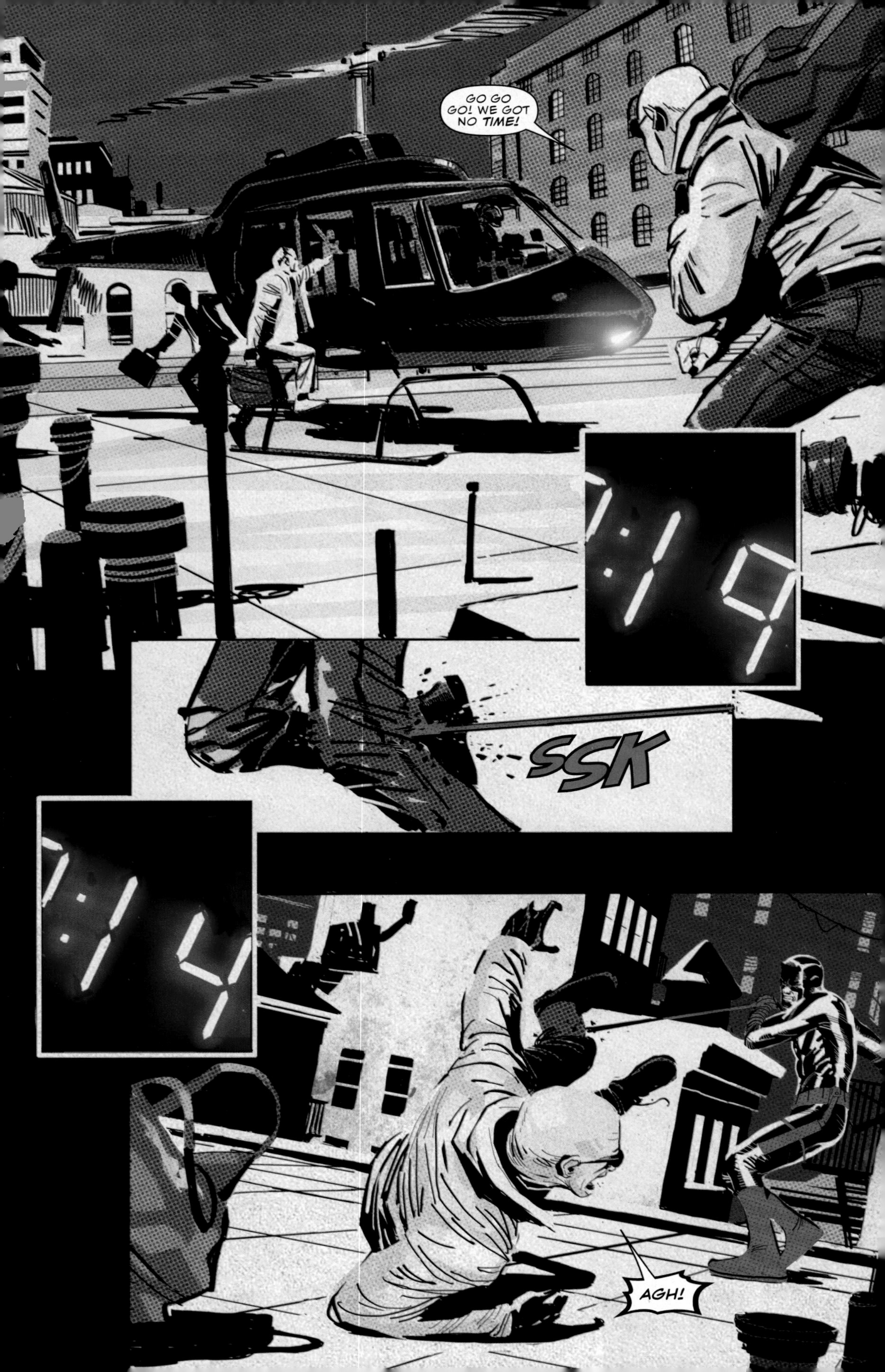
GO GO GO! WE GOT NO TIME!
SSK
AGH!

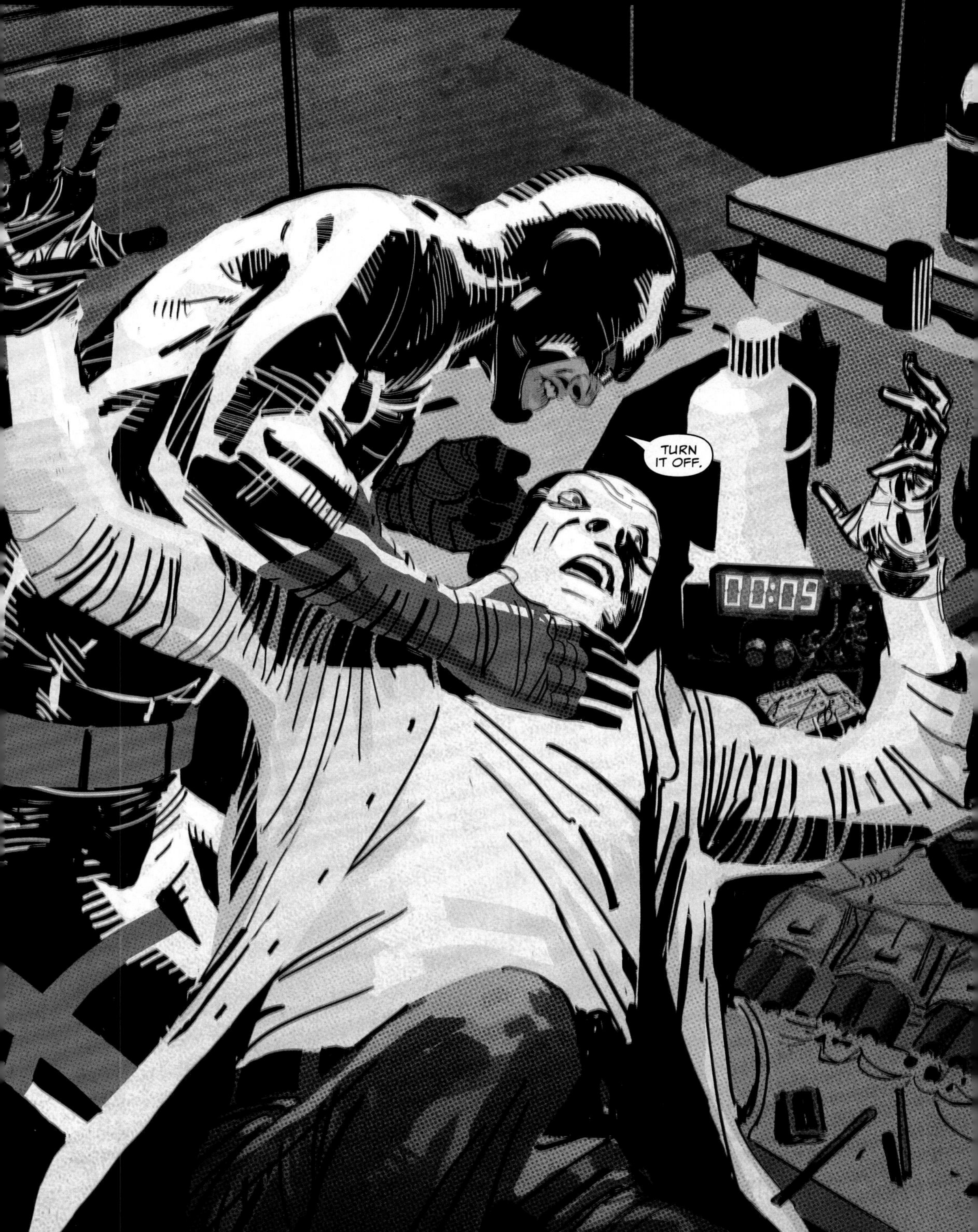
TURN IT OFF.
00:05

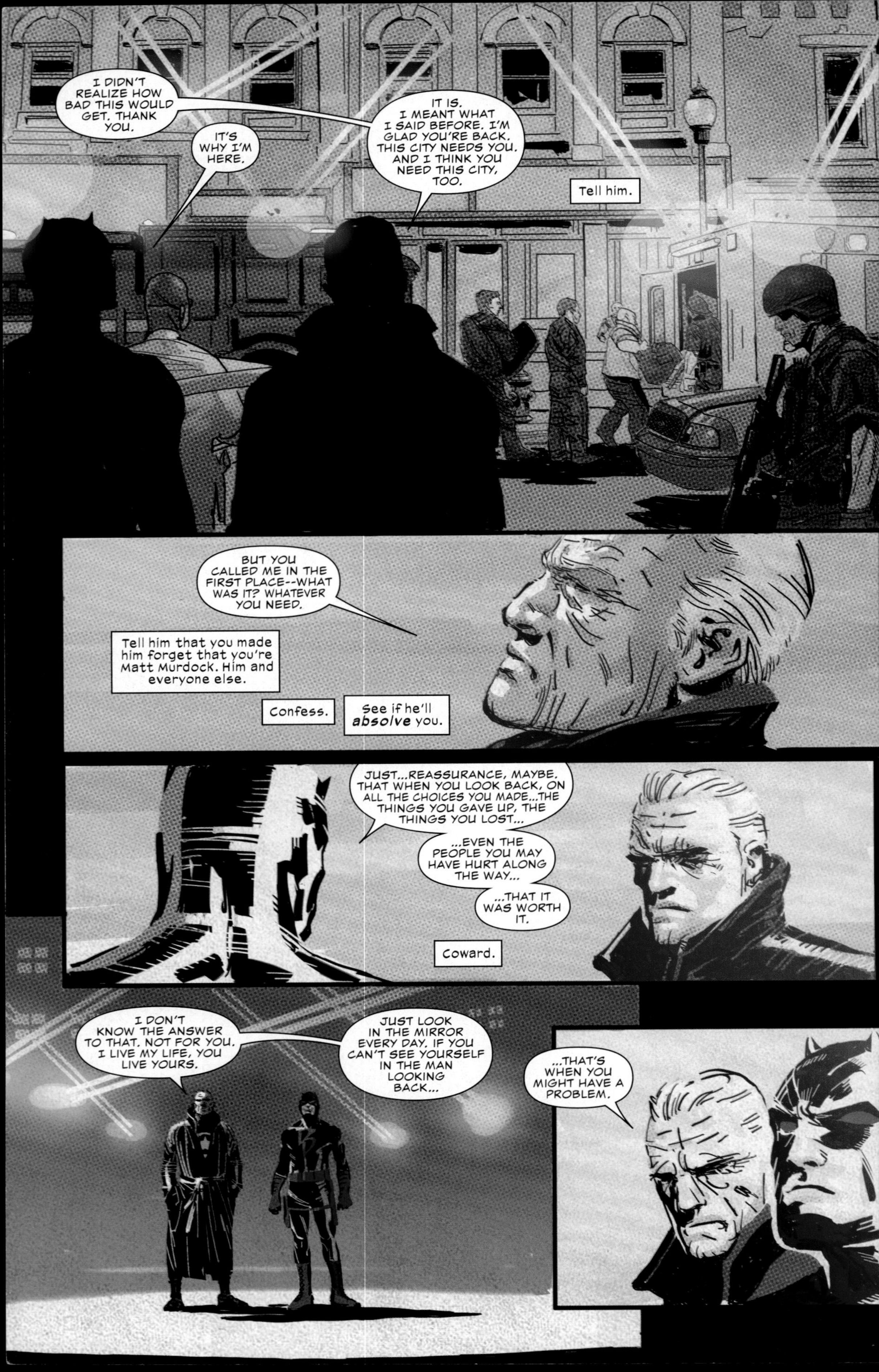

I DIDN'T REALIZE HOW BAD THIS WOULD GET. THANK YOU.
IT'S WHY I'M HERE.
IT IS. I MEANT WHAT I SAID BEFORE. I'M GLAD YOU'RE BACK. THIS CITY NEEDS YOU. AND I THINK YOU NEED THIS CITY, TOO.
Tell him.
BUT YOU CALLED ME IN THE FIRST PLACE--WHAT WAS IT? WHATEVER YOU NEED.
Tell him that you made him forget that you're Matt Murdock. Him and everyone else.
Confess.
See if he'll *absolve* you.
JUST...REASSURANCE, MAYBE. THAT WHEN YOU LOOK BACK, ON ALL THE CHOICES YOU MADE...THE THINGS YOU GAVE UP, THE THINGS YOU LOST...
...EVEN THE PEOPLE YOU MAY HAVE HURT ALONG THE WAY...
...THAT IT WAS WORTH IT.
Coward.
I DON'T KNOW THE ANSWER TO THAT. NOT FOR YOU. I LIVE MY LIFE, YOU LIVE YOURS.
JUST LOOK IN THE MIRROR EVERY DAY. IF YOU CAN'T SEE YOURSELF IN THE MAN LOOKING BACK...
...THAT'S WHEN YOU MIGHT HAVE A PROBLEM.

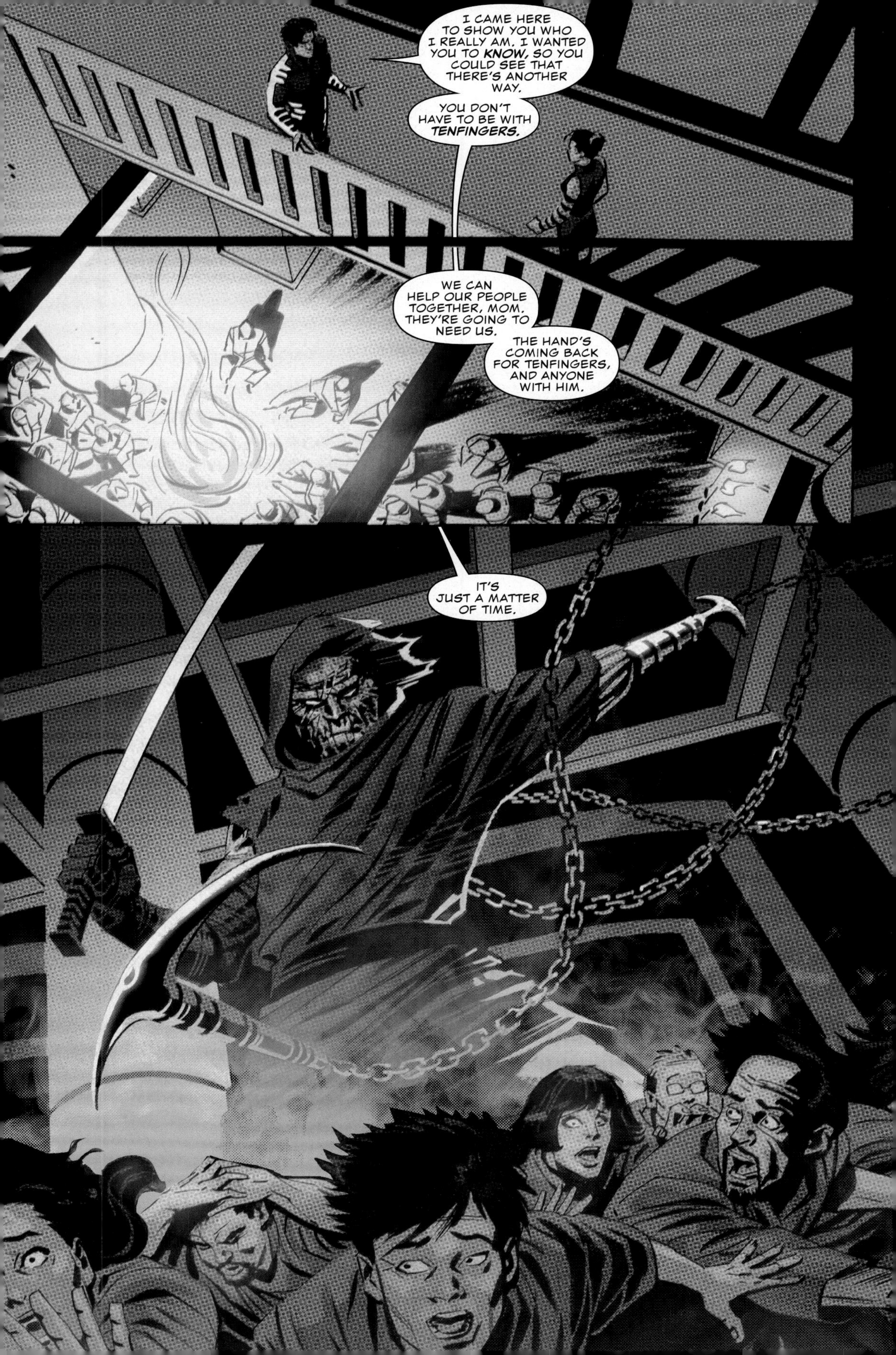
I CAME HERE TO SHOW YOU WHO I REALLY AM. I WANTED YOU TO **KNOW,** SO YOU COULD SEE THAT THERE'S ANOTHER WAY.
YOU DON'T HAVE TO BE WITH ***TENFINGERS.***
WE CAN HELP OUR PEOPLE TOGETHER, MOM. THEY'RE GOING TO NEED US.
THE HAND'S COMING BACK FOR TENFINGERS, AND ANYONE WITH HIM.
IT'S JUST A MATTER OF TIME.

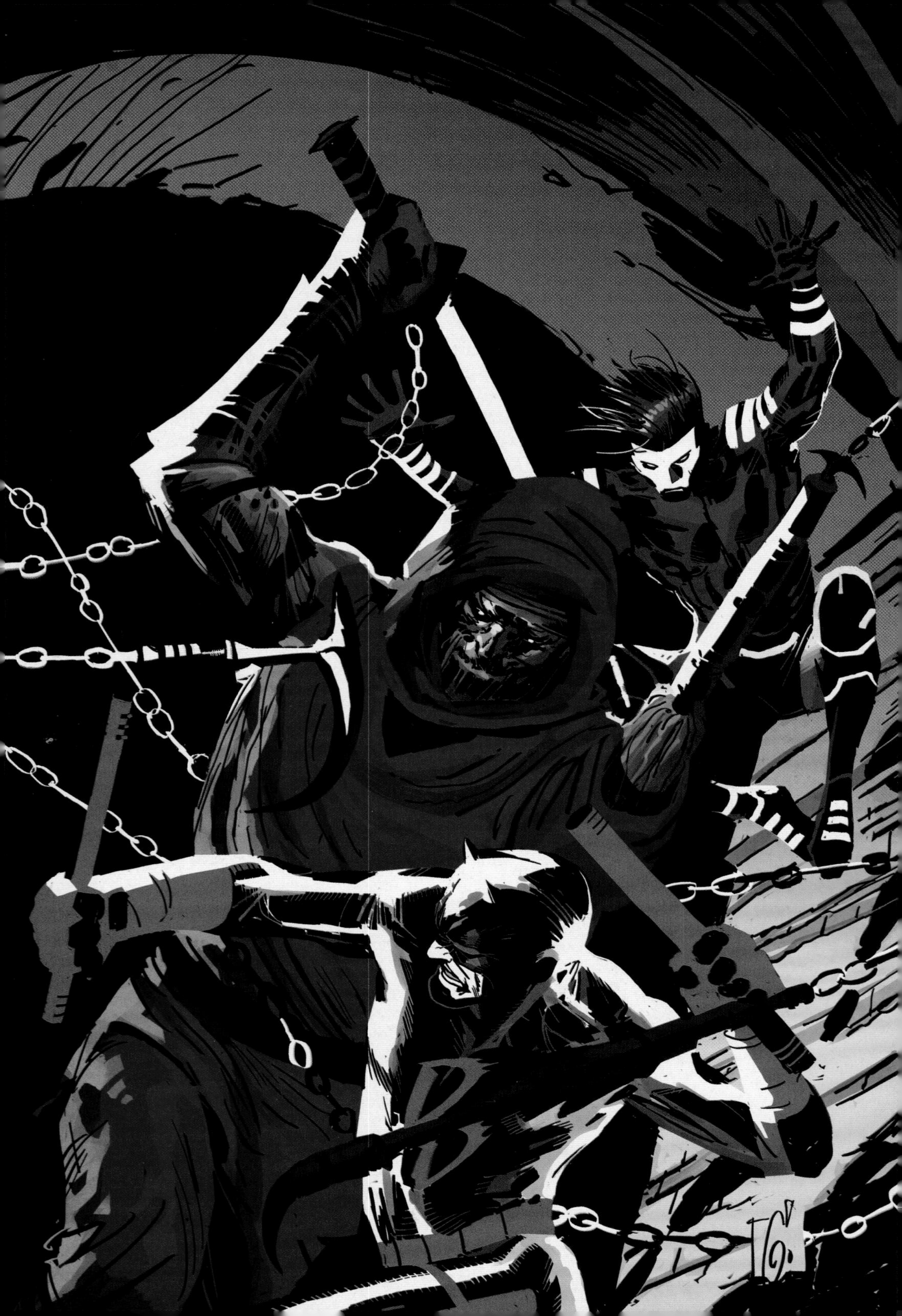

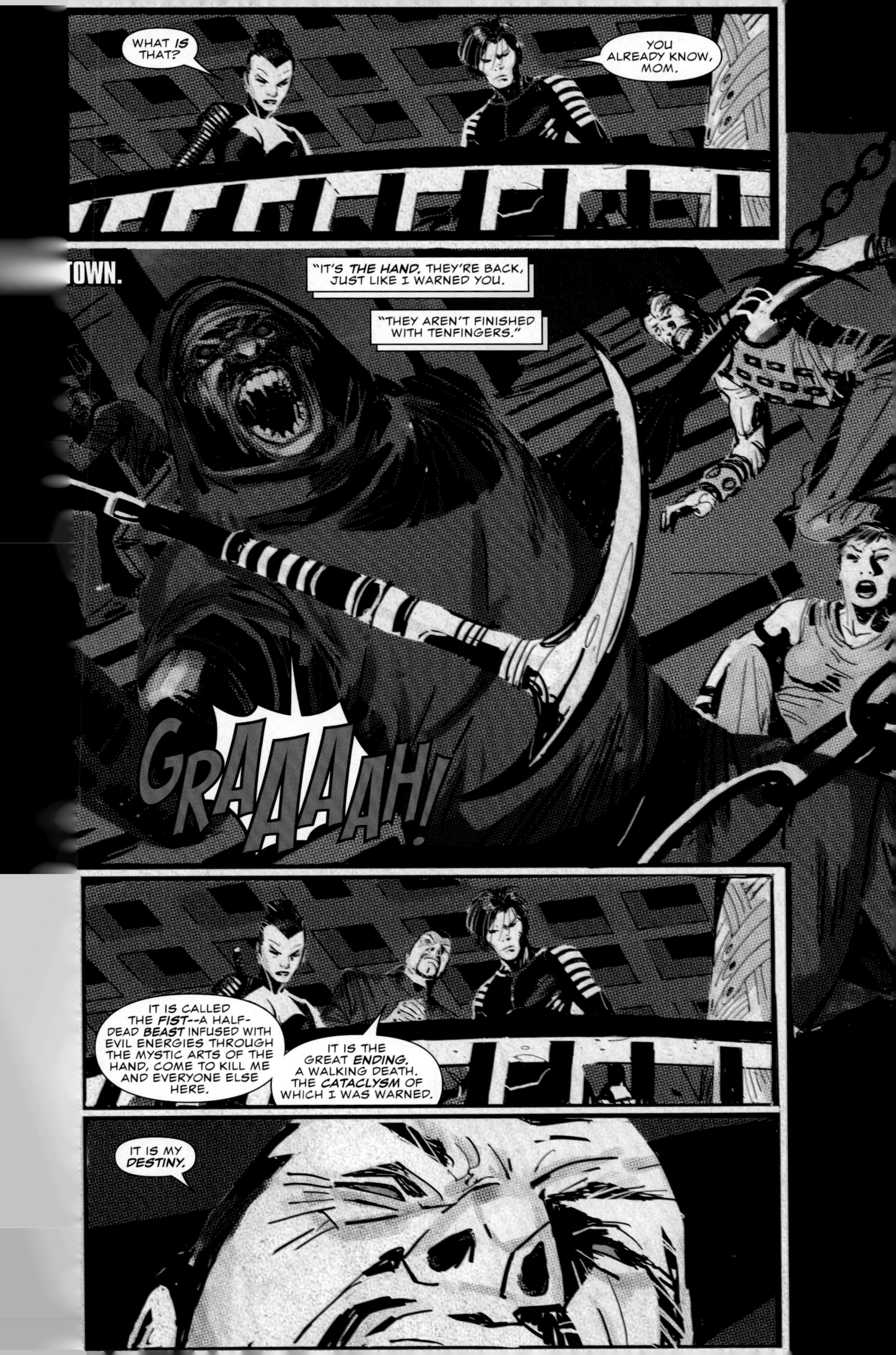
WHAT IS THAT?
YOU ALREADY KNOW, MOM.
TOWN.
"IT'S THE HAND. THEY'RE BACK, JUST LIKE I WARNED YOU.
"THEY AREN'T FINISHED WITH TENFINGERS."
GRAAAAH!
IT IS CALLED THE FIST--A HALF-DEAD BEAST INFUSED WITH EVIL ENERGIES THROUGH THE MYSTIC ARTS OF THE HAND, COME TO KILL ME AND EVERYONE ELSE HERE.
IT IS THE GREAT ENDING. A WALKING DEATH. THE CATACLYSM OF WHICH I WAS WARNED.
IT IS MY DESTINY.

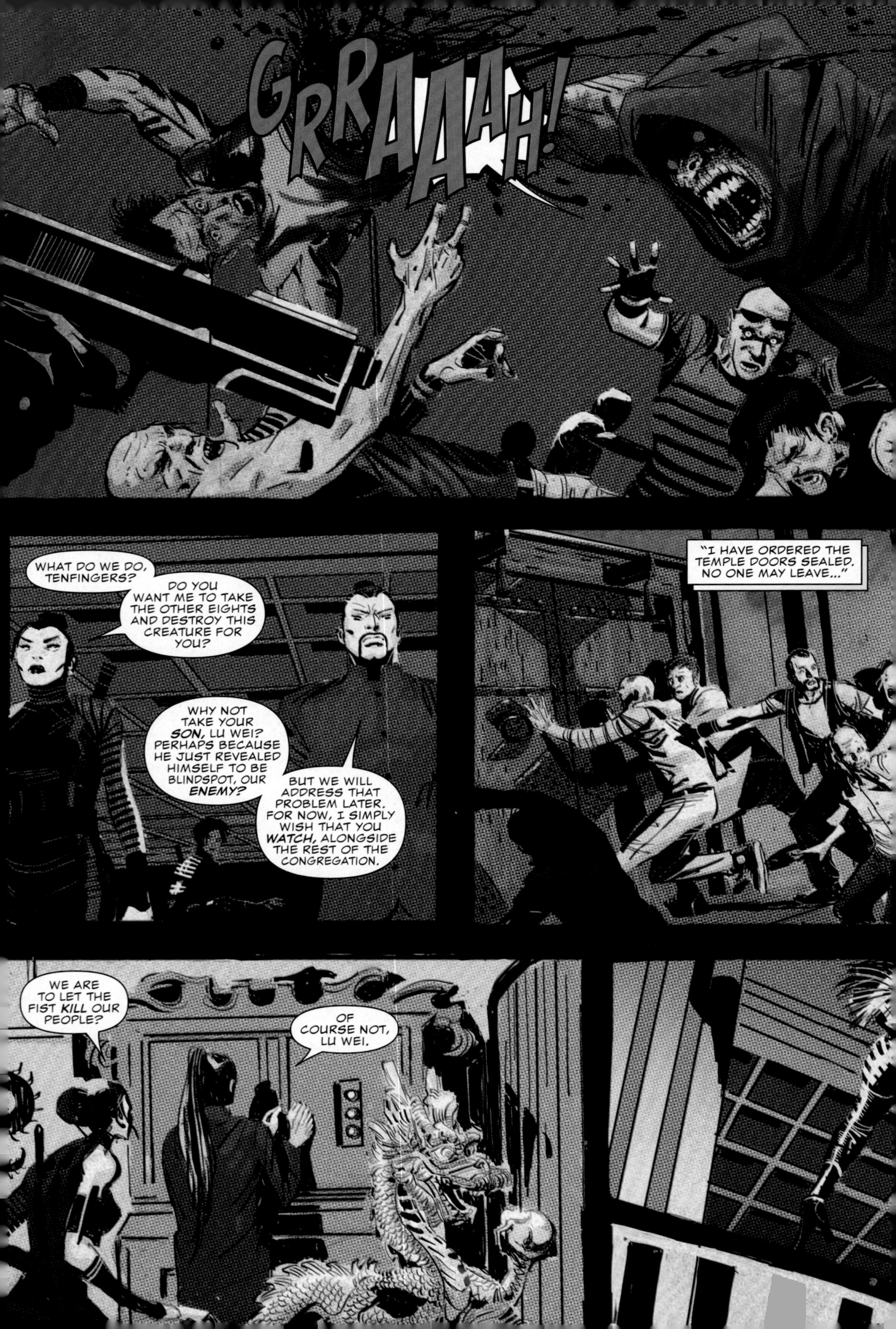
GRRAAAH!
WHAT DO WE DO, TENFINGERS?
DO YOU WANT ME TO TAKE THE OTHER EIGHTS AND DESTROY THIS CREATURE FOR YOU?
WHY NOT TAKE YOUR SON, LU WEI? PERHAPS BECAUSE HE JUST REVEALED HIMSELF TO BE BLINDSPOT, OUR ENEMY?
BUT WE WILL ADDRESS THAT PROBLEM LATER. FOR NOW, I SIMPLY WISH THAT YOU WATCH, ALONGSIDE THE REST OF THE CONGREGATION.
"I HAVE ORDERED THE TEMPLE DOORS SEALED. NO ONE MAY LEAVE..."
WE ARE TO LET THE FIST KILL OUR PEOPLE?
OF COURSE NOT, LU WEI.

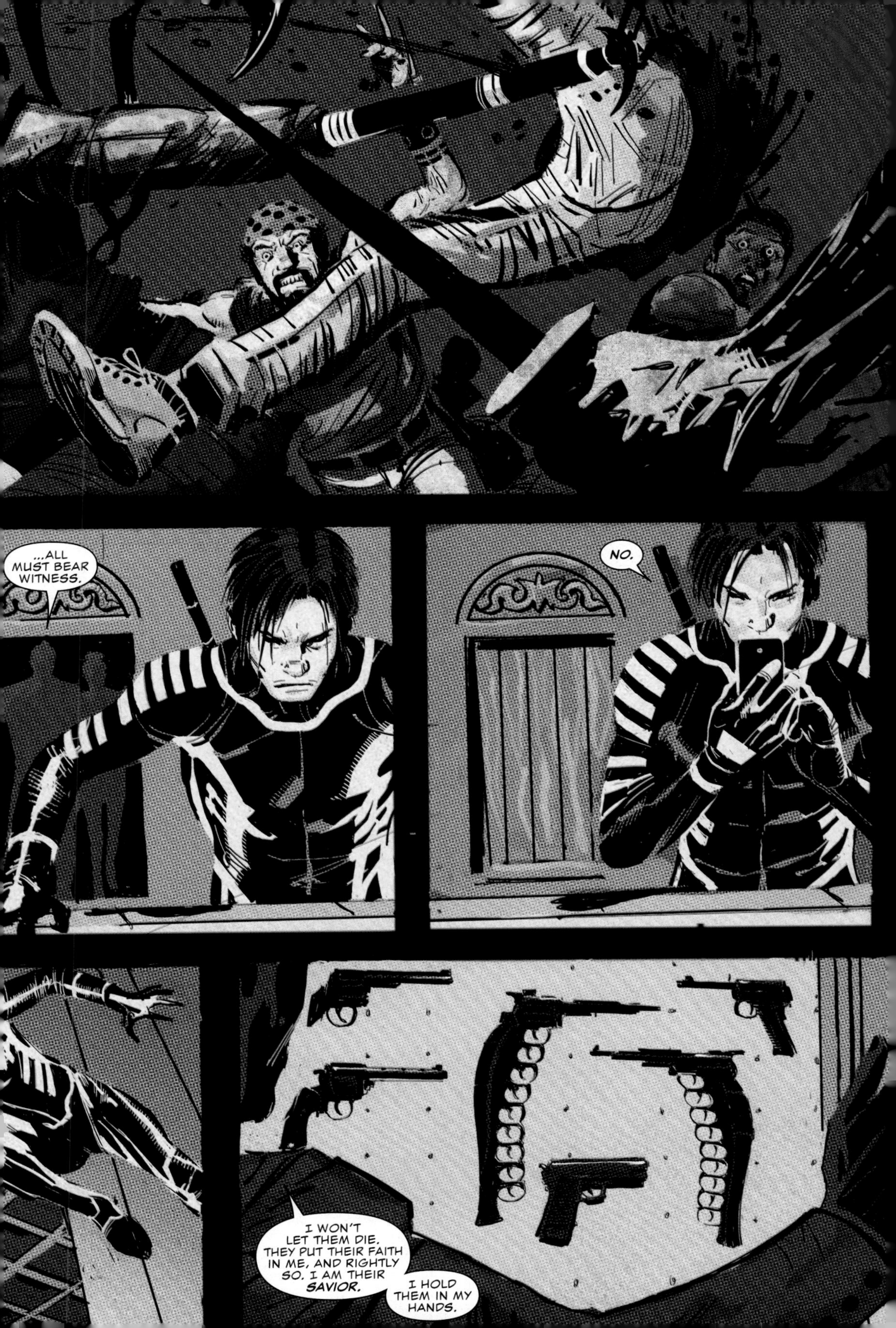
...ALL MUST BEAR WITNESS.
NO.
I WON'T LET THEM DIE. THEY PUT THEIR FAITH IN ME, AND RIGHTLY SO. I AM THEIR *SAVIOR.*
I HOLD THEM IN MY HANDS.

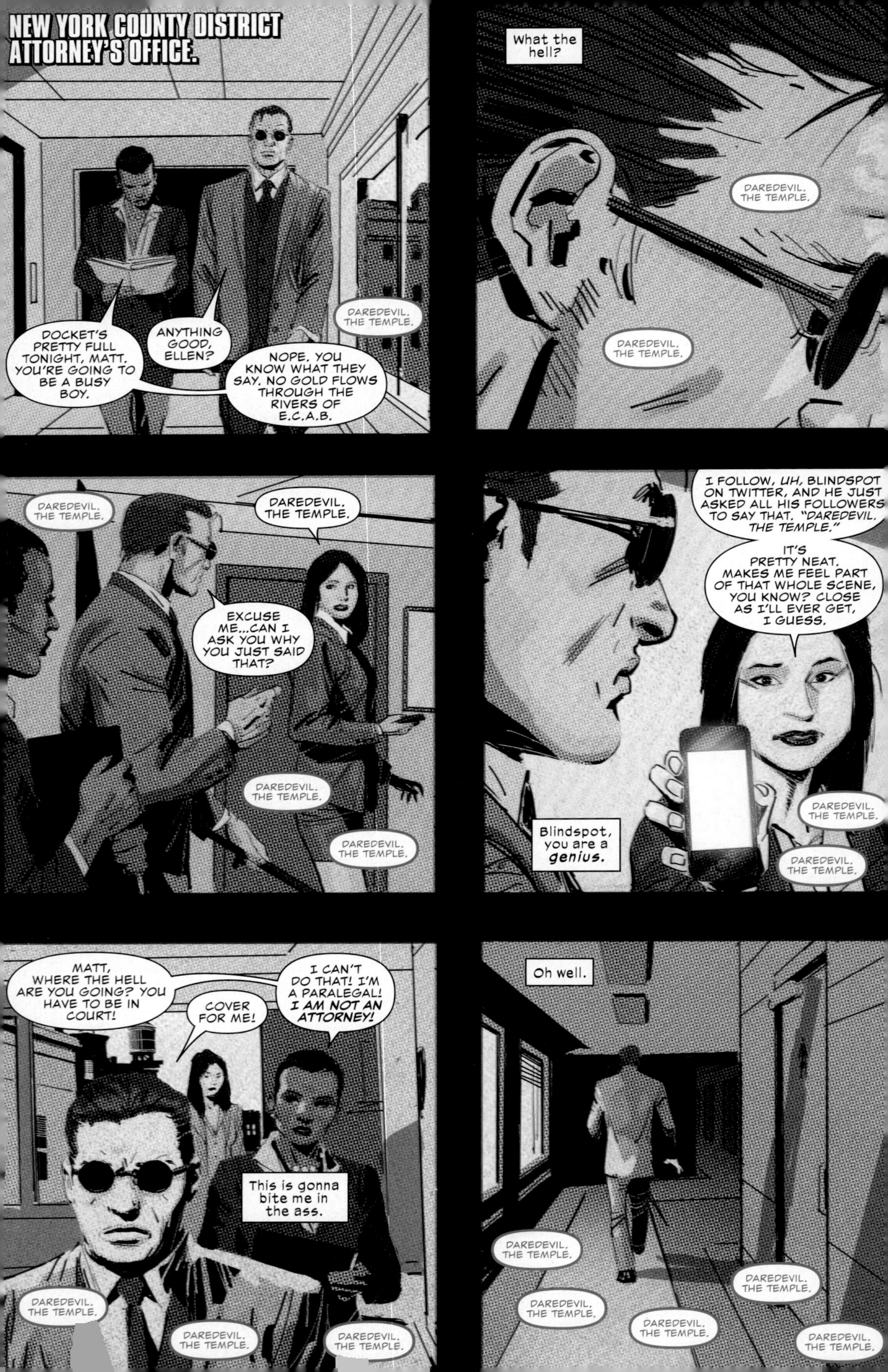
NEW YORK COUNTY DISTRICT ATTORNEY'S OFFICE.
DOCKET'S PRETTY FULL TONIGHT, MATT. YOU'RE GOING TO BE A BUSY BOY.
ANYTHING GOOD, ELLEN?
NOPE. YOU KNOW WHAT THEY SAY. NO GOLD FLOWS THROUGH THE RIVERS OF E.C.A.B.
DAREDEVIL. THE TEMPLE.
What the hell?
DAREDEVIL. THE TEMPLE.
DAREDEVIL. THE TEMPLE.
DAREDEVIL. THE TEMPLE.
DAREDEVIL. THE TEMPLE.
EXCUSE ME...CAN I ASK YOU WHY YOU JUST SAID THAT?
DAREDEVIL. THE TEMPLE.
DAREDEVIL. THE TEMPLE.
I FOLLOW, UH, BLINDSPOT ON TWITTER, AND HE JUST ASKED ALL HIS FOLLOWERS TO SAY THAT. "DAREDEVIL. THE TEMPLE."
IT'S PRETTY NEAT. MAKES ME FEEL PART OF THAT WHOLE SCENE, YOU KNOW? CLOSE AS I'LL EVER GET, I GUESS.
Blindspot, you are a genius.
DAREDEVIL. THE TEMPLE.
DAREDEVIL. THE TEMPLE.
MATT, WHERE THE HELL ARE YOU GOING? YOU HAVE TO BE IN COURT!
COVER FOR ME!
I CAN'T DO THAT! I'M A PARALEGAL! I AM NOT AN ATTORNEY!
This is gonna bite me in the ass.
DAREDEVIL. THE TEMPLE.
DAREDEVIL. THE TEMPLE.
DAREDEVIL. THE TEMPLE.
Oh well.
DAREDEVIL. THE TEMPLE.
DAREDEVIL. THE TEMPLE.
DAREDEVIL. THE TEMPLE.
DAREDEVIL. THE TEMPLE.
DAREDEVIL. THE TEMPLE.

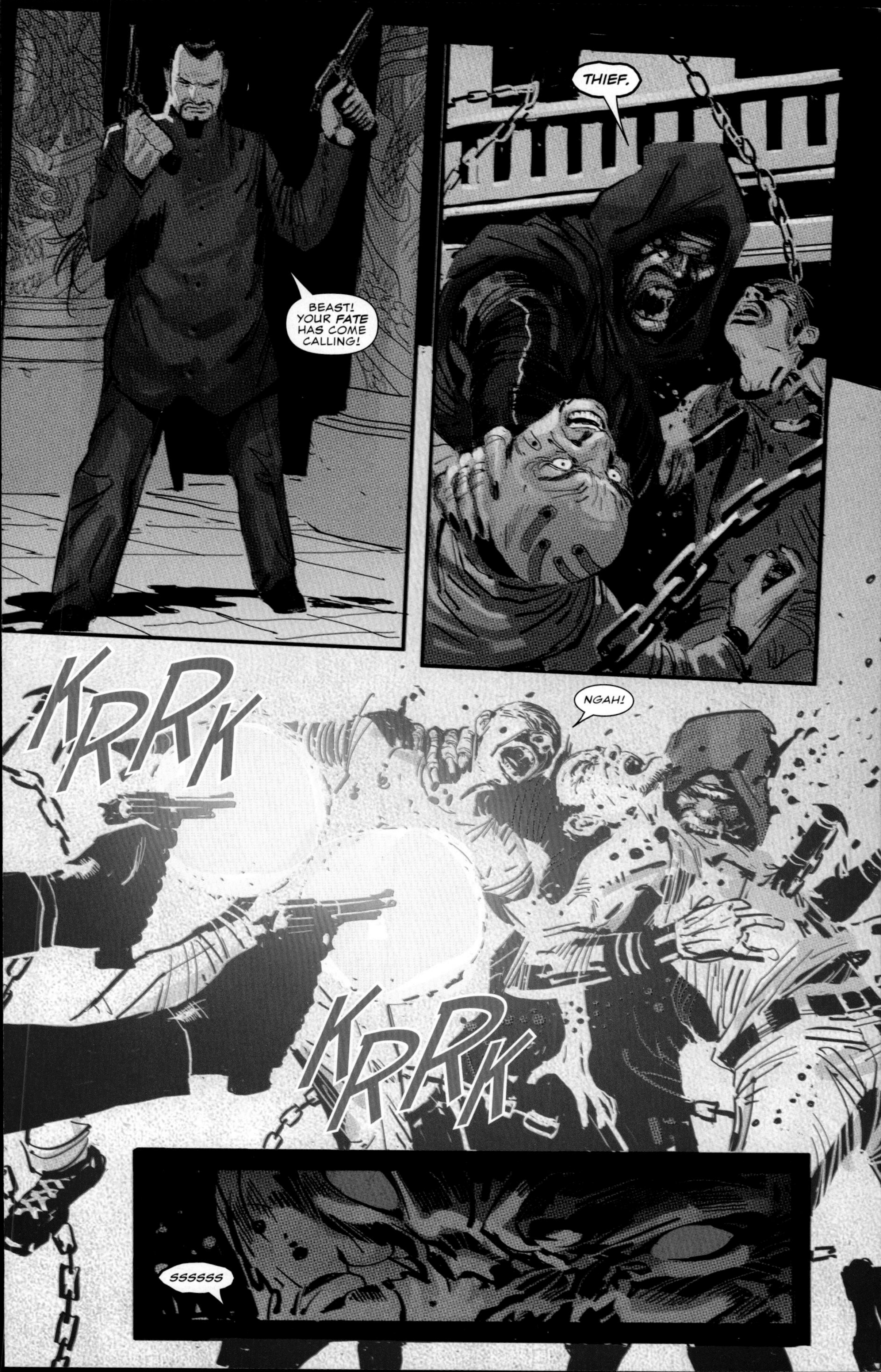

BEAST! YOUR FATE HAS COME CALLING!
THIEF.
KRRK
NGAH!
KRRK
SSSSSS

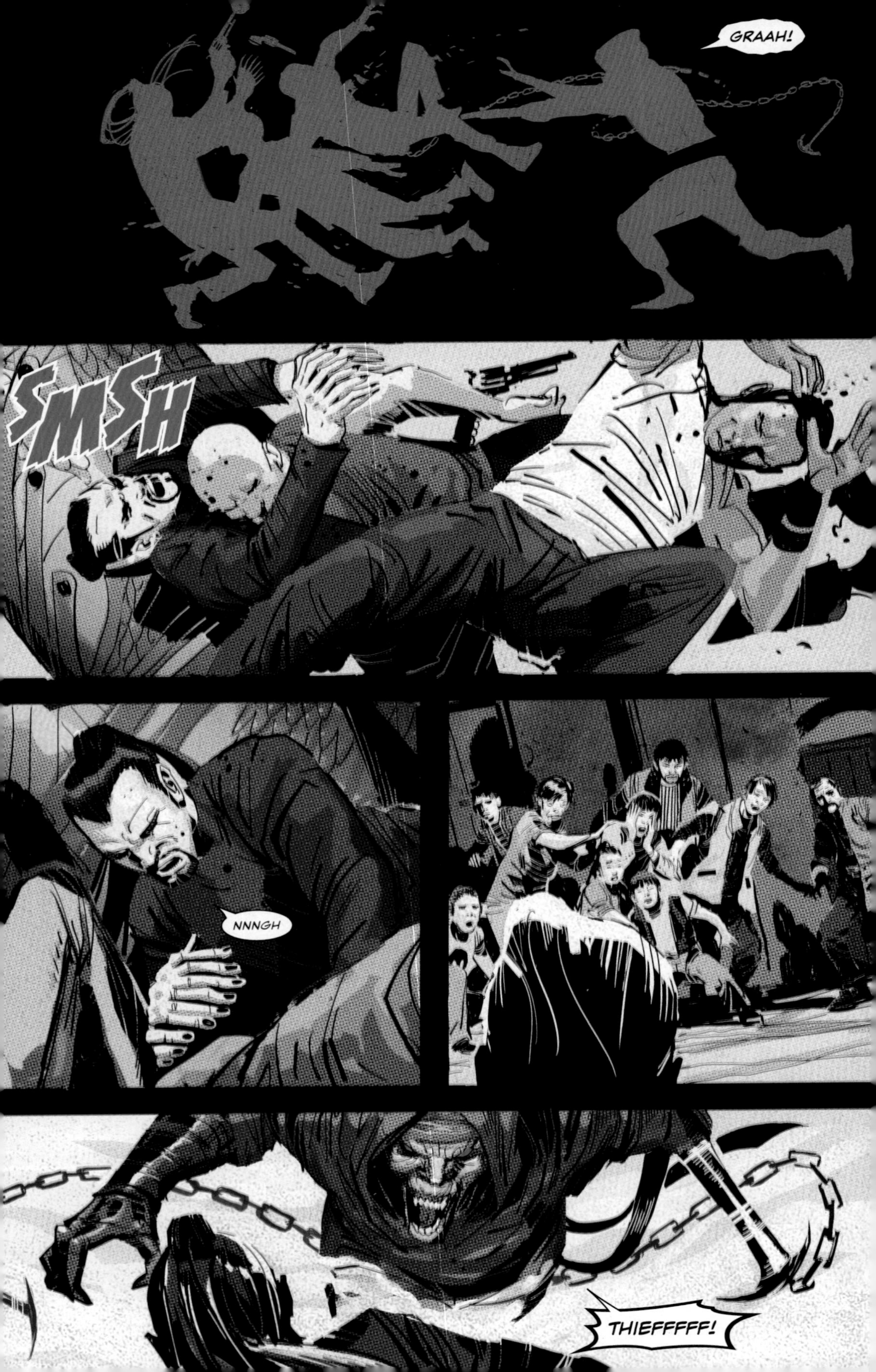
GRAAH!
SMSH
NNNGH
THIEFFFFF!

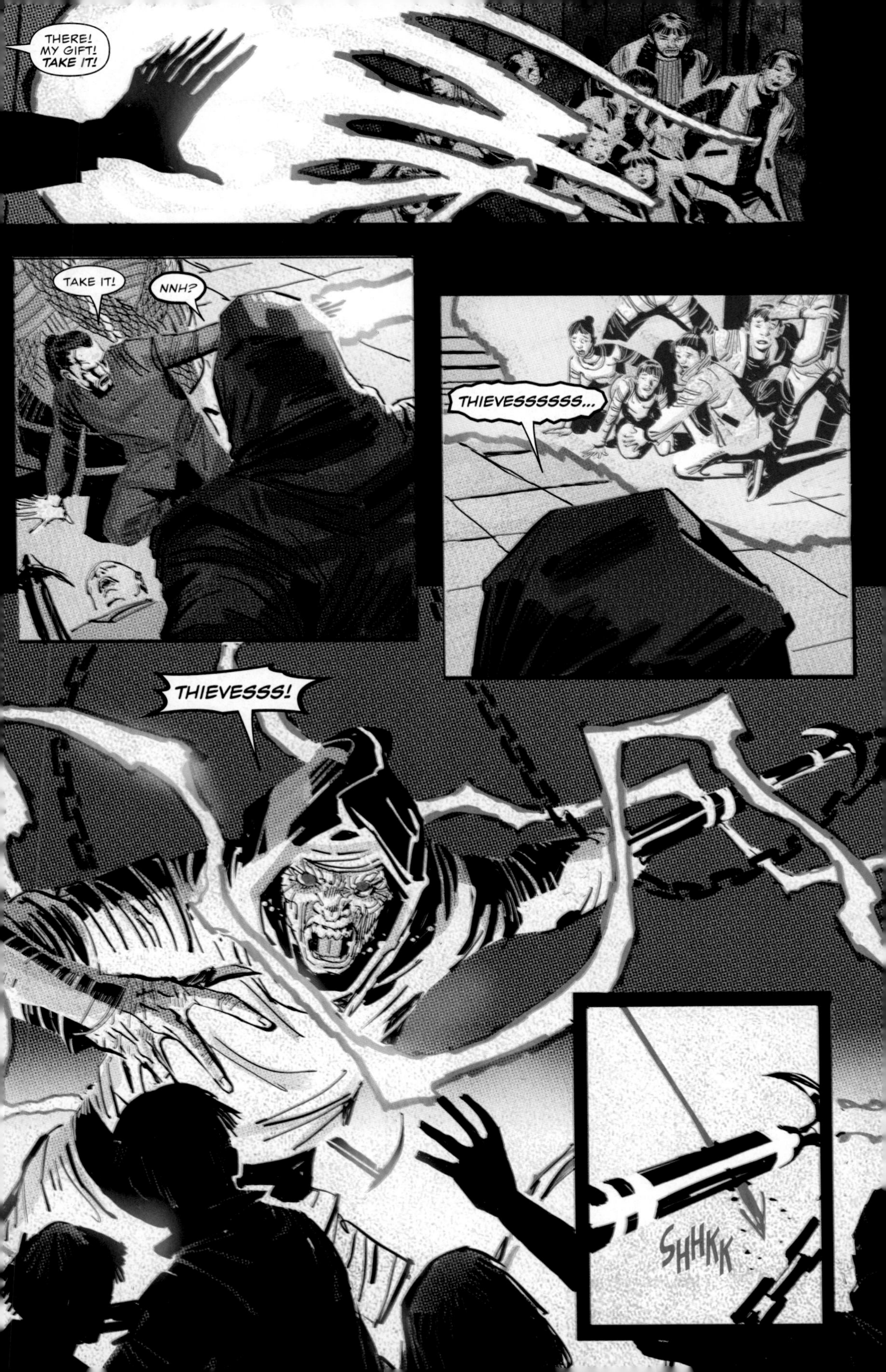

THERE! MY GIFT! TAKE IT!
TAKE IT!
NNH?
THIEVESSSSSS...
THIEVESSS!
SHHKK

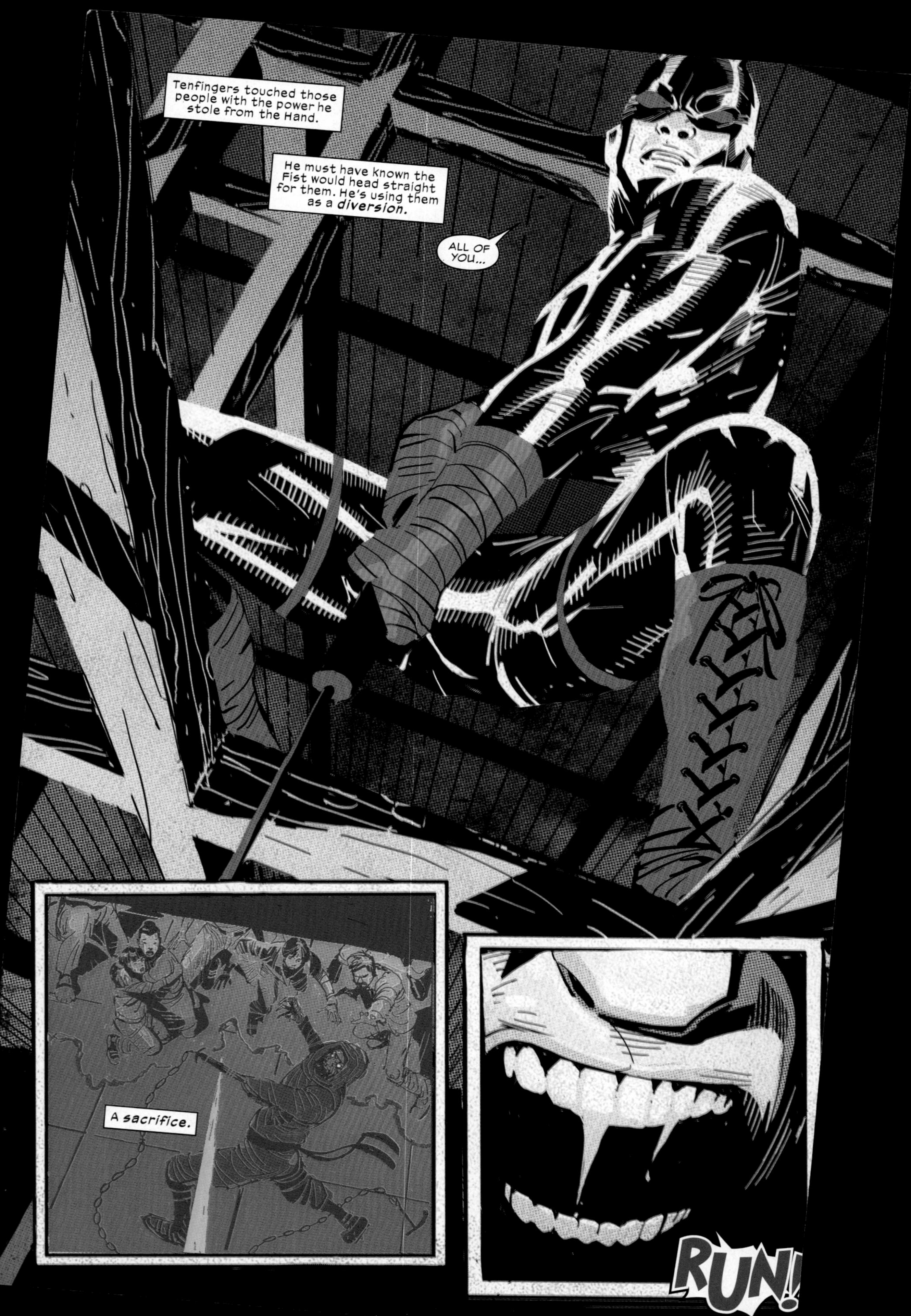
Tenfingers touched those people with the power he stole from the Hand.
He must have known the Fist would head straight for them. He's using them as a *diversion*.
ALL OF YOU...
A *sacrifice*.
RUN!

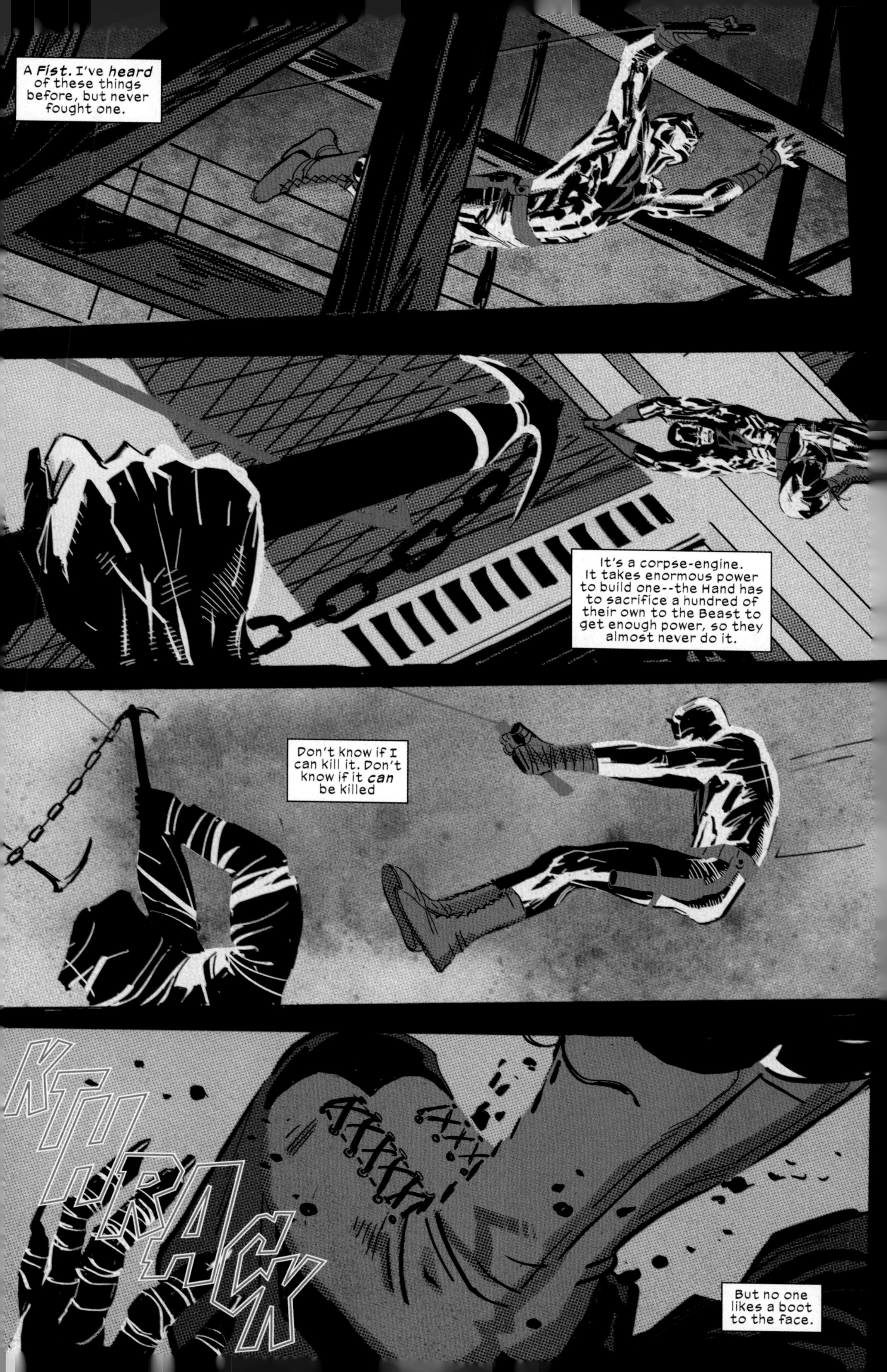
A Fist. I've heard of these things before, but never fought one.
It's a corpse-engine. It takes enormous power to build one--the Hand has to sacrifice a hundred of their own to the Beast to get enough power, so they almost never do it.
Don't know if I can kill it. Don't know if it can be killed
KTHRACK
But no one likes a boot to the face.

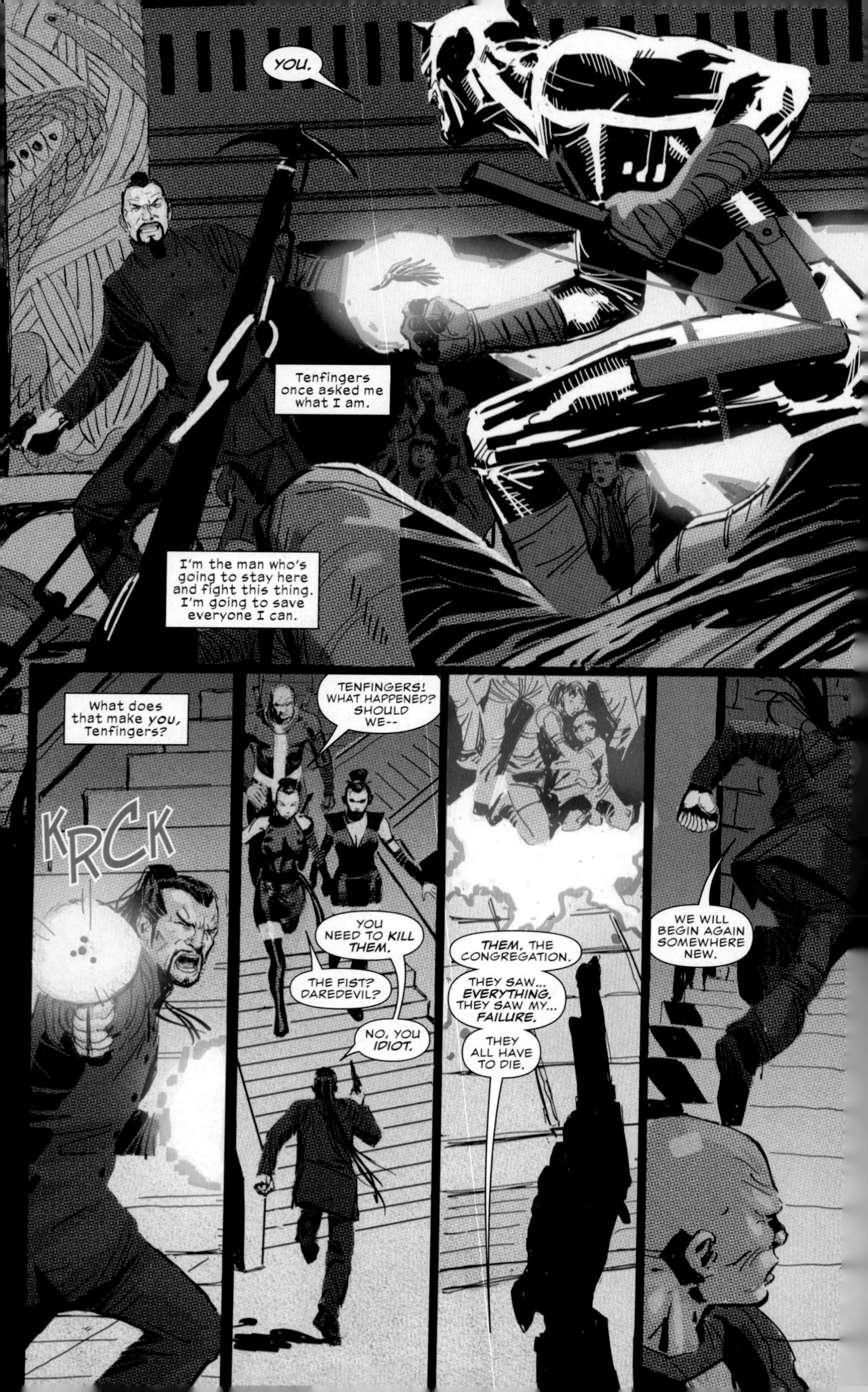

YOU.
Tenfingers once asked me what I am.
I'm the man who's going to stay here and fight this thing. I'm going to save everyone I can.
What does that make *you*, Tenfingers?
KRCK
TENFINGERS! WHAT HAPPENED? SHOULD WE--
YOU NEED TO **KILL THEM.**
THE FIST? DAREDEVIL?
NO, YOU ***IDIOT.***
THEM. THE CONGREGATION.
THEY SAW... ***EVERYTHING.*** THEY SAW MY... ***FAILURE.***
THEY ALL HAVE TO DIE.
WE WILL BEGIN AGAIN SOMEWHERE NEW.

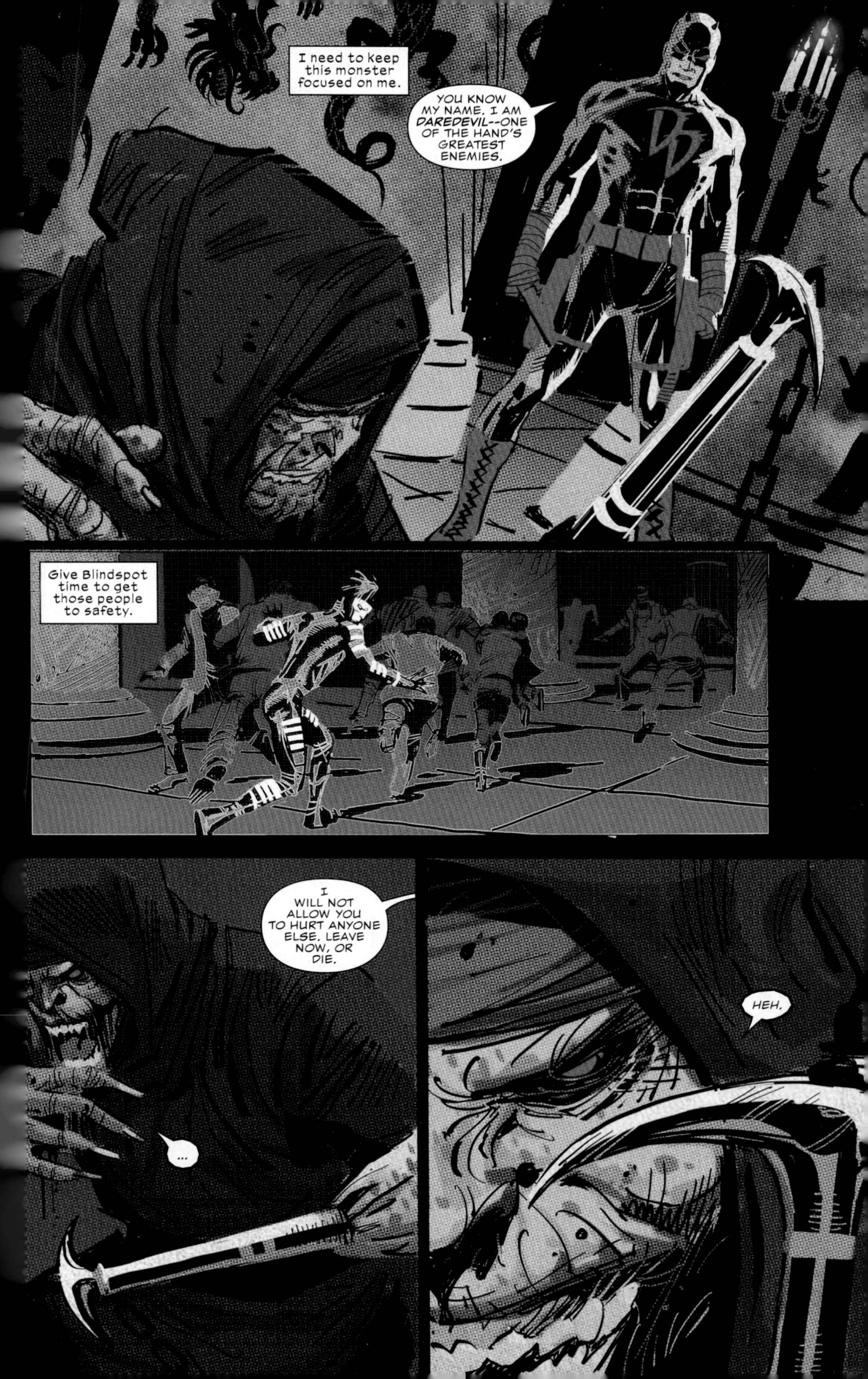
I need to keep this monster focused on me.
YOU KNOW MY NAME. I AM DAREDEVIL--ONE OF THE HAND'S GREATEST ENEMIES.
Give Blindspot time to get those people to safety.
I WILL NOT ALLOW YOU TO HURT ANYONE ELSE. LEAVE NOW, OR DIE.
...
HEH.

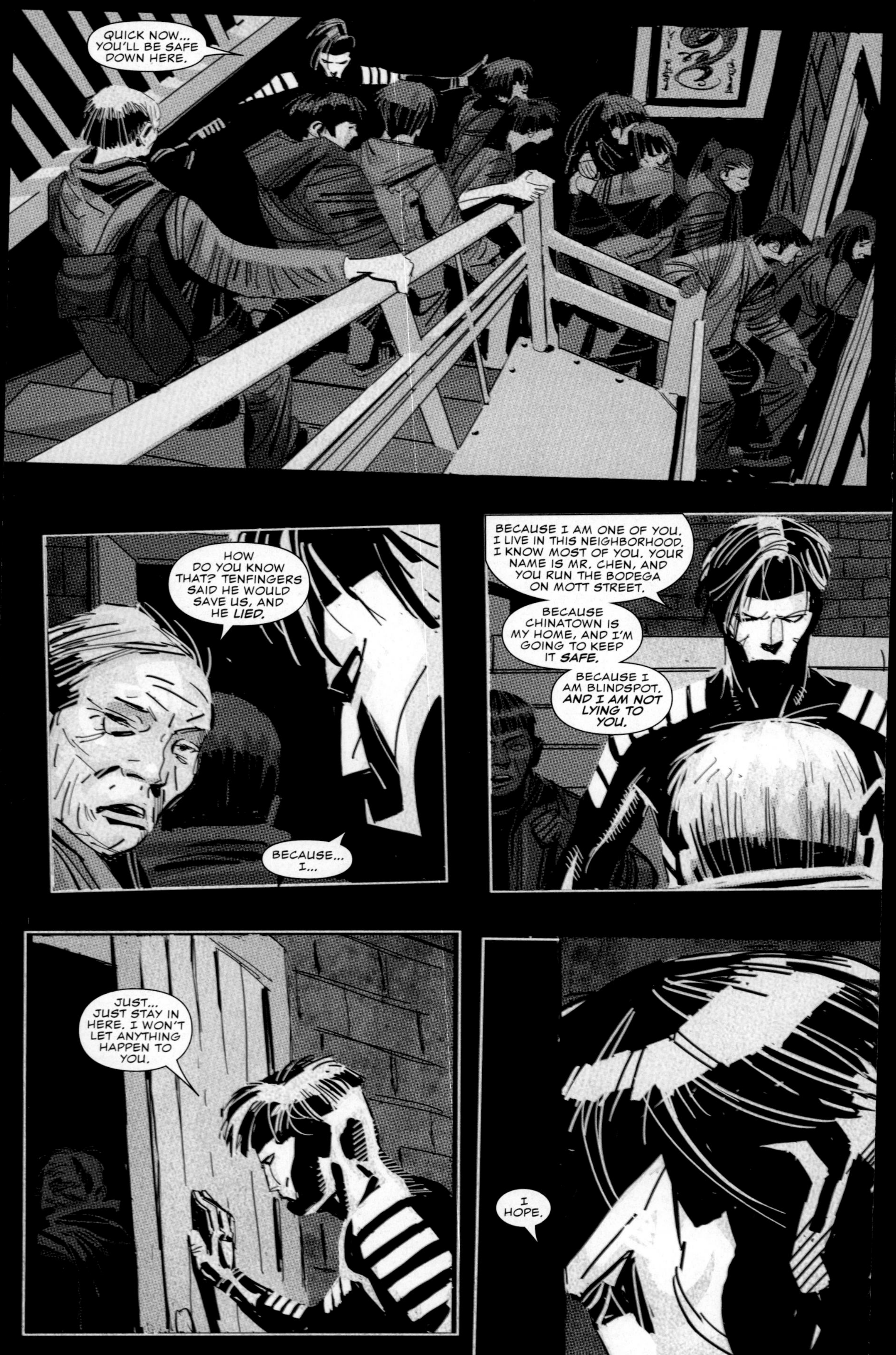
QUICK NOW... YOU'LL BE SAFE DOWN HERE.
HOW DO YOU KNOW THAT? TENFINGERS SAID HE WOULD SAVE US, AND HE LIED.
BECAUSE... I...
BECAUSE I AM ONE OF YOU. I LIVE IN THIS NEIGHBORHOOD. I KNOW MOST OF YOU. YOUR NAME IS MR. CHEN, AND YOU RUN THE BODEGA ON MOTT STREET.
BECAUSE CHINATOWN IS MY HOME, AND I'M GOING TO KEEP IT SAFE.
BECAUSE I AM BLINDSPOT. AND I AM NOT LYING TO YOU.
JUST... JUST STAY IN HERE. I WON'T LET ANYTHING HAPPEN TO YOU.
I HOPE.

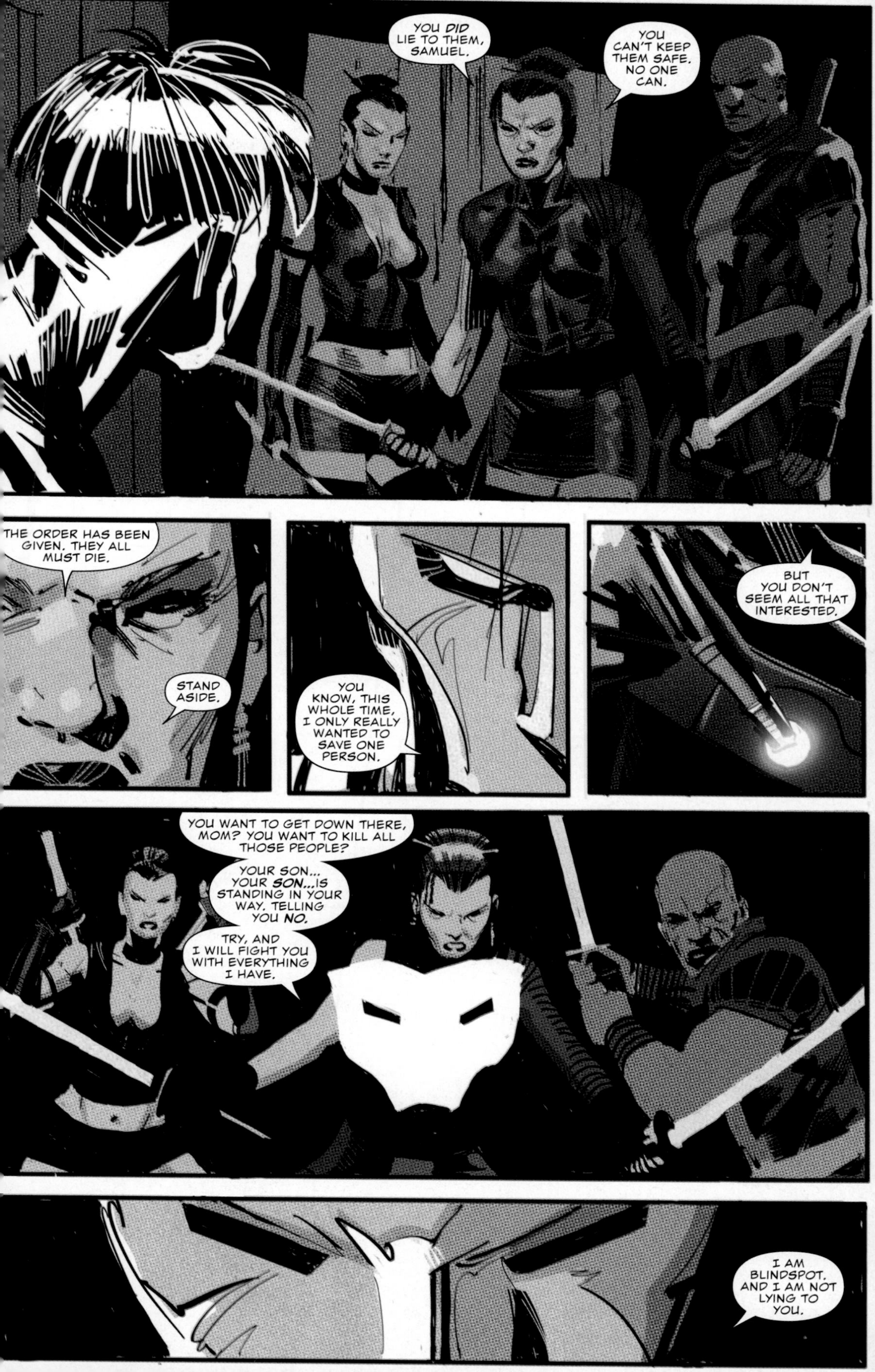
YOU DID LIE TO THEM, SAMUEL.
YOU CAN'T KEEP THEM SAFE. NO ONE CAN.
THE ORDER HAS BEEN GIVEN. THEY ALL MUST DIE.
STAND ASIDE.
YOU KNOW, THIS WHOLE TIME, I ONLY REALLY WANTED TO SAVE ONE PERSON.
BUT YOU DON'T SEEM ALL THAT INTERESTED.
YOU WANT TO GET DOWN THERE, MOM? YOU WANT TO KILL ALL THOSE PEOPLE?
YOUR SON... YOUR SON...IS STANDING IN YOUR WAY. TELLING YOU NO.
TRY, AND I WILL FIGHT YOU WITH EVERYTHING I HAVE.
I AM BLINDSPOT. AND I AM NOT LYING TO YOU.

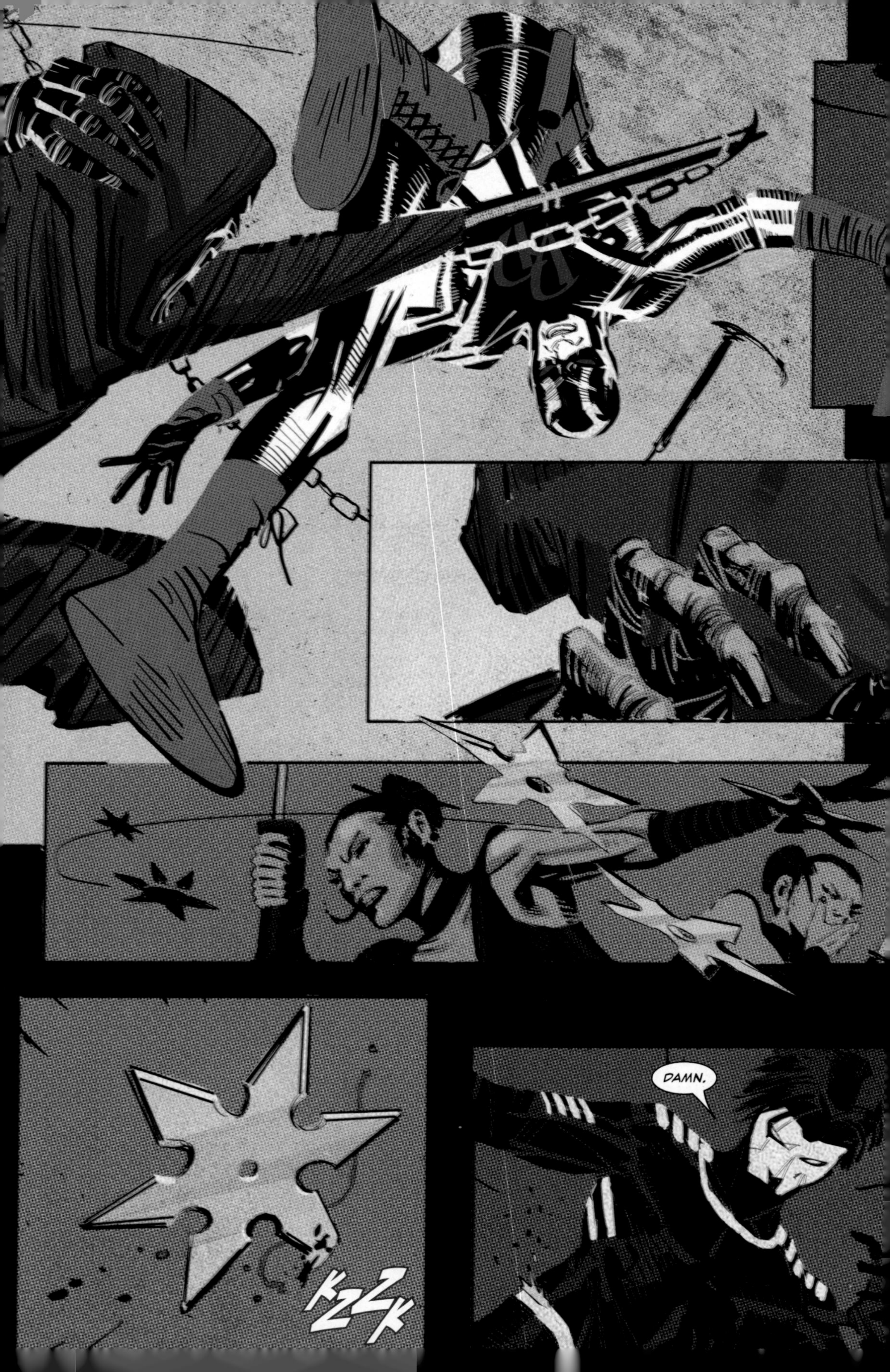
KZZK
DAMN.

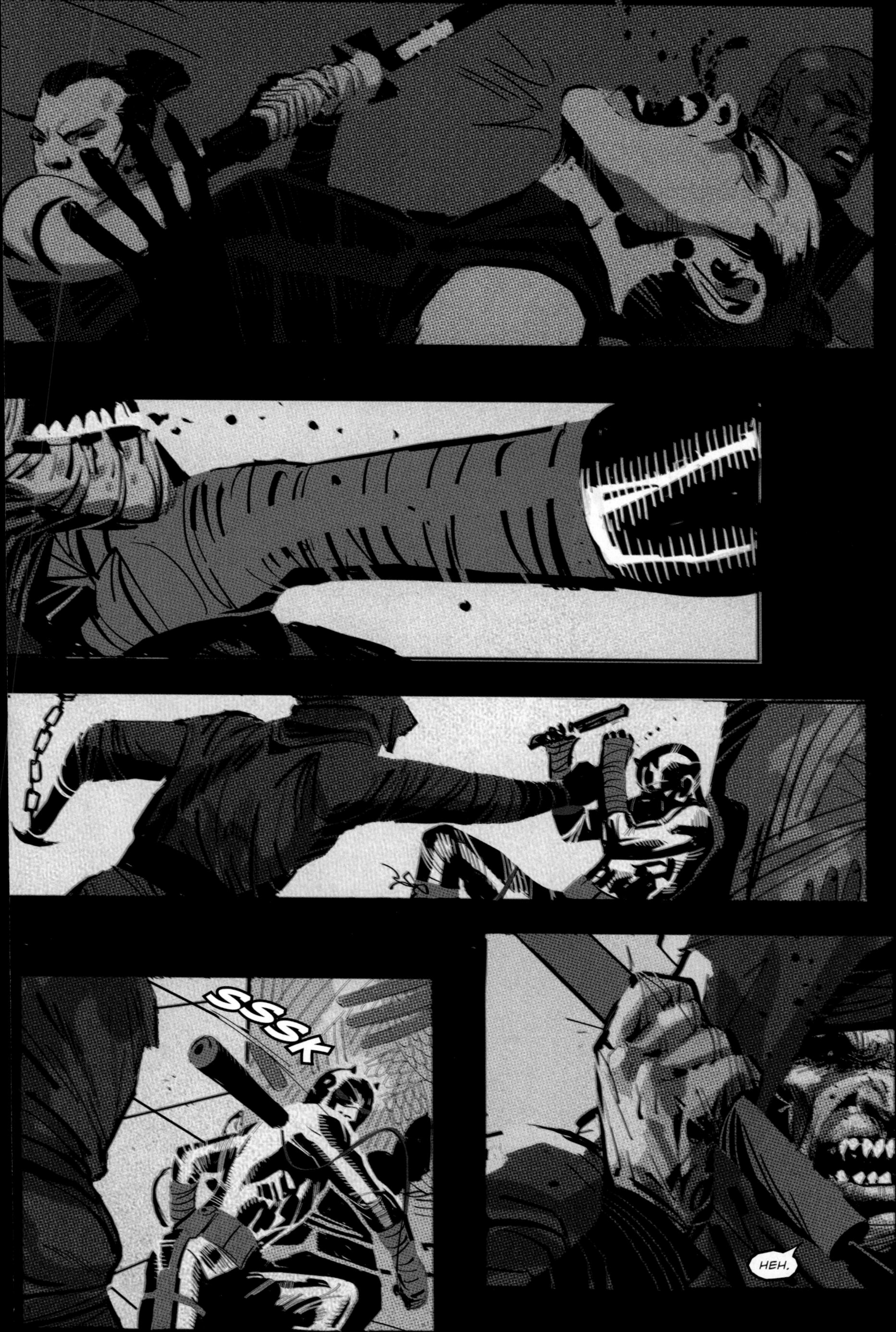
SSSK
HEH.

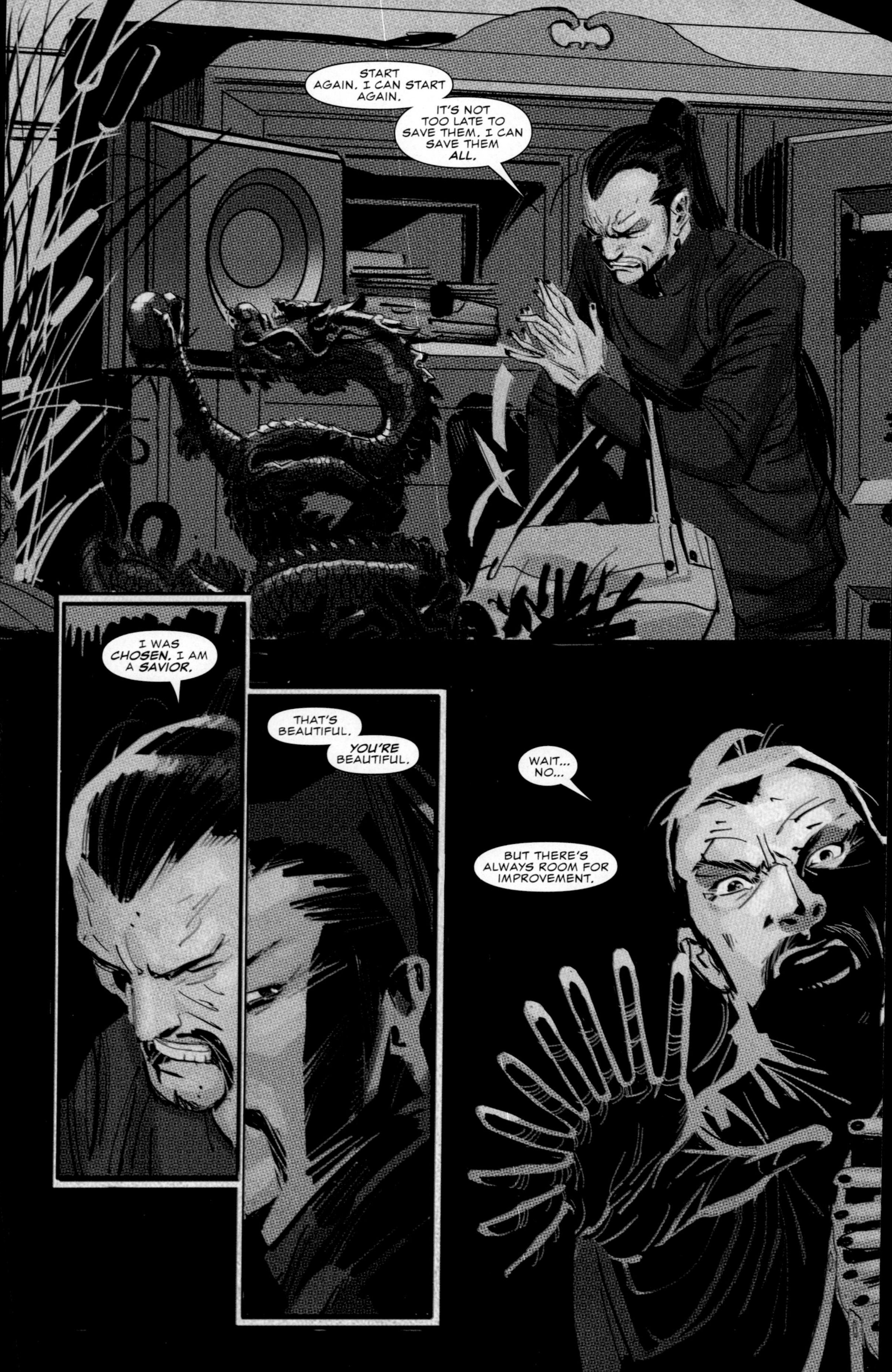
START AGAIN. I CAN START AGAIN.
IT'S NOT TOO LATE TO SAVE THEM. I CAN SAVE THEM ALL.
I WAS CHOSEN. I AM A SAVIOR.
THAT'S BEAUTIFUL. YOU'RE BEAUTIFUL.
WAIT... NO...
BUT THERE'S ALWAYS ROOM FOR IMPROVEMENT.

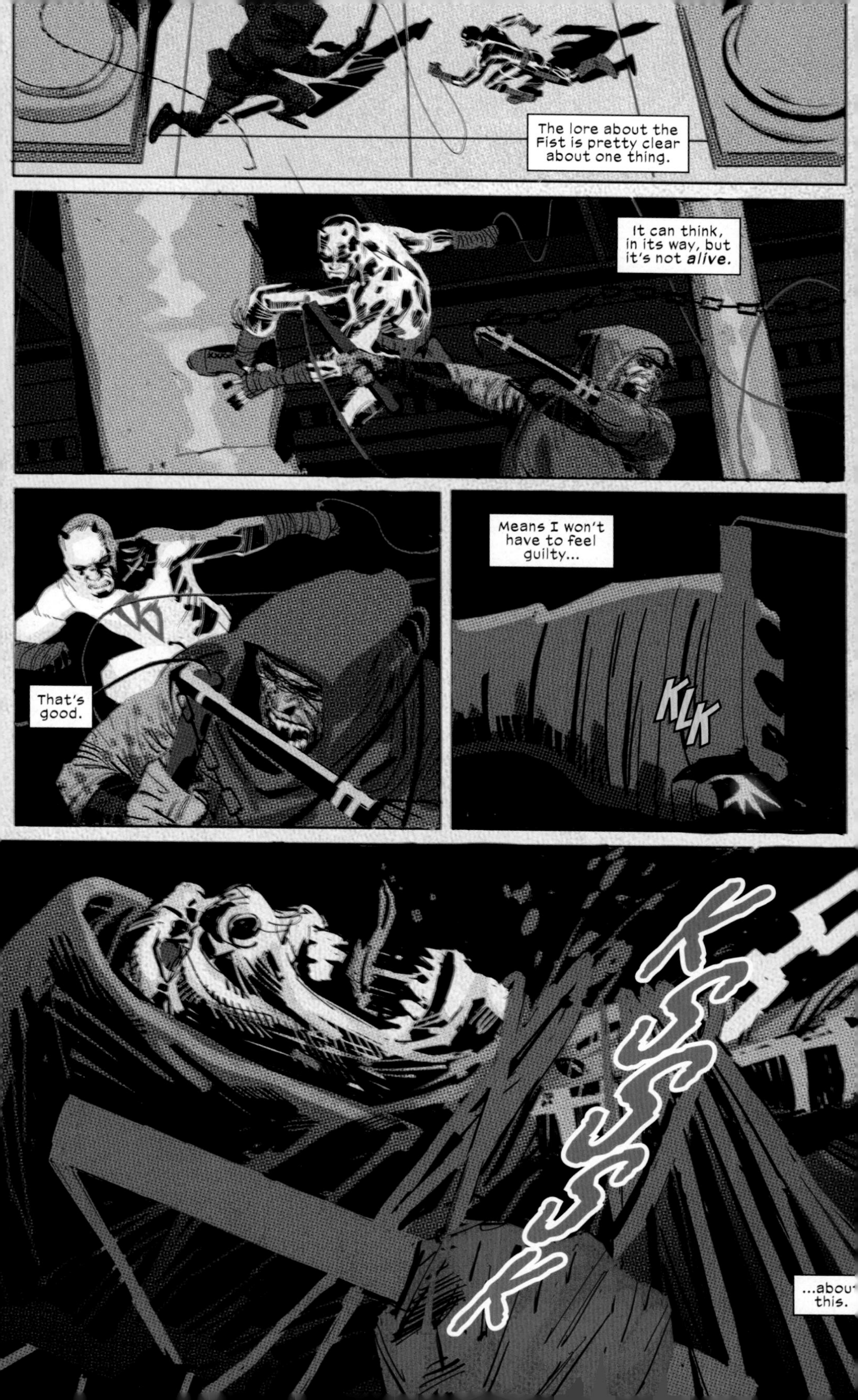
The lore about the Fist is pretty clear about one thing.
It can think, in its way, but it's not *alive.*
That's good.
Means I won't have to feel guilty...
KLK
KSSSSK
...about this.

HOLY--

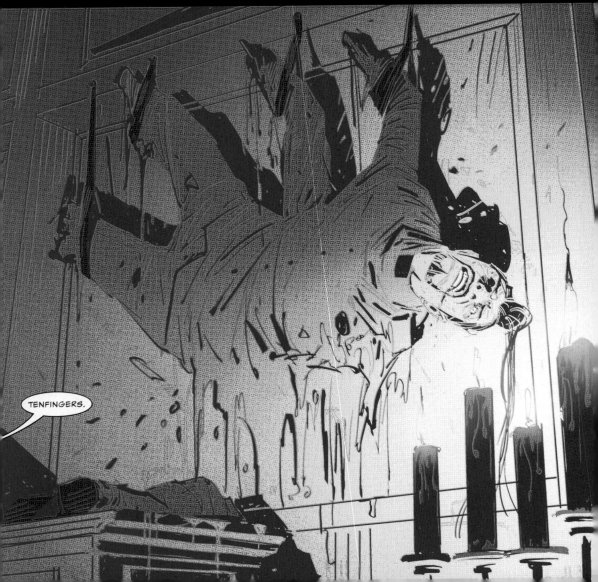

TENFINGERS.

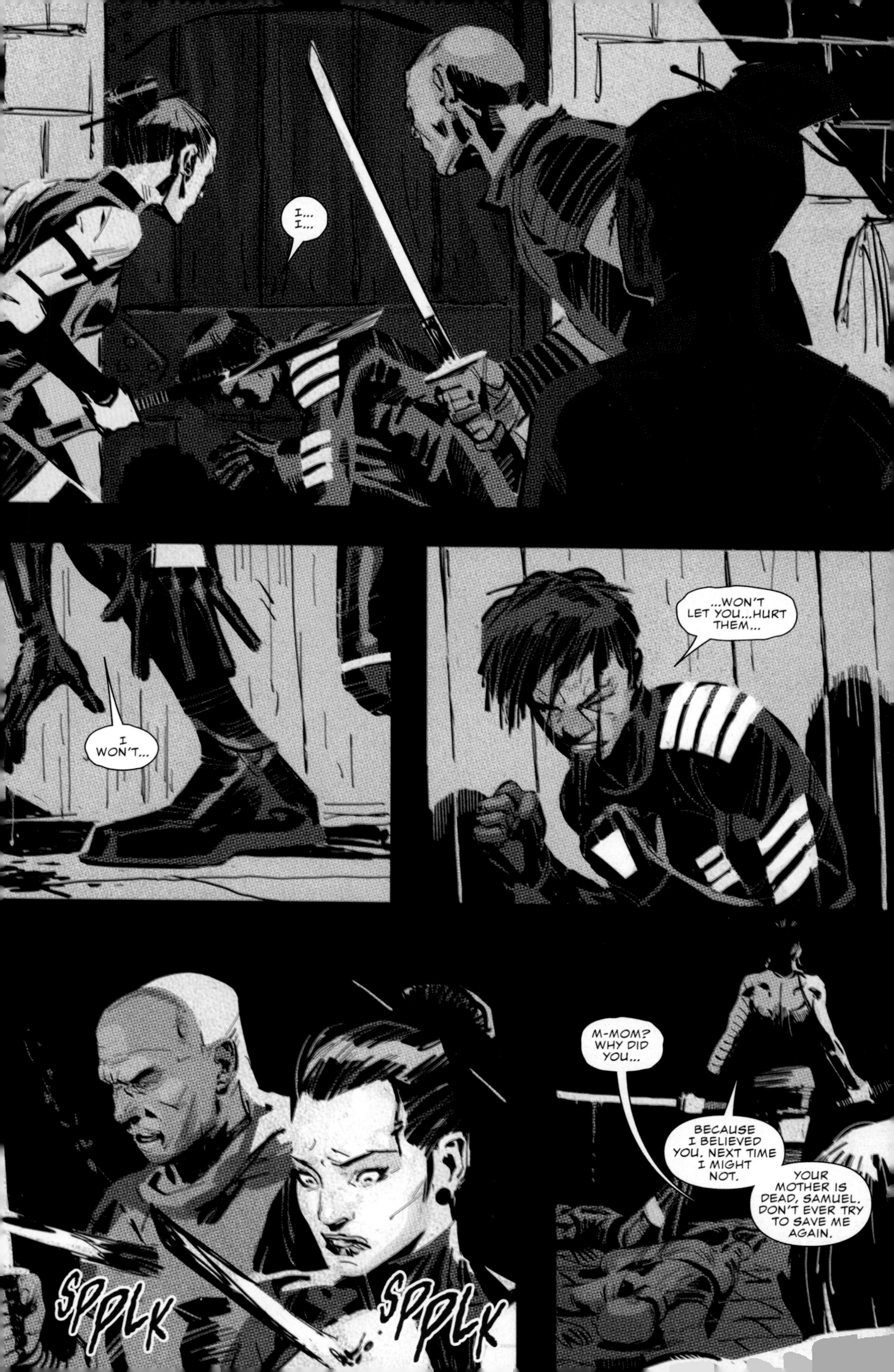
I... I...
I WON'T...
...WON'T LET YOU...HURT THEM...
M-MOM? WHY DID YOU...
BECAUSE I BELIEVED YOU. NEXT TIME I MIGHT NOT.
YOUR MOTHER IS DEAD, SAMUEL. DON'T EVER TRY TO SAVE ME AGAIN.
SPDLK
SPDLK

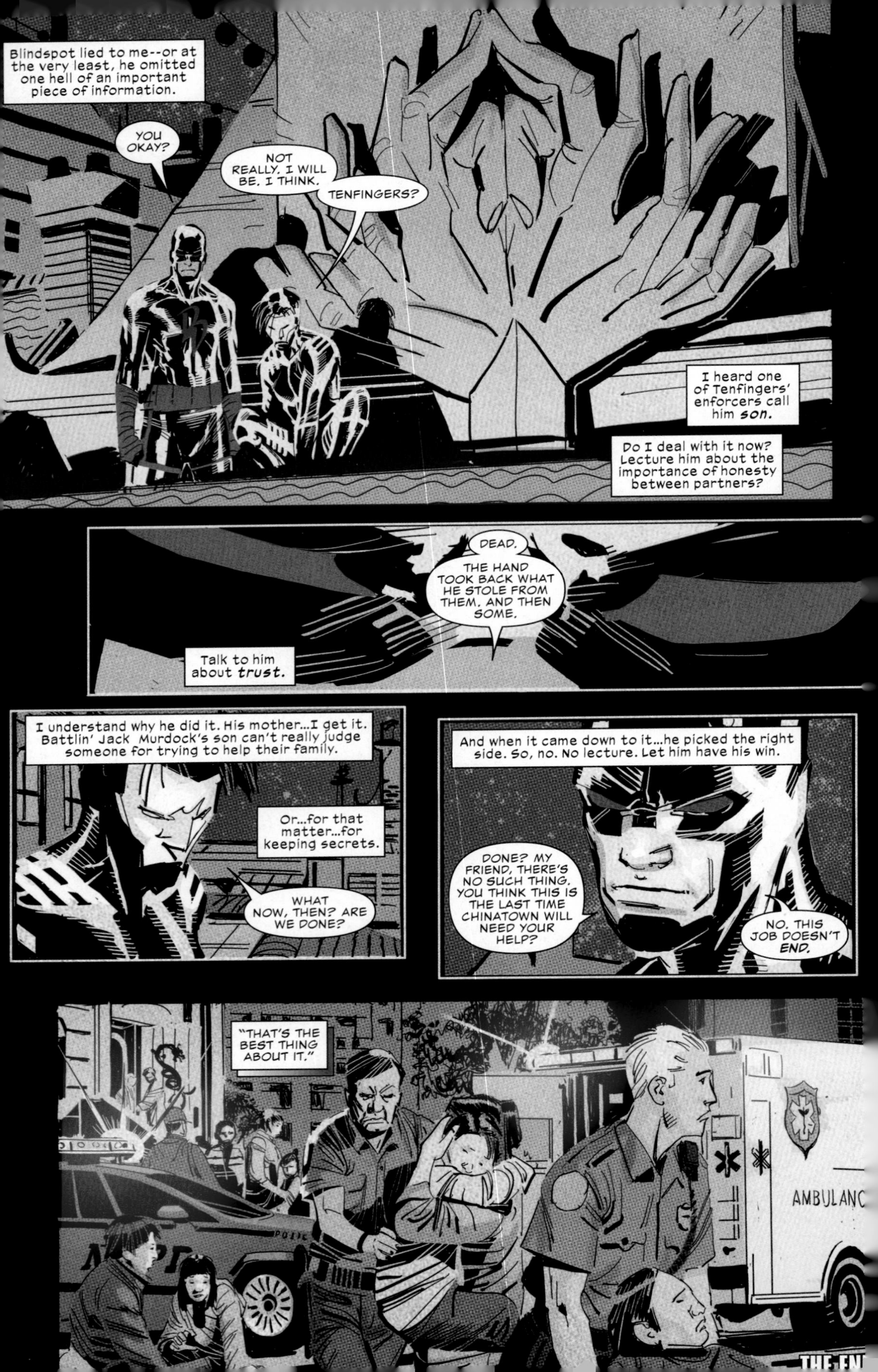
Blindspot lied to me--or at the very least, he omitted one hell of an important piece of information.
YOU OKAY?
NOT REALLY. I WILL BE. I THINK.
TENFINGERS?
I heard one of Tenfingers' enforcers call him *son.*
Do I deal with it now? Lecture him about the importance of honesty between partners?
DEAD.
THE HAND TOOK BACK WHAT HE STOLE FROM THEM, AND THEN SOME.
Talk to him about *trust.*
I understand why he did it. His mother...I get it. Battlin' Jack Murdock's son can't really judge someone for trying to help their family.
Or...for that matter...for keeping secrets.
WHAT NOW, THEN? ARE WE DONE?
And when it came down to it...he picked the right side. So, no. No lecture. Let him have his win.
DONE? MY FRIEND, THERE'S NO SUCH THING. YOU THINK THIS IS THE LAST TIME CHINATOWN WILL NEED YOUR HELP?
NO. THIS JOB DOESN'T *END.*
"THAT'S THE BEST THING ABOUT IT."
AMBULANC
THE EN

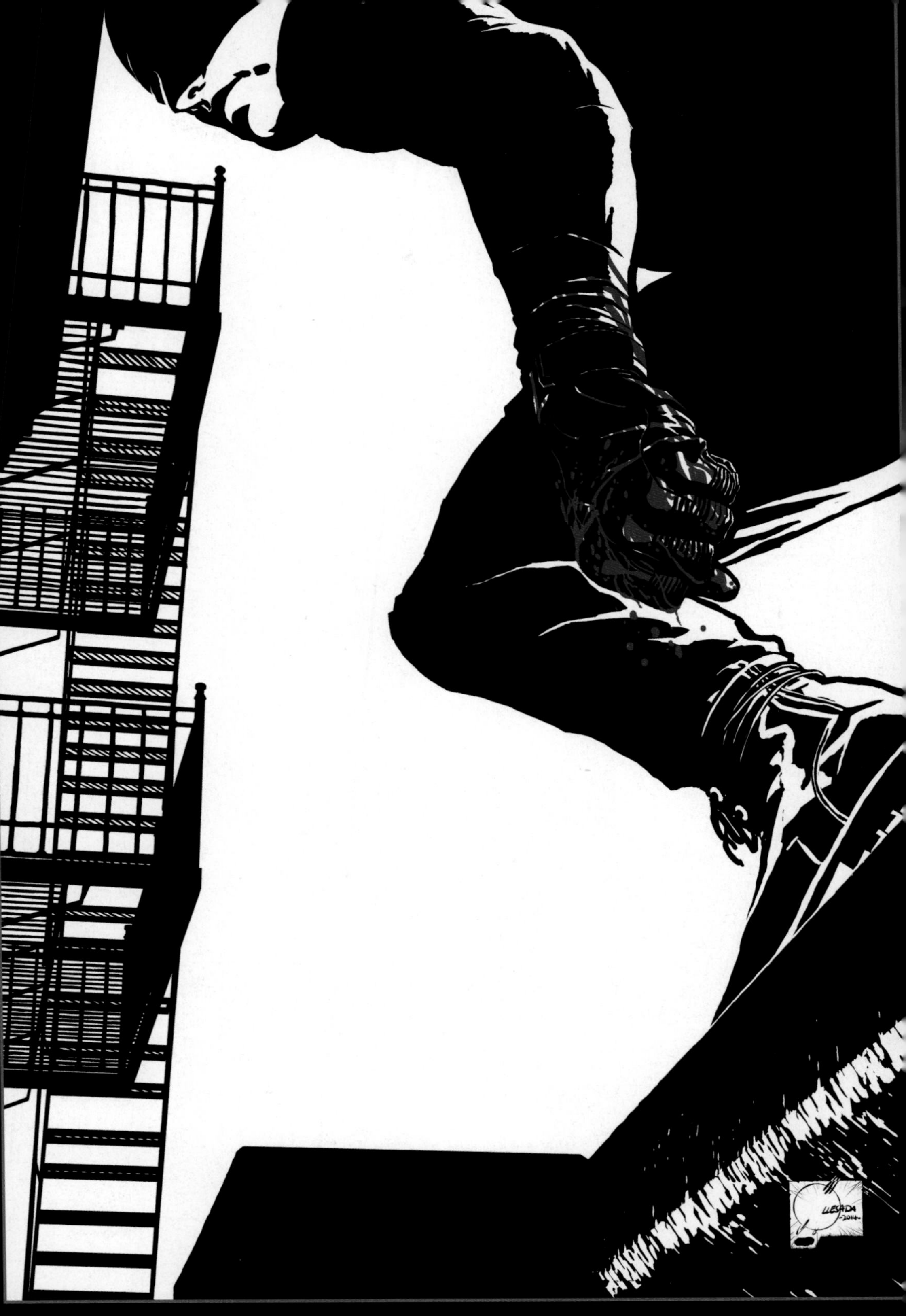
QUESADA 2014

JOE QUESADA
No. 1 VARIANT

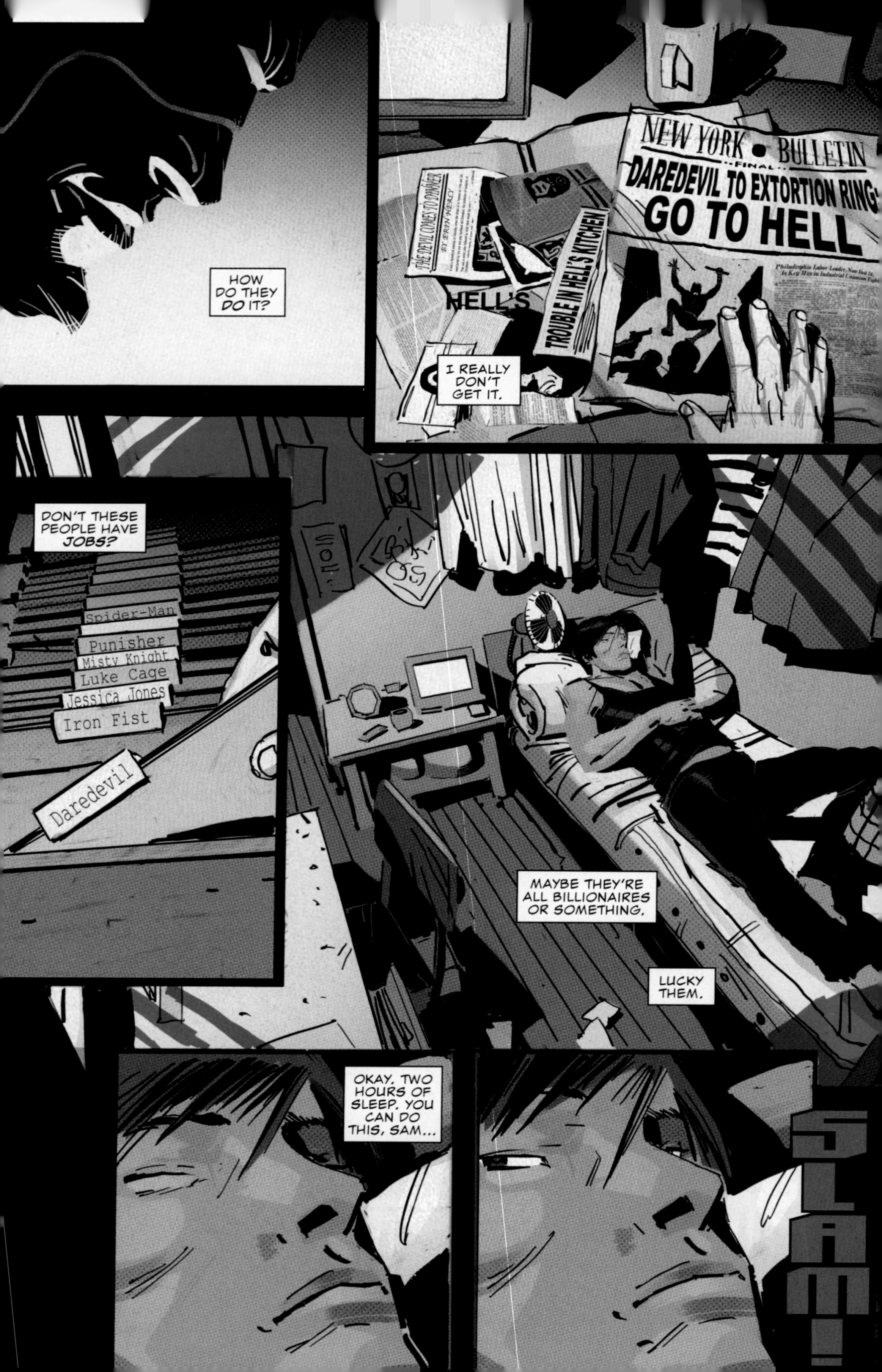
HOW DO THEY DO IT?
NEW YORK • BULLETIN
DAREDEVIL TO EXTORTION RING: GO TO HELL
THE DEVIL COMES TO DINNER
TROUBLE IN HELL'S KITCHEN
HELL'S
I REALLY DON'T GET IT.
DON'T THESE PEOPLE HAVE JOBS?
Spider-Man
Punisher
Misty Knight
Luke Cage
Jessica Jones
Iron Fist
Daredevil
MAYBE THEY'RE ALL BILLIONAIRES OR SOMETHING.
LUCKY THEM.
OKAY. TWO HOURS OF SLEEP. YOU CAN DO THIS, SAM...
SLAM!

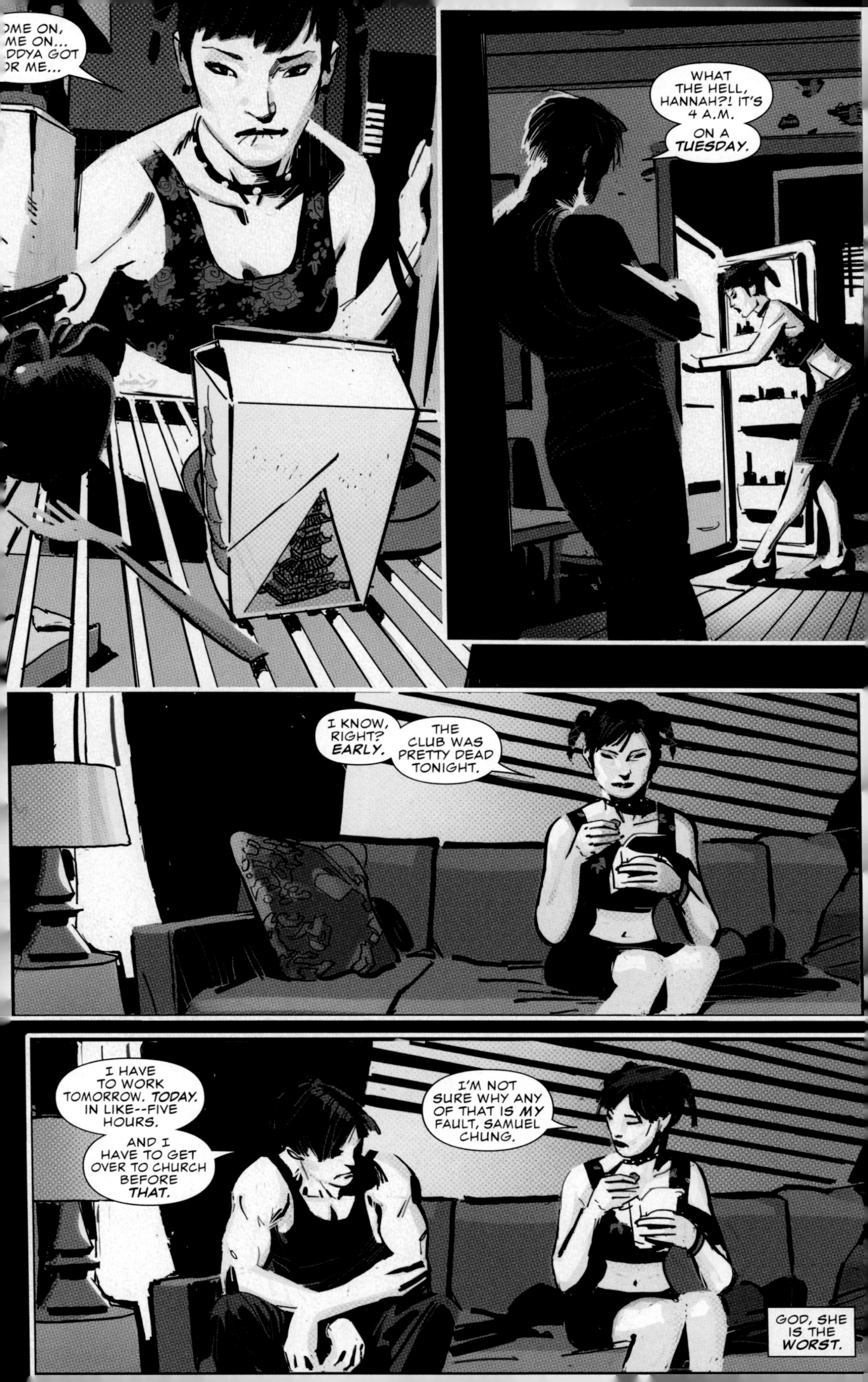

OME ON, ME ON... DDYA GOT OR ME...
WHAT THE HELL, HANNAH?! IT'S 4 A.M.
ON A TUESDAY.
I KNOW, RIGHT? EARLY.
THE CLUB WAS PRETTY DEAD TONIGHT.
I HAVE TO WORK TOMORROW. TODAY. IN LIKE--FIVE HOURS.
AND I HAVE TO GET OVER TO CHURCH BEFORE THAT.
I'M NOT SURE WHY ANY OF THAT IS MY FAULT, SAMUEL CHUNG.
GOD, SHE IS THE WORST.

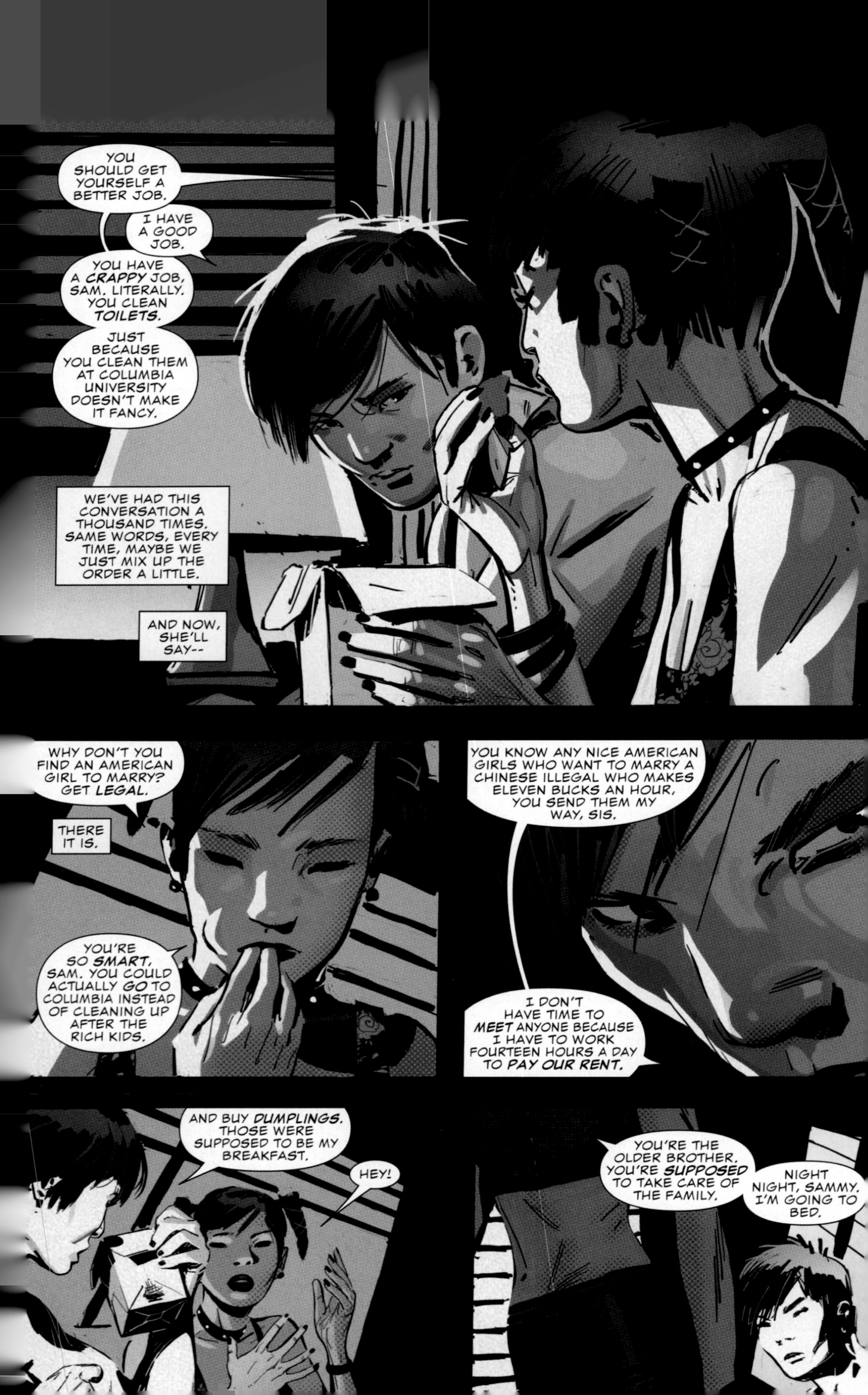
YOU SHOULD GET YOURSELF A BETTER JOB.
I HAVE A GOOD JOB.
YOU HAVE A CRAPPY JOB, SAM. LITERALLY. YOU CLEAN TOILETS.
JUST BECAUSE YOU CLEAN THEM AT COLUMBIA UNIVERSITY DOESN'T MAKE IT FANCY.
WE'VE HAD THIS CONVERSATION A THOUSAND TIMES. SAME WORDS, EVERY TIME, MAYBE WE JUST MIX UP THE ORDER A LITTLE.
AND NOW, SHE'LL SAY--
WHY DON'T YOU FIND AN AMERICAN GIRL TO MARRY? GET LEGAL.
THERE IT IS.
YOU'RE SO SMART, SAM. YOU COULD ACTUALLY GO TO COLUMBIA INSTEAD OF CLEANING UP AFTER THE RICH KIDS.
YOU KNOW ANY NICE AMERICAN GIRLS WHO WANT TO MARRY A CHINESE ILLEGAL WHO MAKES ELEVEN BUCKS AN HOUR, YOU SEND THEM MY WAY, SIS.
I DON'T HAVE TIME TO MEET ANYONE BECAUSE I HAVE TO WORK FOURTEEN HOURS A DAY TO PAY OUR RENT.
AND BUY DUMPLINGS. THOSE WERE SUPPOSED TO BE MY BREAKFAST.
HEY!
YOU'RE THE OLDER BROTHER. YOU'RE SUPPOSED TO TAKE CARE OF THE FAMILY.
NIGHT NIGHT, SAMMY. I'M GOING TO BED.

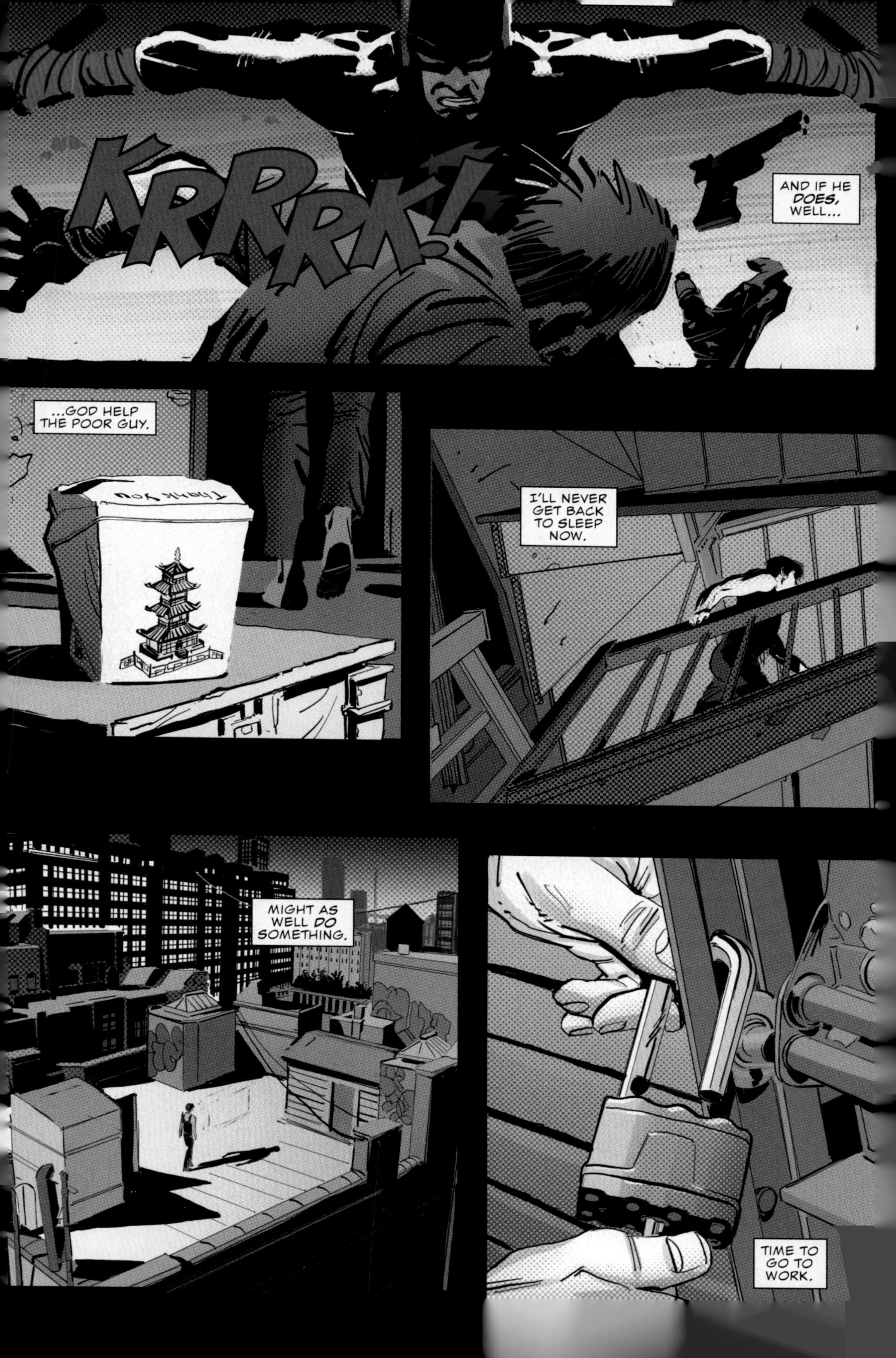
KRRRK!
AND IF HE *DOES,* WELL...
...GOD HELP THE POOR GUY.
I'LL NEVER GET BACK TO SLEEP NOW.
MIGHT AS WELL *DO* SOMETHING.
TIME TO GO TO WORK.

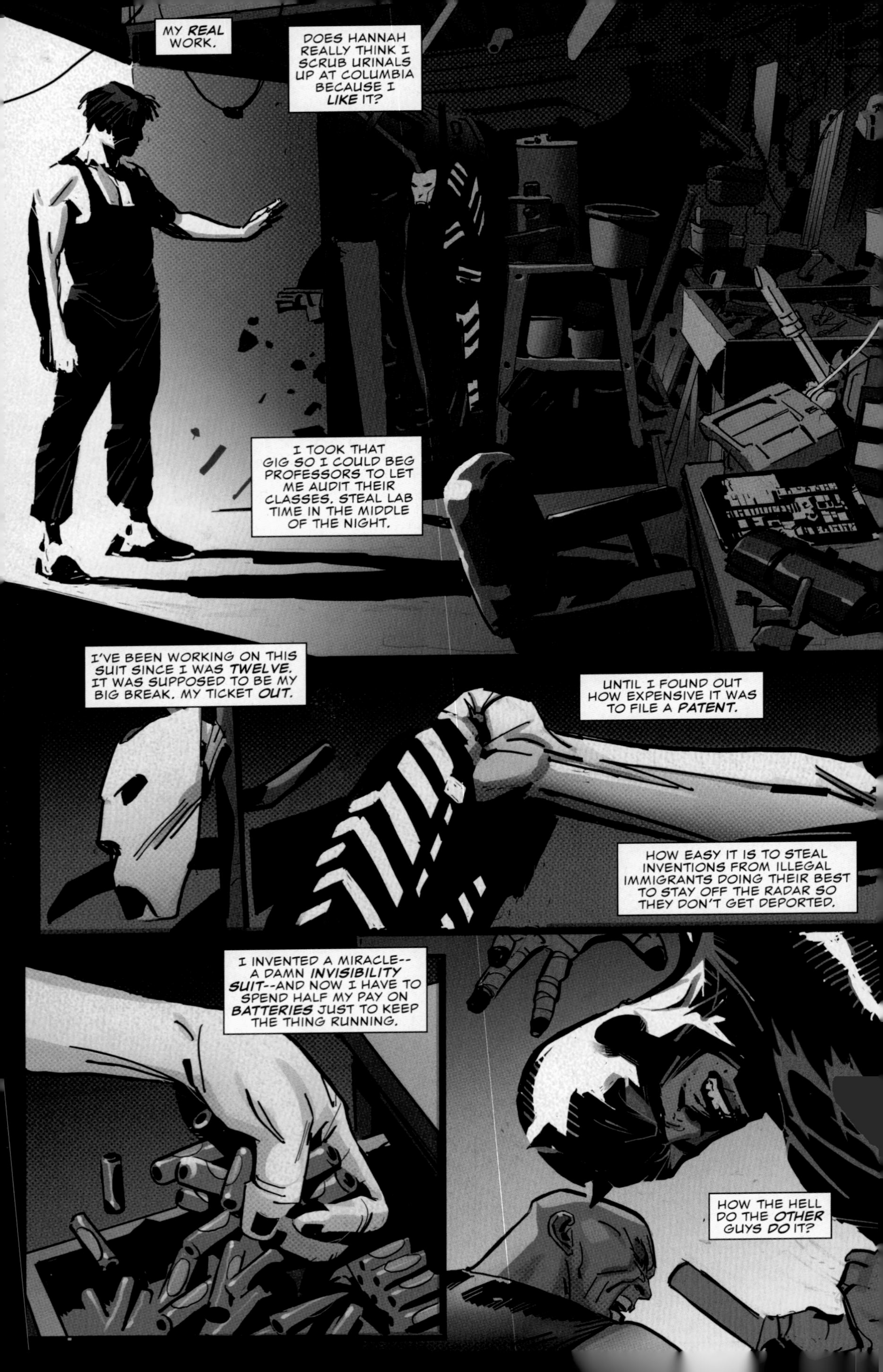
MY REAL WORK.
DOES HANNAH REALLY THINK I SCRUB URINALS UP AT COLUMBIA BECAUSE I LIKE IT?
I TOOK THAT GIG SO I COULD BEG PROFESSORS TO LET ME AUDIT THEIR CLASSES. STEAL LAB TIME IN THE MIDDLE OF THE NIGHT.
I'VE BEEN WORKING ON THIS SUIT SINCE I WAS TWELVE. IT WAS SUPPOSED TO BE MY BIG BREAK. MY TICKET OUT.
UNTIL I FOUND OUT HOW EXPENSIVE IT WAS TO FILE A PATENT.
HOW EASY IT IS TO STEAL INVENTIONS FROM ILLEGAL IMMIGRANTS DOING THEIR BEST TO STAY OFF THE RADAR SO THEY DON'T GET DEPORTED.
I INVENTED A MIRACLE-- A DAMN INVISIBILITY SUIT--AND NOW I HAVE TO SPEND HALF MY PAY ON BATTERIES JUST TO KEEP THE THING RUNNING.
HOW THE HELL DO THE OTHER GUYS DO IT?

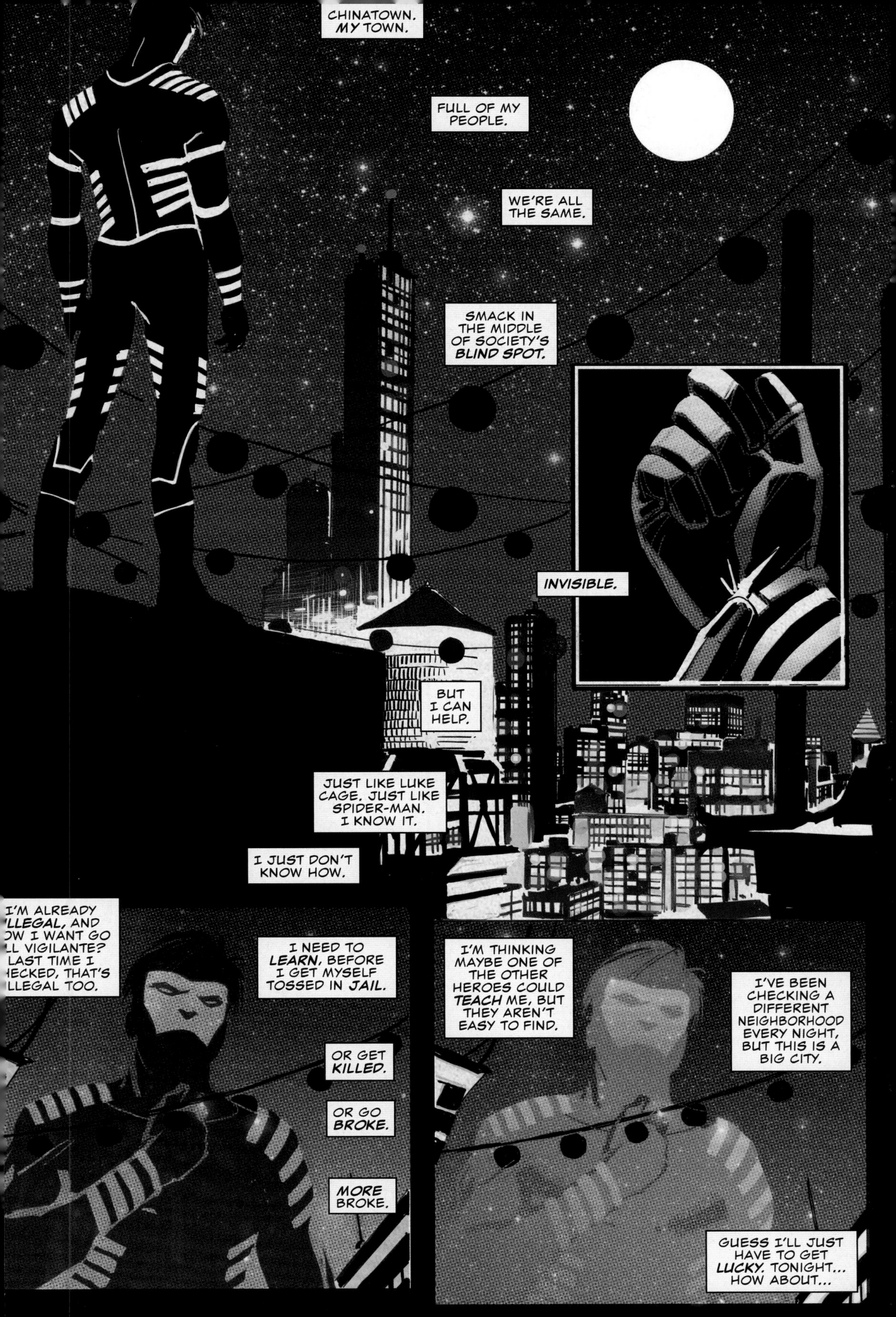
CHINATOWN. MY TOWN.
FULL OF MY PEOPLE.
WE'RE ALL THE SAME.
SMACK IN THE MIDDLE OF SOCIETY'S BLIND SPOT.
INVISIBLE.
BUT I CAN HELP.
JUST LIKE LUKE CAGE. JUST LIKE SPIDER-MAN. I KNOW IT.
I JUST DON'T KNOW HOW.
I'M ALREADY ILLEGAL, AND NOW I WANT GO FULL VIGILANTE? LAST TIME I CHECKED, THAT'S ILLEGAL TOO.
I NEED TO LEARN, BEFORE I GET MYSELF TOSSED IN JAIL.
OR GET KILLED.
OR GO BROKE.
MORE BROKE.
I'M THINKING MAYBE ONE OF THE OTHER HEROES COULD TEACH ME, BUT THEY AREN'T EASY TO FIND.
I'VE BEEN CHECKING A DIFFERENT NEIGHBORHOOD EVERY NIGHT, BUT THIS IS A BIG CITY.
GUESS I'LL JUST HAVE TO GET LUCKY. TONIGHT... HOW ABOUT...

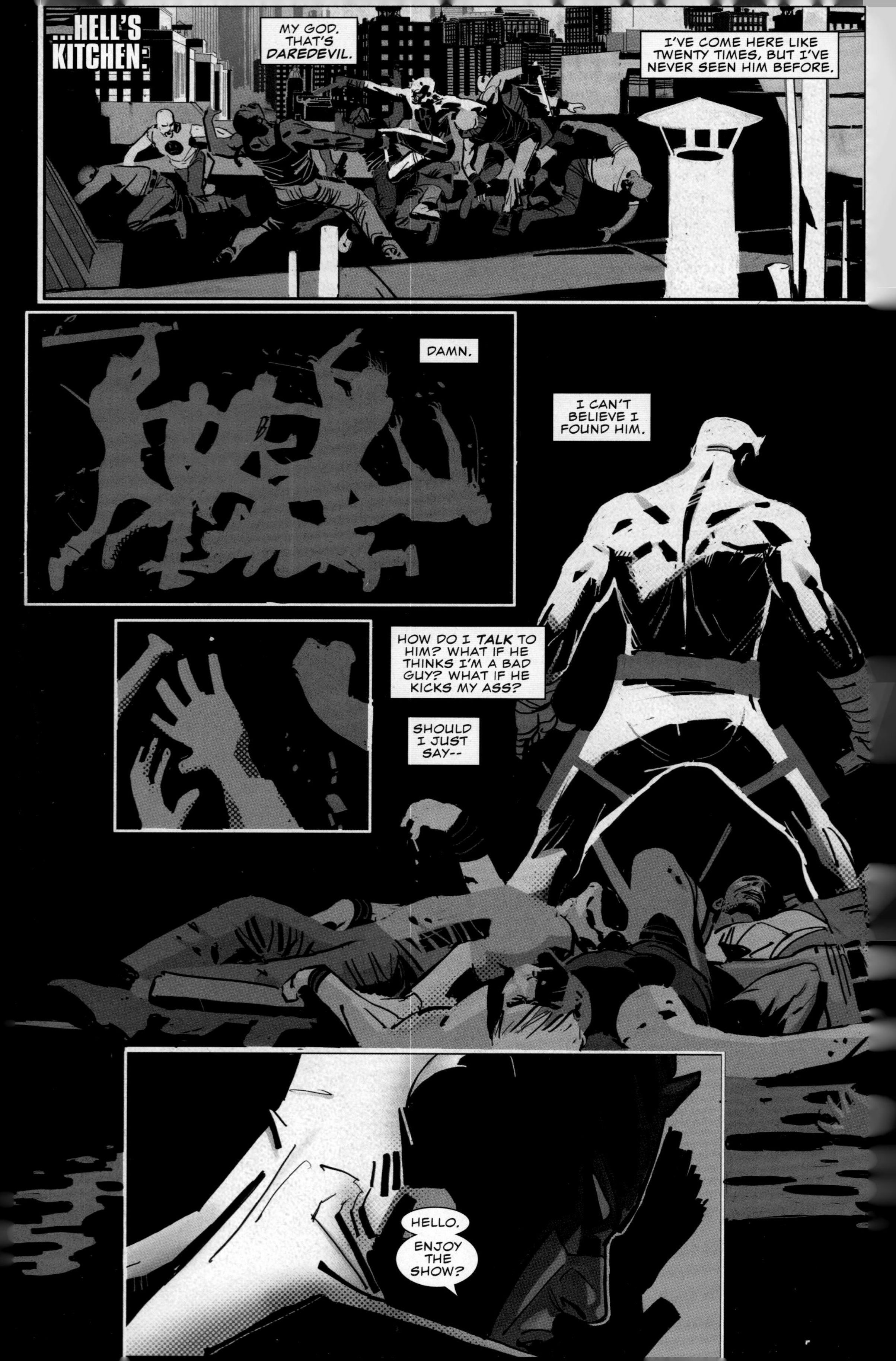

...HELL'S KITCHEN:
MY GOD. THAT'S DAREDEVIL.
I'VE COME HERE LIKE TWENTY TIMES, BUT I'VE NEVER SEEN HIM BEFORE.
DAMN.
I CAN'T BELIEVE I FOUND HIM.
HOW DO I TALK TO HIM? WHAT IF HE THINKS I'M A BAD GUY? WHAT IF HE KICKS MY ASS?
SHOULD I JUST SAY--
HELLO.
ENJOY THE SHOW?

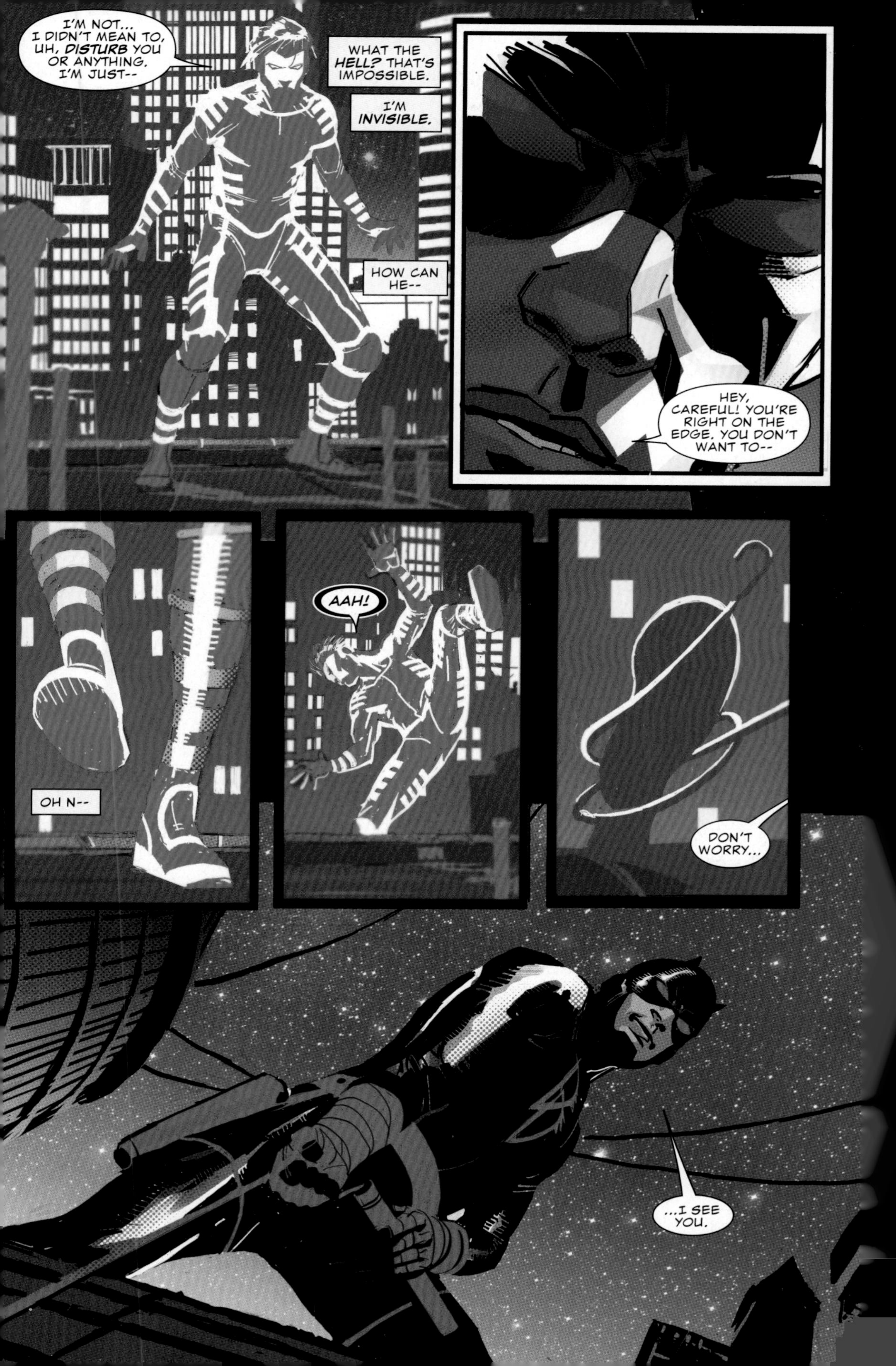
I'M NOT... I DIDN'T MEAN TO, UH, DISTURB YOU OR ANYTHING. I'M JUST--
WHAT THE HELL? THAT'S IMPOSSIBLE.
I'M INVISIBLE.
HOW CAN HE--
HEY, CAREFUL! YOU'RE RIGHT ON THE EDGE. YOU DON'T WANT TO--
OH N--
AAH!
DON'T WORRY...
...I SEE YOU.

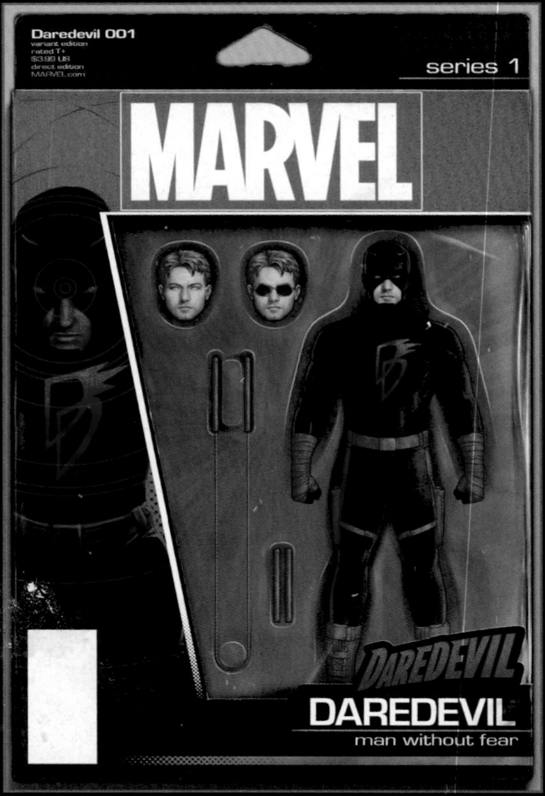
Daredevil 001
variant edition
rated T+
$3.99 US
direct edition
MARVEL.com
series 1
MARVEL
DAREDEVIL
DAREDEVIL
man without fear

JOHN TYLER CHRISTOPHER
No. 1 ACTION FIGURE VARIANT

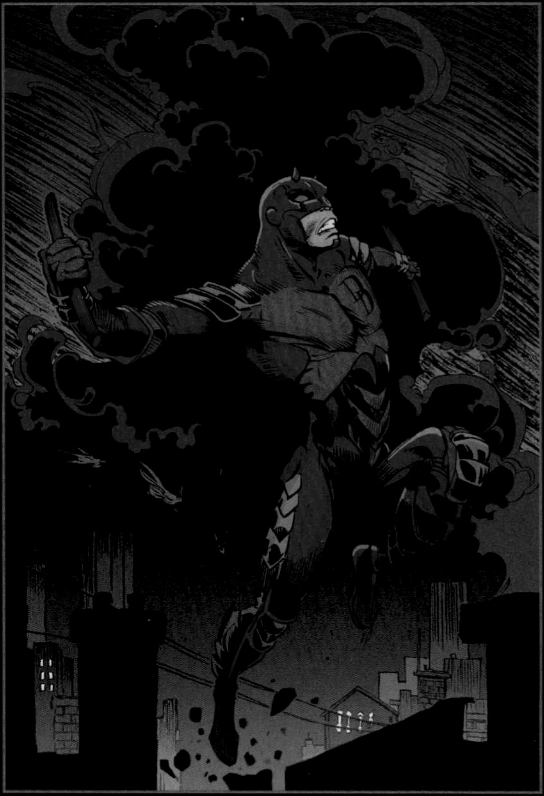

LARRY STROMAN, TOM PALMER & RACHELLE ROSENBERG
No. 1 MARVEL '92 VARIANT

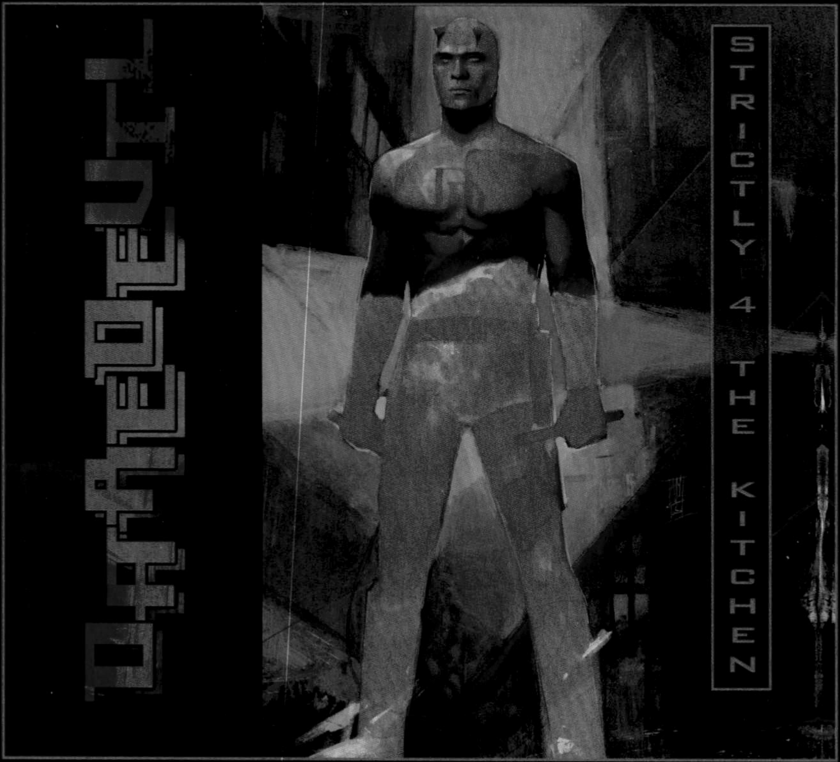
STRICTLY 4 THE KITCHEN

ALEX MALEEV
No. 1 HIP-HOP VARIANT

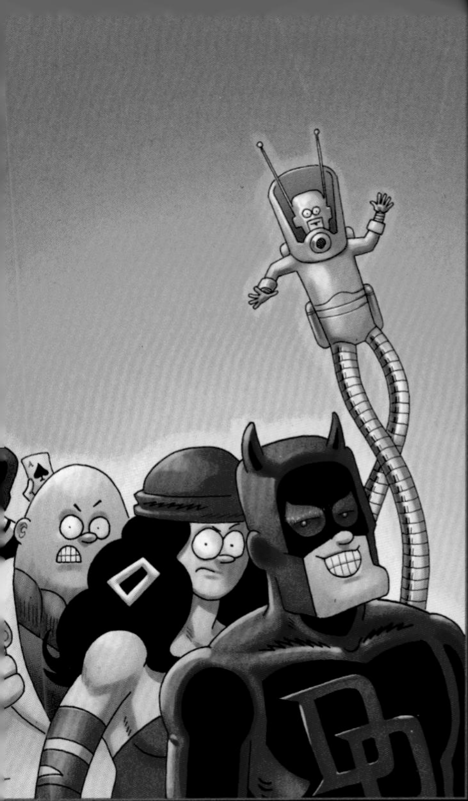

FRED HEMBECK & CHRIS SOTOMAYOR
No. 2 VARIANT

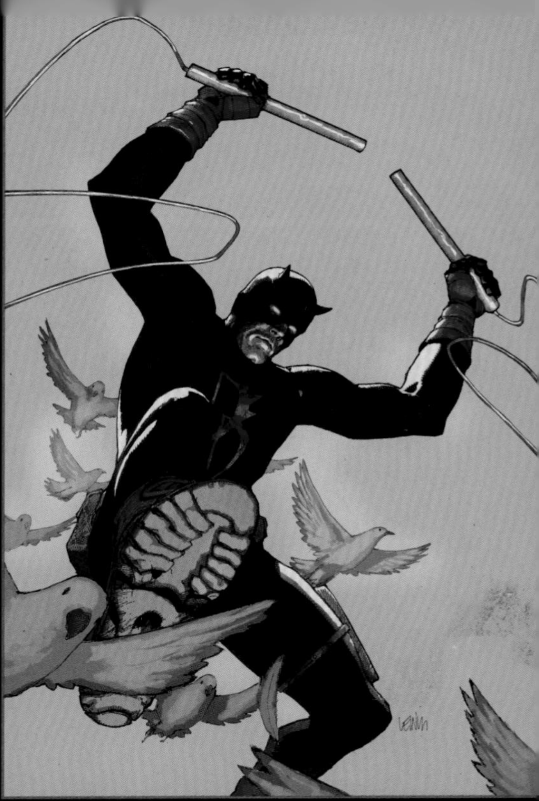

LEINIL YU
No. 2 VARIANT

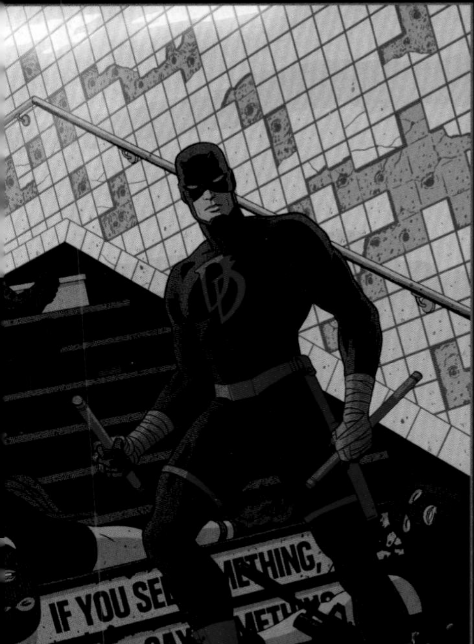

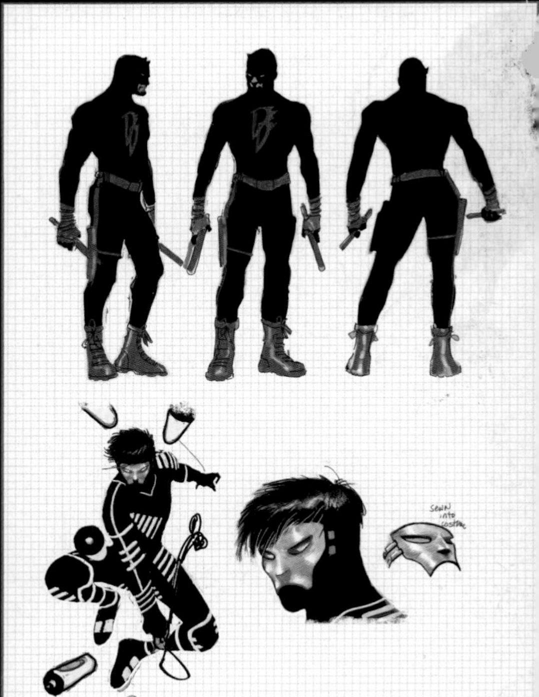

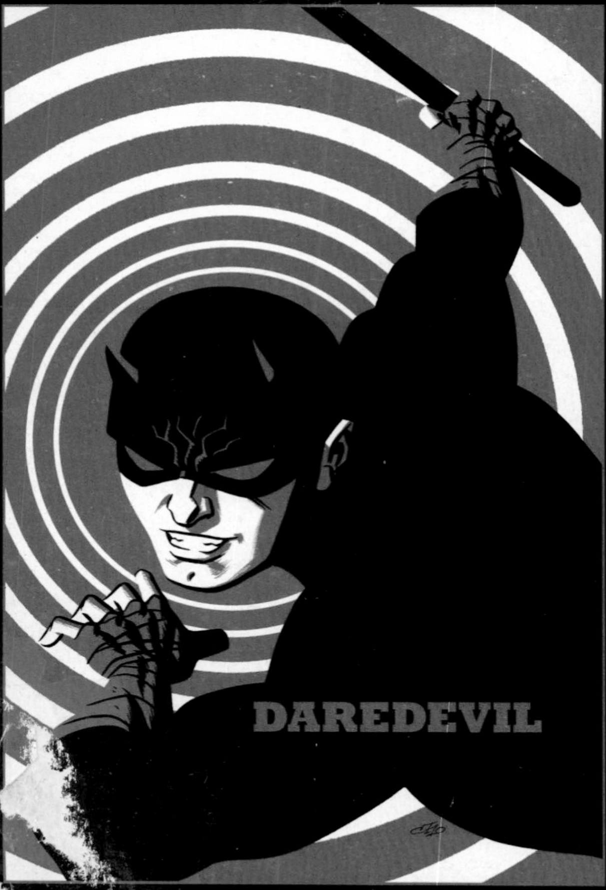
DAREDEVIL

MICHAEL CHO
No. 4 VARIANT

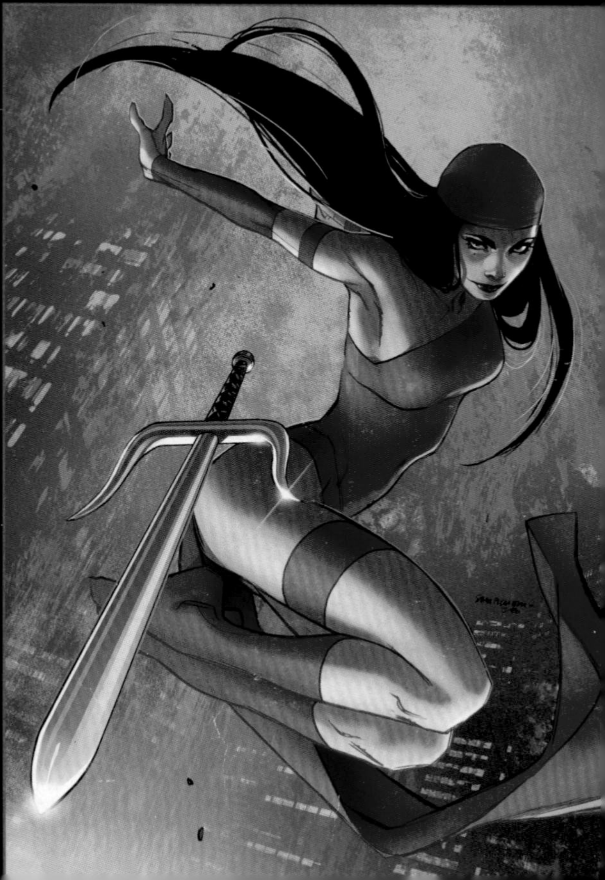

SARA PICHELLI
& JUSTIN PONSOR
No. 5 WOMEN OF POWER VARIANT